Business Maths

Pippa Riley

Viva Books

New Delhi | Mumbai | Chennai | Kolkata | Bengaluru | Hyderabad | Kochi | Guwahati

First Indian Edition 2011

VIVA BOOKS PRIVATE LIMITED

- 4737/23 Ansari Road, Daryaganj, New Delhi 110 002
  E-mail: vivadelhi@vivagroupindia.net, Tel. 42242200
- 76, Service Industries, Shirvane, Sector 1, Nerul, Navi Mumbai 400 706
  E-mail: vivamumbai@vivagroupindia.net, Tel. 27721273, 27721274
- Jamals Fazal Chambers, 26 Greams Road, Chennai 600 006
  E-mail: vivachennai@vivagroupindia.net, Tel. 28290304, 28294241
- B-103, Jindal Towers, 21/1A/3 Darga Road, Kolkata 700 017
  E-mail: vivakolkata@vivagroupindia.net, Tel. 22836381, 22816713
- 7, Sovereign Park Apartments, 56-58, K. R. Road, Basavanagudi, Bengaluru 560 004
  E-mail: vivabangalore@vivagroupindia.net, Tel. 26607409, 26607410
- 101-102 Mughal Marc Aptt., 3-4-637 to 641, Narayanguda, Hyderabad 500 029
  E-mail: vivahyderabad@vivagroupindia.net, Tel. 27564481, 27564482
- First Floor, Beevi Towers, SRM Road, Kaloor, Kochi 682 018, Kerala
  E-mail: vivakochi@vivagroupindia.net, Tel: 0484-2403055, 2403056
- 232, GNB Road, Beside UCO Bank, Silpukhuri, Guwahati 781 003
  E-mail: vivaguwahati@vivagroupindia.net, Tel: 0361-2666386

Published by arrangement with

BPP Learning Media Ltd.
BPP House, Aldine Place
London W12 8AA

ISBN : 978-81-309-1755-9

Published by Vinod Vasishtha for Viva Books Private Limited, 4737/23, Ansari Road, Daryaganj, New Delhi - 110 002.

Printed and bound by Raj Press, R-3, Inderpuri, New Delhi - 110 012.

Contents

Introduction

Viva-BPP Learning Media's Business Essentials range is the ideal learning solution for students studying for business-related qualifications and degrees. The range provides concise and comprehensive coverage of the key areas that are essential to the business student.

Qualifications in business are traditionally very demanding. Students therefore need learning resources which go straight to the core of the topics involved, and which build upon students' pre-existing knowledge and experience. The BPP Learning Media Business Essentials range has been designed to meet exactly that need.

Features include:

- In-depth coverage of essential topics within business-related subjects
- Plenty of activities, quizzes and topics for discussion to help retain the interest of students and ensure progress
- Up-to-date practical illustrations and case studies that really bring the material to life
- A full index, with key terms highlighted in bold

Each chapter contains:

- An introduction and a list of specific study objectives
- Summary diagrams and signposts to guide you through the chapter
- A chapter roundup, quick quiz with answers and answers to activities

Titles in the Series

- Accounts
- Business Decision Making
- Business Environment
- Business Maths
- Business Strategy
- Economics
- Finance: Management Accounting and Financial Reporting
- Human Resource Development and Employee Relations
- Human Resource Management
- Management: Communications and Achieving Results
- Management: Leading People and Professional Development
- Managing Finance
- Marketing and Promotion
- Marketing and Sales Strategy
- Marketing Principles
- Organisations and Behaviour
- Research Project

Study Guide

This Course Book includes features designed specifically to make learning effective and efficient.

- Each chapter begins with a summary diagram which maps out the areas covered by the chapter. There are detailed summary diagrams at the start of each main section of the chapter. You can use the diagrams during revision as a basis for your notes.
- After the main summary diagram there is an introduction, which sets the chapter in context. This is followed by learning objectives, which show you what you will learn as you work through the chapter.
- Throughout the Course Book, there are special aids to learning. These are indicated by symbols in the margin:

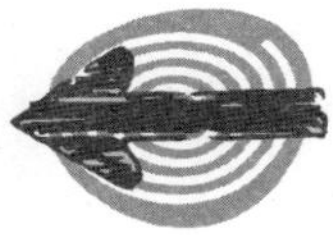

Signposts guide you through the book, showing how each section connects with the next.

Definitions give the meanings of key terms. The *glossary* at the end of the book summarises these.

Activities help you to test how much you have learned. An indication of the time you should take on each is given. Answers are given at the end of each chapter.

Topics for discussion are for use in seminars. They give you a chance to share your views with your fellow students. They allow you to highlight holes in your knowledge and to see how others understand concepts. If you have time, try 'teaching' someone the concepts you have learned in a session. This helps you to remember key points and answering their questions will consolidate your knowledge.

Examples relate what you have learned to the outside world. Try to think up your own examples as you work through the Course Book.

Chapter roundups present the key information from the chapter in a concise format. Useful for revision.

- At the end of each chapter, there is a **chapter roundup** and a **quick quiz** with answers. Use these to revise and consolidate your knowledge. The chapter roundup summarises the chapter. The quick quiz tests what you have learned (the answers often refer you back to the chapter so you can look over subjects again).
- At the end of the book, there is an index.

Business Maths

Chapter 1 :

REVISION OF BASIC MATHEMATICAL TECHNIQUES

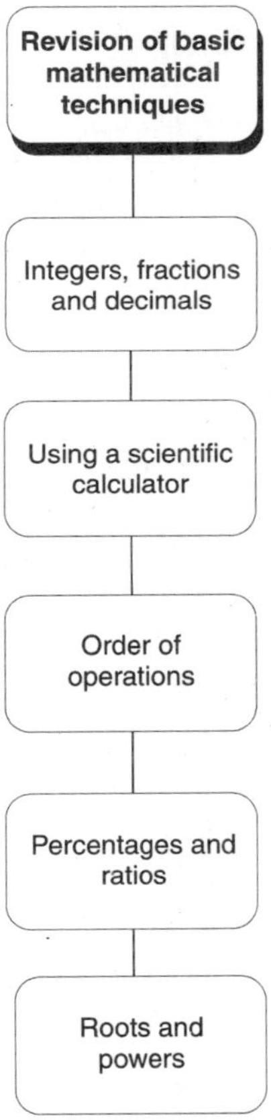

Introduction

This book is designed to provide you with a number of mathematical and statistical concepts and techniques that you will need as you progress through your studies.

Many students do not have a mathematical background and so this chapter is intended to cover the basic mathematics that you will need.

Even if you have done mathematics in the past don't ignore this chapter. Skim through it to make sure that you are aware of all the concepts and techniques covered. Since it provides the foundation for much of what is to follow it is an **extremely important chapter**.

Your objectives

In this chapter you will learn about the following

- Integers, fractions and decimals
- Using a scientific calculator
- Order of operations
- Percentages and ratios
- Roots and powers

1 INTEGERS, FRACTIONS AND DECIMALS

Integers, fractions and decimals
Integers
Fractions
Decimals

1.1 Integers, fractions and decimals

Definition

- An **integer** is a whole number and can be either positive or negative.
- **Fractions** and **decimals** are ways of showing parts of a whole.

Examples of integers are ..., –5, –4 , –3 , –2, –1, 0, 1, 2, 3, 4, 5, ...

Examples of fractions are 1/2, 1/4, 19/35, 10/377, ...

Examples of decimals are 0.1, 0.25, 0.3135, ...

Negative numbers

The negative number rules are as follows:

$$-p + q = q - p$$
$$q - (-p) = q + p$$
$$-p \times -q = pq \text{ and } \frac{-p}{-q} = \frac{p}{q}$$
$$-p \times q = -pq \text{ and } \frac{-p}{q} = -\frac{p}{q}$$

Adding and subtracting negative numbers

When a negative number (–p) is **added** to another number (q), the net effect is to **subtract** p from q.

(a) 10 + (–6) = 10 – 6 = 4 (b) –10 + (–6) = –10 – 6 = –16

When a negative number (–p) is **subtracted** from another number (q), the net effect is to **add** p to q.

(a) 12 – (–8) = 12 + 8 = 20 (b) –12 – (–8) = –12 + 8 = –4

Multiplying and dividing negative numbers

When a negative number is **multiplied** or **divided** by another negative number, the result is a **positive** number.

(a) $-8 \times (-4) = +32$ (b) $\dfrac{-18}{-3} = +6$

If there is only **one negative number** in a multiplication or division, the result is **negative**.

(a) $-8 \times 4 = -32$ (b) $3 \times (-2) = -6$ (c) $\dfrac{12}{-4} = -3$ (d) $\dfrac{-20}{5} = -4$

Activity 1 **(10 minutes)**

Work out the following

(a) $(72 - 8) - (-2 + 1)$

(b) $\dfrac{88+8}{12} + \dfrac{(29-11)}{2}$

(c) $8(2 - 5) - (4 - (-8))$

(d) $\dfrac{-36}{9-3} - \dfrac{84}{3-10} - \dfrac{-81}{3}$

1.2 Fractions

A fraction has a numerator (the number on the top line) and a denominator (the number on the bottom line).

$$\textbf{FRACTION} = \frac{\textbf{NUMERATOR}}{\textbf{DENOMINATOR}}$$

For example, the fraction 1/2 has a numerator equal to 1 and a denominator of 2.

Reciprocals

The reciprocal of a number is 1 divided by that number. For example, the reciprocal of 2 is 1 divided by 2 = 1/2. The reciprocal of 3 is 1 divided by 3 = 1/3.

1.3 Decimals

A fraction can be turned into a decimal by dividing the numerator by the denominator. For example, the fraction 1/2 equates to 0.5, and the fraction 1/4 equates to 0.25. When turning decimals into fractions, you need to remember that places after the decimal point stand for tenths, hundredths, thousandths and so on.

Decimal places

Sometimes a decimal number has too many figures in it for practical use. For example consider the fraction 6/9 which when turned into a decimal = 0.666666 recurring. This problem can be overcome by **rounding** the decimal number to a specific number of **decimal places** by discarding figures using the following rule.

If the first figure to be discarded is greater than or equal to five then add one to the previous figure. Otherwise the previous figure is unchanged.

EXAMPLE

Decimal places

(a) 49.28723 correct to four decimal places is 49.2872
Discarding a 3 causes nothing to be added to the 2.

(b) 49.28723 correct to three decimal places is 49.287
Discarding a 2 causes nothing to be added to the 7.

(c) 49.28723 correct to two decimal places is 49.29
Discarding the 7 causes 1 to be added to the 8.

(d) 49.28723 correct to one decimal place is 49.3
Discarding the 8 causes 1 to be added to the 2.

Significant figures

Another method for giving an approximated answer is to round off using **significant** figures. Significant means important and the closer a digit is to the beginning of a number, the more significant it is.

For example, if we want to express 95,431 to 3 significant figures, '31' will be discarded, leaving 95,400 (3sf).

Zeros have specific rules. All zeros **between** non-zeros are significant. For example, 20,606 has 5 significant figures. Leading zeros in a decimal are **not** significant. For example, 0.025 has 2 significant figures.

Activity 2 **(5 minutes)**

(a) Round off the number 37,649 to one significant figure

(b) Round off the number 0.073184 to one significant figure

(c) Round off the number 0.0073184 to four decimal places

(d) Work out the answer to 974×586 on a calculator and round off the answer to three significant figures

(e) Work out the answer to $23 \div 946$ on a calculator and round off the answer to three decimal places

Extra symbols

We will come across several other mathematical signs in this book but there are five which you should learn **now**:

(a) $>$ means 'greater than'. So $46 > 29$ is true, but $40 > 86$ is false.
(b) $\geq$ means 'is greater than or equal to'. So $4 \geq 3$ and $4 \geq 4$.
(c) $<$ means 'is less than'. So $29 < 46$ is true, but $86 < 40$ is false.
(d) $\leq$ means 'is less than or equal to'. So $7 \leq 8$ and $7 \leq 7$.
(e) $\neq$ means 'is not equal to'. So we could write $100.004 \neq 100$.

We have now been introduced to integers, fractions and decimals. Sitting on the desk of most of us is a calculator with more computing power than was used to put a man on the moon. Let's look at how we can use it!

2 USING A SCIENTIFIC CALCULATOR

Using a scientific calculator
The need for a scientific calculator
A typical scientific calculator

Scientific calculators can make calculations quicker and easier.

2.1 The need for a scientific calculator

For your studies you will need to have an up-to-date scientific calculator. They are not expensive and if you spend time now getting to know what it can do for you, you will have a much better chance of succeeding in your studies.

The calculator can make calculations quicker and easier but it is very important that you show all your workings to numerical calculations.

2.2 A typical scientific calculator

The illustration below shows a typical scientific calculator that is widely available. It has a natural textbook display which allows you to input and display fractions, square roots and other numeric expressions as they appear in your textbook and assessment. Your calculator may be slightly different and it is essential that you read its instruction leaflet and practise using it.

REPLAY

◄ ► This allows you to change any part of the series of keys you have pressed

▲ This lets you go back to previous calculations

COMP mode is the usual setting for calculations. STAT mode lets you do statistical calculations

RECIPROCAL
This recalculates the number displayed as 1 over that number $\left(\frac{1}{x}\right)$

SHIFT
Pressing this key followed by a second key performs the alternative function of the second key

POWER and ROOT
Press the SHIFT button before this button if you want to find a root. This is the same as ^, y^x or x^y

FRACTIONS
This lets you put a fraction into a calculation without having to convert it into a decimal

DELETE
Used with the replay button, this allows you to go back and correct your calculation

NEGATIVE
A very useful button for minus numbers

BRACKETS
These are used just like you write a calculation so that it is done in the right order

ANSWER
This stores the last calculation result

EQUALS
Input the calculation expressions as they are written then press = to execute it

Activity 3 **(10 minutes)**

(a) Put the following calculations into your calculator exactly as it is written:

$3 + 6 \times 5 =$

What does this tell you about how your calculator carries out the order of operation?

(b) Calculate the following using the brackets buttons on your calculator:

$(3 + 5) \times 2$

What happens if you don't use brackets?

(c) Use the fraction button to calculate the following:

$^1/_2 + {^1/_4} + {^1/_8}$

(d) What is $6^{2.75}$?

(e) What is $\sqrt[7]{78{,}125}$?

(f) What is $1/0.2 \times (3 - (1 + 0.7)^5)$?

(g) What is $\dfrac{2.25^4 + 0.025^{-3}}{2.653}$?

3 ORDER OF OPERATIONS

Order of operations
Brackets

3.1 Brackets

Brackets indicate a priority or an order in which calculations should be made.

Brackets are commonly used to indicate which parts of a mathematical expression should be grouped together, and calculated before other parts. The rule for using brackets is as follows:

(a) Do things in brackets before doing things outside them.

(b) Subject to rule (a), do things in this order:

(1) Powers and roots
(2) Multiplications and divisions, working from left to right
(3) Additions and subtractions, working from left to right

Brackets – clarity

Brackets are used for the sake of clarity.

(a) $3 + 6 \times 8 = 51$. This is the same as writing $3 + (6 \times 8) = 51$.

(b) $(3 + 6) \times 8 = 72$. The brackets indicate that we wish to multiply the sum of 3 and 6 by 8.

(c) $12 - 4 \div 2 = 10$. This is the same as writing $12 - (4 \div 2) = 10$ or $12 - (4/2) = 10$.

(d) $(12 - 4) \div 2 = 4$. The brackets tell us to do the subtraction first.

A figure outside a bracket may be multiplied by two or more figures inside a bracket, linked by addition or subtraction signs. Here is an example.

$$5(6 + 8) = 5 \times (6 + 8) = (5 \times 6) + (5 \times 8) = 70$$

This is the same as $5(14) = 5 \times 14 = 70$

The multiplication sign after the 5 can be omitted, as shown here ($5(6 + 8)$), but there is no harm in putting it in ($5 \times (6 + 8)$) if you want to.

Similarly:

$$5(8 - 6) = 5(2) = 10; \text{ or}$$

$$(5 \times 8) - (5 \times 6) = 10$$

Brackets – multiplication

When two sets of figures linked by addition or subtraction signs within brackets are multiplied together, each figure in one bracket is multiplied in turn by every figure in the second bracket. Thus:

$$(8 + 4)(7 + 2) = (12)(9) = 108 \text{ or}$$
$$(8 \times 7) + (8 \times 2) + (4 \times 7) + (4 \times 2) = 56 + 16 + 28 + 8 = 108$$

Brackets on a calculator

A modern scientific calculator will let you do calculations with brackets in the same way they are written. Try doing the examples above using the brackets buttons.

Activity 4 **(10 minutes)**

Work out all answers to four decimal places, using a calculator.

(a) $(43 + 26.705) \times 9.3$

(b) $(844.2 \div 26) - 2.45$

(c) $\dfrac{45.6 - 13.92 + 823.1}{14.3 \times 112.5}$

(d) $\dfrac{303.3 + 7.06 \times 42.11}{1.03 \times 111.03}$

(e) $\dfrac{7.6 \times 1{,}010}{10.1 \times 76{,}000}$

(f) $(43.756 + 26.321) \div 171.036$

(g) $(43.756 + 26.321) \times 171.036$

(h) $171.45 + (-221.36) + 143.22$

(i) $66 - (-43.57) + (-212.36)$

(j) $\dfrac{10.1 \times 76{,}000}{7.6 \times 1{,}010}$

(k) $\dfrac{21.032 + (-31.476)}{3.27 \times 41.201}$

(l) $\dfrac{-33.33 - (-41.37)}{11.21 + (-24.32)}$

(m) $\dfrac{-10.75 \times (-15.44)}{-14.25 \times 17.15} + \left(\dfrac{16.23}{8.4 + 3.002}\right)$

(n) $\dfrac{-7.366 \times 921.3}{10{,}493 - 2{,}422.8} - \left(\dfrac{8.4 + 3.002}{16.23}\right)$

4 PERCENTAGES AND RATIOS

Percentages and ratios
Percentages
Profits
Proportions
Ratios

4.1 Percentages

Percentages are used to indicate the relative size or proportion of items, rather than their absolute size.

If one office employs ten accountants, six secretaries and four supervisors, the **absolute** values of staff numbers and the **percentage** of the total work force in each type would be as follows:

	Accountants	*Secretaries*	*Supervisors*	*Total*
Absolute numbers	10	6	4	20
Percentages	50%	30%	20%	100%

The idea of percentages is that the whole of something can be thought of as 100%. The whole of a cake, for example, is 100%. If you share it out equally with a friend, you will get half each, or 100%/2 = 50% each.

To turn a percentage into a fraction or decimal you divide by 100%. To turn a fraction or decimal back into a percentage you multiply by 100%.

Percentages, fractions and decimals

Consider the following:

(a) $0.16 = 0.16 \times 100\% = 16\%$

(b) $\frac{4}{5} = 4/5 \times 100\% = \frac{400}{5\%} = 80\%$

(c) $40\% = \frac{40}{100\%} = \frac{2}{5} = 0.4$

Situations involving percentages

Find X% of Y

Question: What is 40% of £64?

Answer: 40% of £64 $= \frac{40}{100} \times$ £64 $= 0.4 \times$ £64 = £25.60.

Express X as a percentage of Y

Question: What is £16 as a percentage of £64?

Answer: £16 as a percentage of £64 $= 16/64 \times 100\% = 1/4 \times 100\% = 25\%$

In other words, put the £16 as a fraction of the £64, and then multiply by 100%.

Find the original value of X, given that after a percentage increase of Y% it is equal to X_1

Question:

Fred Bloggs' salary is now £60,000 per annum after an annual increase of 20%. What was his annual salary before the increase?

Answer:

	%
Fred Bloggs' salary *before* increase (original)	100
Salary increase	20
Fred Bloggs' salary after increase (final)	120

We know that Fred's salary after the increase (final) also equals £60,000.

Therefore 120% = £60,000.

We need to find his salary *before* the increase (original), ie 100%.

We can do this as follows:

Step 1 **Calculate 1%**

If 120% = £60,000

$$1\% = \frac{£60,000}{120}$$

1% = £500

Step 2 **Calculate 100% (original)**

If 1% = £500

100% = £500 × 100

100% = £50,000

Therefore, Fred Bloggs' annual salary before the increase was £50,000.

Find the final value of A, given that after a percentage increase/decrease of B% it is equal to A_1

Question:

If sales receipts in year 1 are £500,000 and there was a percentage decrease of 10% in year 2, what are the sales receipts in year 2?

Answer:

Adopt the step-by-step approach used in paragraph 4.2.3 as follows:

	%
Sales receipts – year 1 (original)	100
Percentage decrease	10
Sales receipts – year 2 (final)	90

This question is slightly different to that in paragraph 4.2.3 because we have the original value (100%) and not the final value as in paragraph 4.2.3.

We know that sales receipts in year 1 (original) also equal £500,000.

We need to find the sales receipts in year 2 (final). We can do this as follows:

Step 1 **Calculate 1%**

If 100% = £500,000
1% = £5,000

Step 2 **Calculate 90% (original)**

If 1% = £5,000
90% = £5,000 × 90
90% = £450,000

Therefore, sales receipts in year 2 are £450,000.

Percentage changes

A percentage increase or reduction is calculated as (change ÷ original) × 100%.

You might also be required to calculate the value of the **percentage change,** ie in paragraph 4.2.3 you may have been required to calculate the percentage increase in Fred Bloggs' salary, or in paragraph 4.2.4 you may have been required to calculate the percentage decrease of sales receipts in year 2 (as compared with year 1).

The formula required for calculating the **percentage change** is as follows:

$$\textbf{Percentage change} = \frac{\text{'Change'}}{\text{Original value}} \times 100\%$$

Note that it is the **original value** that the change is compared with and not the final value when calculating the percentage change.

Activity 5 **(5 minutes)**

A television has been reduced from £490.99 to £340.99. What is the percentage reduction in price to three decimal places?

A 30.550 B 30.551 C 43.990 D 43.989

Discounts

A business may offer a discount on a price to encourage sales. The calculation of discounts requires an ability to manipulate percentages. For example, a travel agent is offering a 17% discount on the brochure price of a particular holiday to America. The brochure price of the holiday is £795. What price is being offered by the travel agent?

Solution

$$\text{Discount} = 17\% \text{ of } £795 = \frac{17}{100} \times £795 = £135.15$$

Price offered = £(795 – 135.15) = £659.85

= ∴ 17% = 17 × 1% = 17 × £7.95 = £135.15

Alternatively, price offered = £795 × (100 – 17)% = £795 × 83% = £795 × 0.83 = £659.85

Quicker percentage change calculations

If something is increased by 10%, we can calculate the increased value by multiplying by (1 + 10%) = 1 +0.1 = 1.1. We are multiplying the number by itself plus 10% expressed as a decimal.

For example, a 15% increase to £1,000 = £1,000 × 1.15
= £1,150

In the same way, a 10% decrease can be calculated by multiplying a number by (1 – 10%) = 1 – 0.1 = 0.9. With practice, this method will speed up your percentage calculations and will be very useful in your future studies.

Activity 6 **(5 minutes)**

Three years ago a retailer sold action man toys for £17.50 each. At the end of the first year he increased the price by 6% and at the end of the second year by a further 5%. At the end of the third year the selling price was £20.06. The percentage price change in year three was

A –3% B +3% C –6% D +9%

4.2 Profits

You may be required in your assessment to calculate profit, selling price or cost of sale of an item or number of items from certain information. To do this you need to remember the following crucial formula:

	%
Cost of sales	100
Plus Profit	25
Equals Sales	125

Profit may be expressed either as a percentage of **cost of sales** (such as 25% (25/100) mark-up) or as a percentage of **sales** (such as 20% (25/125) **margin**).

Profit margins

If profit is expressed as a percentage of sales (**margin**) the following formula is also useful:

	%
Selling price	100
Profit	20
Cost of sales	80

It is best to think of the selling price as 100% if profit is expressed as a **margin** (percentage of sales). On the other hand, if profit is expressed as a percentage of cost of sales (**mark-up**) it is best to think of the cost of sales as being 100%. The following examples should help to clarify this point.

EXAMPLE: MARGIN

Delilah's Dresses sells a dress at a 10% margin. The dress cost the shop £100. Calculate the profit made by Delilah's Dresses.

SOLUTION

The margin is 10% (ie 10/100).

$\therefore$ Let selling price = 100%
$\therefore$ Profit = 10%
$\therefore$ Cost = 90% = £100

$$\therefore 1\% = \left(\frac{£100}{90}\right)$$

$$\therefore 10\% = \text{profit} = £\frac{100}{90} \times 10 = £11.11$$

EXAMPLE: MARK-UP

Trevor's Trousers sells a pair of trousers for £80 at a 15% mark-up.

Required

Calculate the profit made by Trevor's Trousers.

SOLUTION

The markup is 15%.

$\therefore$ Let cost of sales = 100%

$\therefore$ Profit = 15%

$\therefore$ Selling price = 115% = £80

$$\therefore 1\% = \left(\frac{£180}{115}\right)$$

$$\therefore 15\% = \text{profit} = \left(\frac{£180}{115}\right) \times 15 = £10.43$$

Activity 7 **(5 minutes)**

A skirt which cost the retailer £75 is sold at a profit of 25% on the selling price. The profit is therefore

A £18.75 B £20.00 C £25.00 D £30.00

4.3 Proportions

A proportion means writing a percentage as a proportion of 1 (that is, as a decimal). 100% can be thought of as the whole, or 1. 50% is half of that, or 0.5.

EXAMPLE: PROPORTIONS

Suppose there are 14 women in an audience of 70. What proportion of the audience are men?

Number of men = 70 – 14 = 56

Proportion of men = $\frac{56}{70} = \frac{8}{10} = 80\% = 0.8$

- The **fraction** of the audience made up of men is 8/10 or 4/5
- The **percentage** of the audience made up of men is 80%
- The **proportion** of the audience made up of men is 0.8

Activity 8 **(5 minutes)**

There are 30 students in a class room, 17 of whom have blonde hair. What proportion of the students (to four decimal places) do not have blonde hair (delete as appropriate)?

0.5667	0.5666
0.4334	0.4333

4.4 Ratios

Ratios show relative shares of a whole.

Suppose Tom has £12 and Dick has £8. The **ratio** of Tom's cash to Dick's cash is 12:8. This can be cancelled down, just like a fraction, to 3:2. Study the following examples carefully.

EXAMPLE: RATIOS

Suppose Tom and Dick wish to share £20 out in the ratio 3:2. How much will each receive?

SOLUTION

Because 3 + 2 = 5, we must divide the whole up into five equal parts, then give Tom three parts and Dick two parts.

£20 ÷ 5 = £4 (so each part is £4)

Tom's share = 3 × £4 = £12

Dick's share = 2 × £4 = £8

Check: £12 + £8 = £20 (adding up the two shares in the answer gets us back to the £20 in the question)

This method of calculating ratios as amounts works no matter how many ratios are involved.

EXAMPLE: RATIOS AGAIN

A, B, C and D wish to share £600 in the ratio 6:1:2:3. How much will each receive?

SOLUTION

Number of parts = 6 + 1 + 2 + 3 = 12

Value of each part = £600 ÷ 12 = £50

A: $6 \times £50 = £300$
B: $1 \times £50 = £50$
C: $2 \times £50 = £100$
D: $3 \times £50 = £150$

Check: £300 + £50 + £100 + £150 = £600

Activity 9 **(10 minutes)**

Tom, Dick and Harry wish to share out £800. Calculate how much each would receive if the ratio used was:

(a) 3 : 2 : 5
(b) 5 : 3 : 2
(c) 3 : 1 : 1

5 ROOTS AND POWERS

Roots and powers
Powers
Root
Rules for powers
Examples

The nth root of a number is a value which, when multiplied by itself (n – 1) times, equals the original number. Powers work the other way round.

Definition

The **square root** of a number is a value which, when multiplied by itself, equals the original number. $\sqrt{9} = 3$, since $3 \times 3 = 9$

The **cube root** of a number is the value which, when multiplied by itself twice, equals the original number. $\sqrt[3]{64} = 4$, since $4 \times 4 \times 4 = 64$

5.1 Powers

A **power** is the result when equal numbers are multiplied together.

The 6th power of 2 = $2^6 = 2 \times 2 \times 2 \times 2 \times 2 \times 2 = 64$.

Similarly, $3^4 = 3 \times 3 \times 3 \times 3 = 81$.

Familiarise yourself with the power button on your calculator. ($x^{■}$, ∧, x^y or y^x). Most calculators will also have separate buttons to square (x^2) and cube a number (x^3).

5.2 Roots

A **root** is the reverse of a power. When 5 is squared, the answer is 25. That is $5^2 = 25$. The reverse of this process is called finding the square root. $\sqrt[2]{25} = \sqrt{25} = 5$. Most calculators have a square root button $\sqrt{\ }$ or $\sqrt{■}$. Higher roots, eg $\sqrt[5]{7,776}$, can be found by using 'shift' before the power ($x^{■}$, ∧, x^y, y^x) button. On a modern scientific calculator, press 5 shift $\times^{■}$ 7,776 = to obtain the answer = 6.

5.3 Rules for powers

Use your calculator to enter each of the following examples to practise this very important topic.

Powers – Rule 1

When a number with a power is multiplied by the **same** number with the same or a different power, the result is that number to the power of the **sum** of the powers.

(a) $5^2 \times 5 = 5^2 \times 5^1 = 5^{(2+1)} = 5^3 = 125$

(b) $4^3 \times 4^3 = 4^{(3+3)} = 4^6 = 4,096$

Powers – Rule 2

Similarly, when a number with a power is divided by the **same** number with the same or a different power, the result is that number to the power of the first index **minus** the second power.

(a) $6^4 \div 6^3 = 6^{(4-3)} = 6^1 = 6$
(b) $7^8 \div 7^6 = 7^{(8-6)} = 7^2 = 49$

Powers – Rule 3

When a number x with a power is raised to the power y, the result is the number raised to the power xy.

The powers are simply multiplied together:

(a) $(2^2)^3 = 2^{2\times3} = 2^6 = 64$
(b) $(5^3)^3 = 5^{3\times3} = 5^9 = 1,953,125$

Powers – Rule 4

Any figure to the power of one always equals itself: $2^1 = 2$, $3^1 = 3$, $4^1 = 4$ and so on.

Powers – Rule 5

Any figure to the power of **zero** always equals **one**: $1^0 = 1$, $2^0 = 1$, $3^0 = 1$, $4^0 = 1$ and so on.

Powers – Rule 6

One to any power always equals one: $1^2 = 1$, $1^3 = 1$, $1^4 = 1$ and so on.

Powers – Rule 7

A power can be a **fraction,** as in $16^{\frac{1}{2}}$. What $16^{\frac{1}{2}}$ means is the square root of 16 $\left(\sqrt{16} \text{ or } 4\right)$.
If we multiply $16^{\frac{1}{2}}$ by $16^{\frac{1}{2}}$ we get $16^{\left(\frac{1}{2}+\frac{1}{2}\right)}$ which equals 16^1 and thus 16.
Similarly, $216^{\frac{1}{3}}$ is the cube root of 216 (which is 6) because $216^{\frac{1}{3}} \times 216^{\frac{1}{3}} \times 216^{\frac{1}{3}} = 216^{\left(\frac{1}{3}+\frac{1}{3}+\frac{1}{3}\right)} = 216^1 = 216$.

Powers – Rule 8

A power can be a **negative** value. The negative sign represents a **reciprocal.** Thus 2^{-1} is the reciprocal of, or one over, 2^1.

$$2^{-1} = \frac{1}{2^1} = \frac{1}{2}$$

Likewise $2^{-2} = \frac{1}{2^2} = \frac{1}{4}$

$$2^{-3} = \frac{1}{2^3} = \frac{1}{8}$$

$$5^{-6} = \frac{1}{5^6} = \frac{1}{15{,}625}$$

EXAMPLES

When we multiply or divide by a number with a negative power, the rules previously stated still apply:

(a) $9^2 \times 9^{-2} = 9^{(2+(-2))} = 9^0 = 1$ (That is, $9^2 \times \frac{1}{9^2} = 1$)

(b) $4^5 \div 4^{-2} = 4^{(5-(-2))} = 4^7 = 16{,}384$

(c) $3^8 \times 3^{-5} = 3^{(8-5)} = 3^3 = 27$

(d) $3^{-5} \div 3^{-2} = 3^{-5-(-2)} = 3^{-3} = \frac{1}{3^3} = \frac{1}{27}$.

(This could be re-expressed as $\frac{1}{3^3} \div \frac{1}{3^2} = \frac{1}{3^5} \times 3^2 = \frac{1}{3^3}$.)

A fraction might have a power applied to it. In this situation, the main point to remember is that the power must be applied to both the top and the bottom of the fraction:

(a) $\left(2\frac{1}{3}\right)^3 = \left(\frac{7}{3}\right)^3 = \frac{7^3}{3^3} = \frac{343}{27}$

(b) $\left(5\frac{2}{5}\right)^{-4} = \left(\frac{27}{5}\right)^{4} = \frac{1}{\left(\frac{27}{5}\right)^4} = \frac{1}{\frac{27^4}{5^4}} = \frac{5^4}{27^4} = \frac{625}{531{,}441}$

Summary

The **main rules** to apply when dealing with powers and roots are as follows:

- $2^x \times 2^y = 2^{x+y}$
- $2^x \div 2^y = 2^{x-y}$
- $(2^x)^y = 2^{x \times y} = 2^{xy}$
- $x^0 = 1$
- $x^1 = x$
- $1^x = 1$
- $2^{-x} = \frac{1}{2^x}$
- $\left(1\frac{1}{2}\right)^x = \left(\frac{3}{2}\right)^x = \frac{3_x}{2_x}$

Activity 10 **(10 minutes)**

Work out the following, using your calculator as necessary:

(a) $(18.6)^{2.6}$

(b) $(18.6)^{-2.6}$

(c) $\sqrt[2.6]{18.6}$

(d) $(14.2)^4 \times (14.2)^{\frac{1}{4}}$

(e) $(14.2)^4 + (14.2)^{\frac{1}{4}}$

Chapter roundup

- An integer is a whole number and can be either positive or negative.
- **Fractions** and **decimals** are ways of showing parts of a whole.
- The **negative number rules** are as follows:

  $-p + q = q - p$
  $q - (-p) = q + p$
  $-p \times -q = pq$ and $\frac{-p}{-q} = \frac{p}{q}$
  $-p \times q = -pq$ and $\frac{-p}{q} = -\frac{p}{q}$

- Scientific calculators can make calculations quicker and easier.
- **Brackets** indicate a priority or an order in which calculations should be made.
- The **reciprocal** of a number is 1 divided by that number.
- **Percentages** are used to indicate the **relative size** or **proportion** of items, rather than their **absolute** size. To turn a percentage into a fraction or decimal you **divide by 100%**.
- To turn a fraction or decimal back into a percentage you **multiply by 100%**.
- A **percentage increase** or **reduction** is calculated as (change ÷ original value) × 100%.
- A **proportion** means writing a percentage as a proportion of 1 (that is, as a decimal). 100% can be thought of as the whole, or 1. 50% is half of that, or 0.5.
- **Ratios** show relative shares of a whole.
- The nth **root** of a number is a value which, when multiplied by itself (n–1) times, equals the original number. **Powers** work the other way round.
- The **main rules** to apply when dealing with powers and roots are as follows:
  - $2^x \times 2^y = 2^{x+y}$
  - $2^x \div 2^y = 2^{x-y}$
  - $(2^x)^y = 2^{x \times y} = 2^{xy}$
  - $x^0 = 1$
  - $x^1 = x$
  - $1^x = 1$
  - $2^{-x} = \frac{1}{2^x}$
  - $\left(1\frac{1}{2}\right)^x = \left(\frac{3}{2}\right)^x = \frac{3^x}{2^x}$

Quick quiz

1 $3\frac{3}{4}$ is an integer/fraction/decimal

2 1004.002955 to nine significant figures is …………

3 The product of a negative number and a negative number is

Positive ☐

Negative ☐

4 $217 \leq 217$

True ☐

False ☐

5 To turn a percentage into a fraction or decimal you must

A Divide by 100%
B Multiply by 100%
C Divide by 100
D Multiply by 100

6 3^{-1} can also be written as

A 3^{-1}

B 3^{1}

C $\frac{1}{3}$

D -1^{3}

Answers to quick quiz

1 Fraction

2 1004.00296

3 Positive

4 True

5 A

6 C = $\frac{1}{3}$

Answers to activities

1 (a) 64 – (–1) = 64 + 1 = 65

(b) 8 + (–9) = –1

(c) –24 – (12) = –36

(d) –6 – (–12 – (–27) = –6 + 12 + 27 = 33

2 (a) 40,000

(b) 0.07

(c) 0.0073

(d) 974 × 586 = 570,764
= 571,000 (3 sf)

(e) 23 ÷ 946 = 0.02431289641
= 0.024 (3 dp)

3 (a) 33

This tells you that the calculator carries out mathematical operations in the correct order (see section 3 below).

(b) 16

If brackets are not used the answer is 13. The calculator has done the multiplication before the addition.

(c) $\frac{7}{8}$

(d) 138.0117105

(e) 1,956.55948

(f) –55.99285

(g) 24,133.29397

4 (a) 648.2565

(b) 30.0192

(c) 0.5313

(d) 5.2518

(e) 0.01

(f) 0.4097

(g) 11,985.6898

(h) 93.31

(i) –102.79

(j) 100 (Note that this question is the reciprocal of part (e), and so the answer is the reciprocal of the answer to part (e).)

(k) –0.0775

(l) –0.6133

(m) 0.7443

(n) –1.5434

5 Difference in price = £(490.99 – 340.99) = £150.00

$$\text{Percentage reduction} = \frac{\text{change}}{\text{original price}} \times 100\% = \frac{150}{490.99} \times 100\% = 30.551\%$$

The correct answer is B.

6 Selling price at end of year 1 = £17.50 × 1.06 = £18.55
Selling price at end of year 2 = £18.55 × 1.05 = £19.48
Change in selling price in year 3 = £(20.06 – 19.48) = £0.58

$\therefore$ Percentage change in year 3 was $\frac{£0.58}{£19.48} \times 100\% =$ 2.97%, say 3%

The correct answer is B.

7 Let selling price = 100%

Profit = 25% of selling price

$\therefore$ Cost = 75% of selling price

Cost = £75 = 75%

$\therefore 1\% = \frac{£75}{75}$

$\therefore 25\% = \text{profit} = \frac{£75}{75} \times 25 = £25$

The correct answer is C.

8

~~0.5667~~	~~0.5666~~
~~0.4334~~	0.4333

$\frac{(30-17)}{30} \times 100\% = 43.33\% = 0.4333$

9 (a) Total parts = 10

Each part is worth £800 ÷ 10 = £80

Tom gets 3 × £80 = £240
Dick gets 2 × £80 = £160
Harry gets 5 × £80 = £400

(b) Same parts as (a) but in a different order.

Tom gets £400
Dick gets £240
Harry gets £160

(c) Total parts = 5

Each part is worth £800 ÷ 5 = £160
Therefore Tom gets £480
Dick and Harry each get £160

10 (a) $(18.6)^{2.6} = 1{,}998.6358$

(b) $(18.6)^{-2.6} = \left(\frac{1}{18.6}\right)^{2.6} = 0.0005$

(c) $\sqrt[2.6]{18.6} = 3.078$

(d) $(14.2)^4 \times (14.2)^{\frac{1}{4}} = (14.2)^{4.25} = 78{,}926.976$

(e) $(14.2)^4 + (14.2)^{\frac{1}{4}} = 40{,}658.6896 + 1.9412 = 40{,}660.6308$

Chapter 2 :

EQUATIONS AND GRAPHS

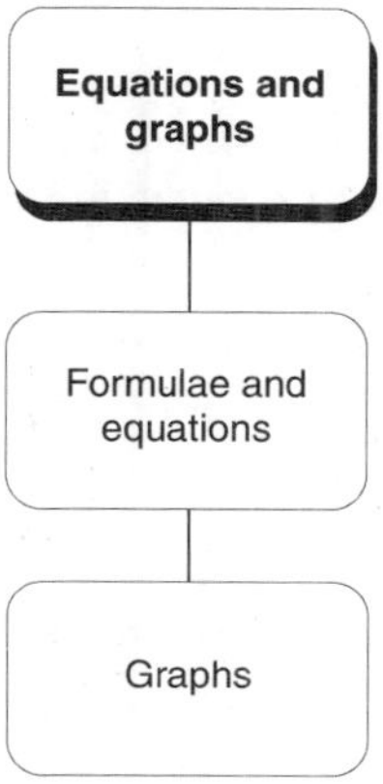

Introduction

You are over the moon. You have just been awarded a £1,000 pay rise. If the man on the Clapham omnibus asks you to explain your new salary in terms of your old salary, what would you say? You might say something like 'my new salary equals my old salary plus £1,000'. Easy. What would you say, on the other hand, to the mathematics professor who asks you to give a mathematical equation which describes your new salary in terms of your old salary? Like many students, you may be perfectly capable of answering the man on the omnibus, but not the professor. Your reply to the professor should be something like '$y = x + 1{,}000$' but many students get completely confused when they have to deal with mathematical symbols and letters instead of simple words. There is, however, no need to worry about equations: they are simply a shorthand method of expressing words.

In the second part of this chapter we look at an introduction to graphs. Put simply graphs are just a way of showing data to make it visually appealing and, hopefully, easier to understand.

Your objectives

In this chapter you will learn about the following:

- Equations and how to manipulate them
- Graphs and the lines on graphs

1 FORMULAE AND EQUATIONS

Equations
Formulae
Equations
Manipulating inequalities
Linear equations

1.1 Formulae

So far all our problems have been formulated entirely in terms of specific numbers. However, we also need to be able to use letters to represent numbers in formulae and equations.

A formula enables us to calculate the value of one variable from the value(s) of one or more other variables.

Use of variables

The use of variables enables us to state general truths about mathematics.

For example

- $x = x$
- $x^2 = x \times x$
- If $y = 0.5 \times x$, then $x = 2 \times y$

These will be true **whatever** values x and y have. For example, let $y = 0.5 \times x$

- If $y = 3, x = 2 \times y = 6$
- If $y = 7, x = 2 \times y = 14$
- If $y = 1, x = 2 \times y = 2$, and so on for any other choice of a value for y.

We can use **variables** to build up useful **formulae**, we can then put in values for the variables, and get out a value for something we are interested in. It is usual when writing formulae to leave out multiplication signs between letters. Thus $p \times u - c$ can be written as $pu - c$. We will also write (for example) 2x instead of $2 \times x$.

EXAMPLE: VARIABLES

For a business, profit = revenue – costs. Since revenue = selling price × units sold, we can say that

profit = (selling price × units sold) – costs.

'(Selling price × units sold) – costs' is a formula for profit.

Notice the use of brackets to help with the order of operations.

We can then use single letters to make the formula quicker to write.

Let p = profit
s = selling price
u = units sold
c = cost

Then p = (s × u) – c.

If we are then told that in a particular month, s = £5, u = 30 and c = £118 we can find out the month's profit.

Profit = p = (s × u) – c = (£5 × 30) – £118
= £150 – £118 = £32

1.2 Equations

In the above example, su – c was a formula for profit. If we write p = su – c, we have written an **equation**. It says that one thing (profit, p) is **equal** to another (su – c).

Solving the equation

Sometimes, we are given an equation with numbers filled in for all but one of the variables. The problem is then to find the number which should be filled in for the last variable. This is called **solving the equation.**

(a) Returning to p = su – c, we could be told that for a particular month s = £4, u = 60 and c = £208. We would then have the **equation** p = (£4 × 60) – £208. We can solve this easily by working out (£4 × 60) – £208 = £240 – £208 = £32. Thus p = £32.

(b) On the other hand, we might have been told that in a month when profits were £172, 50 units were sold and the selling price was £7. The thing we have not been told is the month's costs, c. We can work out c by writing out the equation:

£172 = (£7 × 50) – c
£172 = £350 – c

(c) We need c to be such that when it is taken away from £350 we have £172 left. With a bit of trial and error, we can get to c = £178.

The rule for solving equations

The general rule for solving equations is that you must always do the same thing to both sides of the equal sign so the 'scales' stay balanced.

(a) To solve an equation, we need to get it into the following form:

Unknown variable = something with just numbers in it, which we can work out.

We therefore want to get the unknown variable on one side of the = sign, and everything else on the other side.

(b) **The rule is that you must always do the same thing to both sides of the equal sign so the 'scales' stay balanced. The two sides are equal, and they will stay equal so long as you treat them in the same way.**

$$£172 + c = £350$$

Take £172 from both sides: $£172 + c - £172 = £350 - £172$

$$c = £350 - £172$$

$$c = £178$$

EXAMPLE: SOLVING THE EQUATION

For example, you can do any of the following: add 37 to both sides; subtract 3x from both sides; multiply both sides by –4.329; divide both sides by (x + 2); take the reciprocal of both sides; square both sides; take the cube root of both sides.

We can do any of these things to an equation either before or after filling in numbers for the variables for which we have values.

(a)

If $£172$	=	$£350 - c$	(as in paragraph 1.2.1) we can then get
$£172 + c$	=	$£350$	(add c to each side)
c	=	$£350 - £172$	(subtract £172 from each side)
c	=	$£178$	(work out the right hand side)

(b)

450	=	$3x + 72$	(initial equation: x unknown)
$450 - 72$	=	$3x$	(subtract 72 from each side)
$\frac{450-72}{3}$	=	x	(divide each side by 3)
126	=	x	(work out the left hand side)

(c)

$3y + 2$	=	$5y - 7$	(initial equation: y unknown)
$3y + 9$	=	$5y$	(add 7 to each side)
9	=	$2y$	(subtract 3y from each side)
4.5	=	y	(divide each side by 2)

(d)

$\frac{\sqrt{3x^2+x}}{2\sqrt{x}}$	=	7	(initial equation: x unknown)
$\frac{3x^2+x}{4x}$	=	49	(square each side)
$\frac{(3x+1)}{4}$	=	49	(cancel x in the numerator and the denominator of the left hand side: this does not affect the value of the left hand side, so we do not need to change the right hand side)
$3x + 1$	=	196	(multiply each side by 4)

$$3x = 195 \qquad \text{(subtract 1 from each side)}$$

$$x = 65 \qquad \text{(divide each side by 3)}$$

(e) Our example in Paragraph 1.2 was p = su – c. We could change this, so as to give a formula for s.

$$s = su - c$$

$$p + c = su \qquad \text{(add c to each side)}$$

$$\frac{p+c}{u} = s \qquad \text{(divide each side by u)}$$

$$s = \frac{p+c}{u} \qquad \text{(swap the sides for ease of reading)}$$

Given values for p, c and u we can now find s. We have rearranged the equation to give s in terms of p, c and u.

(f) Given that $y = \sqrt{3x+7}$, we can get an equation giving x in terms of y.

$$y = \sqrt{3x+7}$$

$$y^2 = 3x + 7 \qquad \text{(square each side)}$$

$$y^2 - 7 = 3x \qquad \text{(subtract 7 from each side)}$$

$$x = \frac{y^2 - 7}{3} \qquad \text{(divide each side by 3, and swap the sides for ease of reading)}$$

Solving the equation and brackets

In equations, you may come across expressions such as 3(x + 4y – 2) (that is, 3 × (x + 4y – 2)). These can be re-written in separate bits without the brackets, simply by multiplying the number outside the brackets by each item inside them. Thus 3(x + 4y – 2) = 3x + 12y – 6.

Activity 1 **(10 minutes)**

Solve the equation

(a) If 47x + 256 = 52x, then x = ☐

(b) If $4\sqrt{x} + 32 = 40.6718$, then x = ☐

(c) If $\frac{1}{3x+4} = \frac{5}{2.7\times-2}$, then x = ☐

Activity 2 **(10 minutes)**

Solve the equation

(a) Rearrange $x = (3y - 20)^2$ to get an expression for y in terms of x.
(b) Rearrange $2(y - 4) - 4(x^2 + 3) = 0$ to get an expression for x in terms of y.

1.3 Manipulating inequalities

Definition

An inequality is a statement that shows the relationship between two (or more) expressions with one of the following signs: >, ⩾, <, ⩽ We can solve inequalities in the same way that we can solve equations

Inequality symbols

Equations are called inequalities when the '=' sign is replaced by one of the following.

(a) > means 'greater than'
(b) ⩾ means 'is greater than or equal to'
(c) < means 'is less than'
(d) ⩽ means 'is less than or equal to'

Using inequalities

Inequalities are used in a short-term decision-making technique called linear programming which you will come across in your managerial studies. It involves using inequalities to represent situations where resources are limited.

EXAMPLE: USING INEQUALITIES 1

If a product needs 3kg of material and 700 kg is available, express this as an inequality

SOLUTION

If the number of units of the product = X

$3X \leqslant 700$

EXAMPLE: USING INEQUALITIES 2

Product Z needs three minutes of machining time and product Y needs two minutes of machining time. There are ten hours of machining time available. Express this as an inequality.

SOLUTION

Ten hours of machining time = 600 minutes

The total machining time must be less than or equal to 600 minutes.

$3Z + 2Y \leqslant 600$

where Z = no of units of product Z
Y = no of units of product Y

Solving inequalities

We can solve inequalities in the same way we can solve equations. For example, the inequality $7x - 2 > 0$ can be solved by getting x on its own, but the answer will be a range of values rather than a specific number.

$7x - 2 > 0$

$7x > 2$ (add 2 to both sides)

$x > \frac{2}{7}$ (divide both sides by 7)

Rules for manipulating inequalities

(i) Adding or subtracting the same quantity from both sides of an inequality leaves the inequality symbol unchanged.

(ii) Multiplying or dividing both sides by a **positive** number leaves the inequality symbol unchanged.

(iii) Multiplying or dividing both sides by a **negative** number **reverses** the inequality so $<$ changes to $>$.

EXAMPLE: SOLVING INEQUALITIES

Find the range of values of x satisfying $x - 5 < 2x + 7$

$x - 5 < 2x + 7$

$x < 2x + 12$ (add 5 to both sides)

$-x < 12$ (subtract 2x from both sides)

$x > -12$ (multiply both sides by −1 and so reverse the inequality)

Activity 3 **(15 minutes)**

Solve the following inequalities:

(a) $2x > 11$
(b) $x + 3 > 15$
(c) $-3x < 7$
(d) $7x + 11 > 2x + 5$
(e) $2(x + 3) < x + 1$

1.4 Linear equations

A **linear equation** has the general form y = a + bx

where y is the **dependent variable,** depending for its value on the value of x

x is the **independent variable** whose value helps to determine the corresponding value of y

a is a **constant,** that is, a fixed amount

b is also a **constant,** being the **coefficient** of x (that is, the number by which the value of x should be multiplied to derive the value of y)

EXAMPLE: ESTABLISHING BASIC LINEAR EQUATIONS

Let us establish some basic linear equations. Suppose that it takes Joe Bloggs 15 minutes to walk one mile. How long does it take Joe to walk two miles? Obviously it takes him 30 minutes. How did you calculate the time? You probably thought that if the distance is doubled then the time must be doubled. How do you explain (in words) the relationships between the distance walked and the time taken? One explanation would be that every mile walked takes 15 minutes. Now let us try to explain the relationship with an equation.

(a) First you must decide which is the **dependent variable** and which is the **independent variable.** In other words, does the time taken depend on the number of miles walked or does the number of miles walked depend on the time it takes to walk a mile? Obviously the time depends on the distance. We can therefore let y be the dependent variable (time taken in minutes) and x be the independent variable (distance walked in miles).

(b) We now need to determine the **constants a** and **b**. There is no fixed amount so a = 0. To ascertain b, we need to establish the number of times by which the value of x should be multiplied to derive the value of y. Obviously y = 15x where y is in minutes. If y were in hours then y = x/4.

EXAMPLE: DERIVING A LINEAR EQUATION

A salesman's weekly wage is made up of a basic weekly wage of £100 and commission of £5 for every item he sells. Derive an equation which describes this scenario.

SOLUTION

x = number of items sold and y = weekly wage

a = £100 (fixed weekly wage paid however many items he sells) and b = £5 (variable element of wage, depending on how many items he sells)

$\therefore$ y = 5x + 100

Note that the letters used in an equation do not have to be x and y. It may be sensible to use other letters, for example we could use p and q if we are describing the relationship between the price of an item and the quantity demanded.

Having looked at formulae and equations we will now look at graphs. Wherever your studies lead it is almost certain that you will need to understand and interpret graphical information.

2 GRAPHS

Graphs
Linear equations
and graphs
Simultaneous equations
Non-linear equations

2.1 Linear equations and graphs

The **graph of a linear equation is a straight line**. The intercept of the line on the y axis is

y = a + bx

where a = the intercept of the line on the y axis

and b = the slope of the line.

One of the clearest ways of presenting the relationship between two variables is by plotting a **linear equation** as a **straight line** on a graph.

The rules for drawing graphs

A graph has a **horizontal axis**, the **x axis** and a **vertical axis**, the **y axis**. The x axis is used to represent the **independent variable** and the y axis is used to represent the **dependent variable**. If calendar time is one variable, it is always treated as the independent variable. When time is represented on the x axis of a graph, we have the graph of a **time series**.

(a) If the data to be plotted are derived from calculations, rather than given in the question, make sure that there is a neat table in your workings.

(b) The scales on each axis should be selected so as to use as much of the graph paper as possible. Do not cramp a graph into one corner.

(c) In some cases it is best not to start a scale at zero so as to avoid having a large area of wasted paper. This is perfectly acceptable as long as the scale adopted is clearly shown on the axis. One way of avoiding confusion is to break the axis concerned, as shown below.

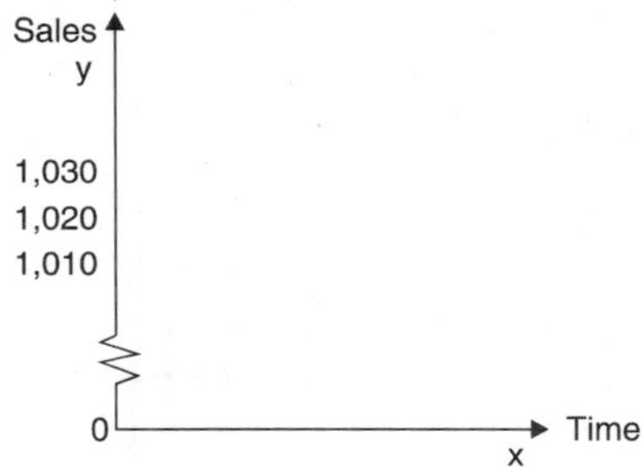

(d) The scales on the x axis and the y axis should be marked. For example, if the y axis relates to amounts of money, the axis should be marked at every £1, or £100 or £1,000 interval or at whatever other interval is appropriate. The axes must be marked with values to give the reader an idea of how big the values on the graph are.

(e) A graph should not be overcrowded with too many lines. Graphs should always give a clear, neat impression.

(f) A graph must always be given a **title**, and, where appropriate, a reference should be made to the **source** of data.

EXAMPLE: DRAWING GRAPHS

Plot the graph for y = 4x + 5.

Consider the range of values from x = 0 to x = 10.

SOLUTION

The first step is to draw up a table for the equation. Although the problem mentions x = 0 to x = 10, it is not necessary to calculate values of y for x = 1, 2, 3 etc. A graph of a linear equation can actually be drawn from just two (x, y) values but it is always best to calculate a number of values in case you make an arithmetical error. We have calculated five values, but three would be enough in your assessment.

x	*y*
0	5
2	13
4	21
6	29
8	37
10	45

Graph of y = 4x +5

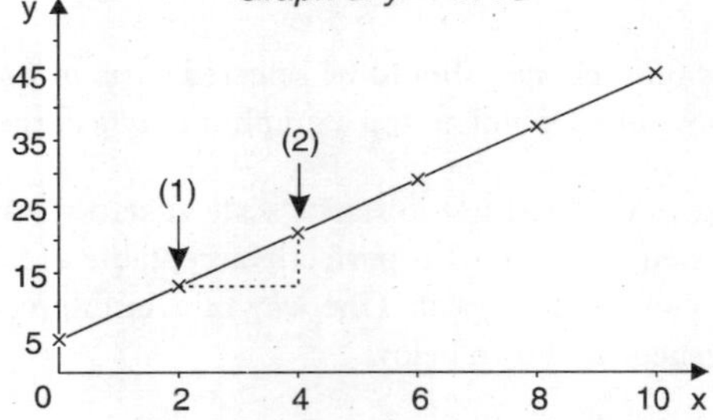

The intercept and the gradient

The graph of a linear equation is determined by two things:

- The gradient (or slope) of the straight line
- The point at which the straight line crosses the y axis

Definitions

- The **intercept** is the point at which a straight line crosses the y-axis.
- The **gradient** of the graph of a linear equation is $\frac{\text{change in y}}{\text{change in x}} = (y_2 - y_1)/(x_2 - x_1)$ where (x_1, y_1) and (x_2, y_2) are two points on the straight line.

The intercept

The intercept of $y = 4x + 5$ is where $y = 5$. It is no coincidence that the intercept is the same as the constant represented by a in the general form of the equation $y = a + bx$. a is the value y takes when $x = 0$, in other words a constant.

The gradient

If we take two points on the line (see graph above)

(1) $x = 2, y = 13$
(2) $x = 4, y = 21$

The gradient of $y = 4x + 5 = \frac{\text{change in y}}{\text{change in x}} = \frac{(21-13)}{(4-2)} = \frac{8}{2} = 4$

Notice that the gradient is also given by the number multiplied by x in the equation (b in the general form of the equation).

Activity 4 **(2 minutes)**

If $y = 10 - x$, the gradient = ☐

Activity 5 **(5 minutes)**

If $y = 10 - x$, the gradient = ☐

What is the intercept and gradient of the graph of $4y = 16x - 12$?

	Intercept	*Gradient*
A	– 3	+ 4
B	– 4	+ 3
C	+ 3	– 4
D	+ 4	– 3

Positive and negative gradients

Note that the gradient of $y = 4x + 5$ is positive whereas the gradient of $y = 10 - x$ is negative.

- A positive gradient slopes upwards from left to right
- A negative gradient slopes downwards from left to right
- The greater the value of the gradient, the steeper the slope

Activity 6 **(15 minutes)**

A company manufactures a product. The total fixed costs are £75 and the variable cost per unit is £5.

Required

(a) Find an expression for total costs (c) in terms of q, the quantity produced.

(b) Use your answer to (a) to determine the total costs if 100 units are produced.

(c) Prepare a graph of the expression for total costs.

(d) Use your graph to determine the total cost if 75 units are produced.

2.2 Simultaneous equations

Definition

Simultaneous equations are two or more equations which are satisfied by the same variable values. They can be solved graphically or algebraically.

EXAMPLE: SIMULTANEOUS EQUATIONS

The following two linear equations both involve the unknown values x and y. There are as many equations as there are unknowns and so we can find the values of x and y.

$$y = 3x + 16$$
$$2y = x + 72$$

SOLUTION: GRAPHICAL APPROACH

One way of finding a solution is by a **graph**. If both equations are satisfied together, the values of x and y must be those where the straight line graphs of the two equations **intersect**.

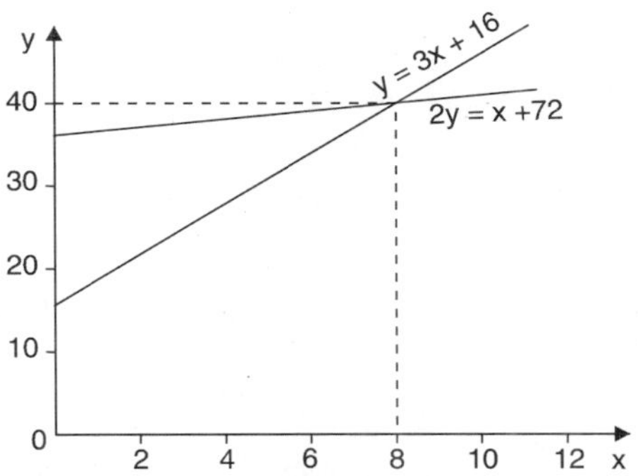

Since both equations are satisfied, the values of x and y must lie on both the lines. Since this happens only once, at the intersection of the lines, the value of x must be 8, and of y 40.

SOLUTION: ALGEBRAIC APPROACH

A more common method of solving simultaneous equations is by **algebra**:

(a) Returning to the original equations, we have

$$y = 3x + 16 \qquad (1)$$
$$2y = x + 72 \qquad (2)$$

(b) Rearranging these, we have

$$y - 3x = 16 \qquad (3)$$
$$2y - x = 72 \qquad (4)$$

(c) If we now multiply equation (4) by 3, so that the coefficient for x becomes the same as in equation (3) we get

$$6y - 3x = 216 \qquad (5)$$
$$y - 3x = 16 \qquad (3)$$

(d) Subtracting (3) from (5) we get

$$5y = 200$$
$$y = 40$$

(e) Substituting 40 for y in any equation, we can derive a value for x. Thus substituting in equation (4) we get

$$2(40) - x = 72$$
$$80 - 72 = x$$
$$8 = x$$

(f) The solution is $y = 40$, $x = 8$.

Activity 7 **(10 minutes)**

Solve the following simultaneous equations using algebra.

$5x + 2y = 34$
$x + 3y = 25$

2.3 Non-linear equations

So far we have looked at equations in which the highest power of the unknown variable(s) is one (that is, the equation contains x, y but not x^2, y^3 and so on). We are now going to turn our attention to **non-linear equations**.

EXAMPLES – NON-LINEAR EQUATIONS

(a) $y = x^2$; $y = 3x^3 + 2$; $2y = 5x^4 - 6$; $y = -x^{12} + 3$

(b) It is common for a non-linear equation to include a number of terms, all to different powers. Here are some examples.

$y = x^2 + 6x + 10$ $\qquad y = -12x^9 + 3x^6 + 6x^3 + 3x^2 - 1$

$2y = 3x^3 - 4x^2 - 8x + 10$ $\qquad 3y = 22x^8 + 7x^7 + 3x^4 - 12$

Graphing non-linear equations

The graph of a **linear equation**, as we saw earlier, is a **straight line**. The graph of a **non-linear equation**, on the other hand, **is not a straight line**. Let us consider an example.

EXAMPLE: GRAPHING NON-LINEAR EQUATIONS

Graph the equation $y = -2x^3 + x^2 - 2x + 10$.

SOLUTION

The graph of this equation can be plotted in the same way as the graph of a linear equation is plotted. Take a selection of values of x, calculate the corresponding values of y, plot the pairs of values and join the points together. The joining must be done using as smooth a curve as possible.

x	*–3*	*–2*	*–1*	*0*	*1*	*2*	*3*
$-2x$	6	4	2	0	–2	–4	–6
x^2	9	4	1	0	1	4	9
$-2x^3$	54	16	2	0	–2	–16	–54
10	10	10	10	10	10	10	10
y	79	34	15	10	7	–6	–41

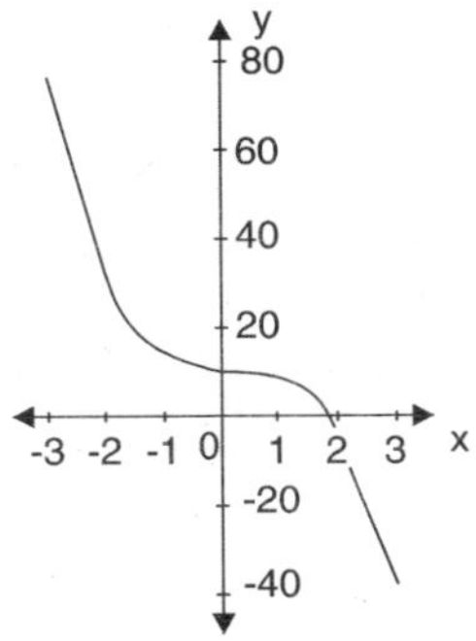

Quadratic equations

Definition

> **Quadratic equations** are a type of **non-linear equation** in which one variable varies with the square (or second power) of the other variable. They can be expressed in the form $y = ax^2 + bx + c$.

A **quadratic equation** may include both a term involving the square and also a term involving the **first power** of a variable. Here are some examples.

$y = x^2$ $\quad$ $y = x^2 + 6x + 10$ $\quad$ $2y = 3x^2 - 4x - 8$ $\quad$ $y = 5x^2 + 7$

In the equation $y = 3x^2 + 2x - 6$, $a = 3$, $b = 2$, $c = -6$.

Graphing a quadratic equation

The graph of a quadratic equation can be plotted using the same method as that illustrated above.

EXAMPLE: GRAPHING A QUADRATIC EQUATION

Graph the equation $y = -2x^2 + x - 3$

SOLUTION

x	*−3*	*−2*	*−1*	*0*	*1*	*2*	*3*
$-2x^2$	−18	−8	−2	0	−2	−8	−18
−3	−3	−3	−3	−3	−3	−3	−3
y	−24	−13	−6	−3	−4	−9	−18

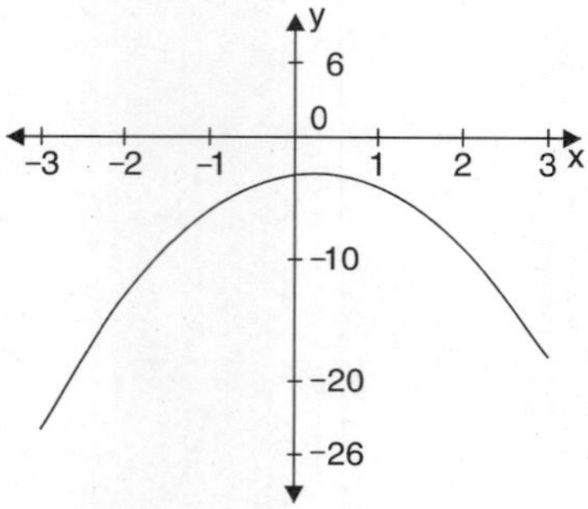

Parabolas

The graphs of quadratic equations are **parabolas**, the sign of 'a' in the general form of the quadratic equation ($y = ax^2 + bx + c$) determining the way up the curve appears.

(a) The constant term 'c' determines the value of y at the point where the curve crosses the y axis (the intercept). In the graph above, $c = -3$ and the curve crosses the y axis at $y = -3$.

(b) The sign of 'a' determines the way up the curve appears:

- If 'a' is positive, the curve is shaped like a ditch.
- If 'a' is negative, as illustrated above, the curve is shaped like a bell.

A ditch-shaped curve is said to have a **minimum point** whereas a bell-shaped curve is said to have a **maximum point**.

(c) The graph enables us to find the values of x when $y = 0$ (if there are any). In other words the graph allows us to solve the quadratic equation $0 = ax^2 + bx + c$. For the curve above we see that there are no such values (that is, $0 = -2x^2 + x - 3$ cannot be solved).

Solving quadratic equations

The graphical method is not, in practice, the most efficient way to determine the solution of a quadratic equation. Many quadratic equations have two values of x (called '**solutions for x**' or '**roots of the equation**') which satisfy the equation for any particular value of y.

Quadratic equations can be solved by the formula

$$x = \frac{-b \pm \sqrt{(b^2 - 4ac)}}{2a} \quad \text{when } ax^2 + bx + c = 0$$

EXAMPLE: QUADRATIC EQUATIONS

Solve $x^2 + x - 2 = 0$.

SOLUTION

For the equation $x^2 + x - 2 = 0$

$a = 1$
$b = 1$
$c = -2$

We can insert these values into the quadratic equation formula.

$$x = \frac{-b \pm \sqrt{(b^2 - 4ac)}}{2a}$$

$$x = \frac{-1 \pm \sqrt{(1^2 - (4 \times 1 \times (-2)))}}{2 \times 1} = \frac{-1 \pm \sqrt{(1+8)}}{2} = \frac{-1 \pm 3}{2}$$

$$\therefore x = \frac{-4}{2} \text{ or } \frac{2}{2} \text{ ie } x = -2 \text{ or } x = 1$$

Quadratic equations with a single value for x

Sometimes, $b^2 - 4ac = 0$, and so there is only one solution to the quadratic equation. Let us solve $x^2 + 2x + 1 = 0$ using the formula above where $a = 1, b = 2$ and $c = 1$.

$$x = \frac{-2 \pm \sqrt{(2^2 - (4 \times 1 \times 1))}}{2} = \frac{-2 \pm 0}{2} = -1$$

This quadratic equation can only be solved by one value of x.

Activity 8 **(15 minutes)**

Non-linear graphs

A company manufactures a product, the total cost function for the product being given by $C = 25q - q^2$, where q is the quantity produced and C is in £.

Required

(a) Calculate the total costs if 15 units are produced.

(b) Draw a graph of the total cost function and use it to calculate the total cost if 23 units are produced.

Chapter roundup

- A formula enables us to calculate the value of one variable from the value(s) of one or more other variables.
- The **general rule for solving equations** is that you must always do the same thing to both sides of the equal sign so the scales stay balanced.
- An inequality is a statement that shows the relationship between two (or more) expressions with one of the following signs: >, ≥, <, ≤. We can solve inequalities in the same way that we can solve equations.
- A **linear equation** has the general form **y = a + bx**, where x is the independent variable and y the dependent variable, and a and b are fixed amounts.
- The **graph of a linear equation is a straight** line, where y = a + bx. The intercept of the line on the y axis = a and the gradient of the line = b.
- **Simultaneous equations** are two or more equations which are satisfied by the same variable values. They can be solved graphically or algebraically.
- In **non-linear equations**, one variable varies with the nth power of another, where n > 1. The graph of a non-linear equation is *not* a straight line.
- **Quadratic equations** are a type of **non-linear equation** in which one variable varies with the square (or second power) of the other variable. They can be expressed in the form $y = ax^2 + bx + c$.
- The graphs of quadratic equations are **parabolas**, the sign of 'a' in the general form of the quadratic equation ($y = ax^2 + bx + c$) determining the way up the curve appears.
- **Quadratic equations** can be solved by the formula

$$x = \frac{-b \pm \sqrt{(b^2 - 4ac)}}{2a} \text{ when } ax^2 + bx + c = 0$$

Quick quiz

1 A linear equation has the general form y = a + bx where

y		independent variable
x	?	constant (fixed amount)
b		constant (coefficient of x)
a		dependent variable

2 The horizontal axis on a graph is known as the y axis.

True ☐

False ☐

3 The intercept is ....

		True	False
4	(a) A positive gradient slopes upwards from right to left	☐	☐
	(b) A negative gradient slopes downwards from left to right	☐	☐
	(c) The greater the value of the gradient, the steeper the slope	☐	☐

5 What are simultaneous equations?

6 In what form are quadratic equations usually expressed?

7 Consider the equation $\mathbf{y = -4x^2 + 3x - 2}$

(a) The graph of the equation is shaped like a ditch/bell

(b) The graph of the equation has a minimum/maximum point

(c) The point at which the curve crosses the y axis is ....

8 Use the symbols and numbers below to construct the formula for solving a quadratic equation.

x, –b, –4, a, a, √, =, ±, b^2, c, 2

Answers to quick quiz

1 y = dependent variable

x = independent variable

b = constant (coefficient of x)

a = constant (fixed amount)

2 False

3 The point at which a straight line crosses the y-axis

4 (a) False

(b) True

(c) True

5 Two or more equations which are satisfied by the same variable values

6 $y = ax^2 + bx + c$

7 (a) bell

(b) maximum point

(c) –2

8 $x = \frac{-b \pm \sqrt{(b^2 - 4ac)}}{2a}$

Answers to activities

1 (a) $\boxed{x = 51.2}$

$$\begin{aligned} 47x + 256 &= 52x \\ 256 &= 5x && \text{(subtract 47x from each side)} \\ 51.2 &= x && \text{(divide each side by 5)} \end{aligned}$$

(b) $\boxed{x = 4.7}$

$$\begin{aligned} 4\sqrt{x} + 32 &= 40.6718 \\ 4\sqrt{x} &= 8.6718 && \text{(subtract 32 from each side)} \\ \sqrt{x} &= 2.16795 && \text{(divide each side by 4)} \\ x &= 4.7 && \text{(square each side)} \end{aligned}$$

(c) $\boxed{x = -1.789}$

$$\begin{aligned} \frac{1}{3x+4} &= \frac{5}{2.7x-2} \\ 3x + 4 &= \frac{2.7x-2}{5} && \text{(take the reciprocal of each side)} \\ 15x + 20 &= 2.7x - 2 && \text{(multiply each side by 5)} \\ 12.3x &= -22 && \text{(subtract 20 and subtract 2.7x from each side)} \\ x &= -1.789 && \text{(divide each side by 12.3)} \end{aligned}$$

2 (a)

$$\begin{aligned} x &= (3y - 20)^2 \\ \sqrt{x} &= 3y - 20 && \text{(take the square root of each side)} \\ 20 + \sqrt{x} &= 3y && \text{(add 20 to each side)} \\ y &= \frac{20 + \sqrt{x}}{3} && \text{(divide each side by 3, and swap the sides for ease of reading)} \end{aligned}$$

(b)

$$\begin{aligned} 2(y - 4) - 4(x^2 + 3) &= 0 \\ 2(y - 4) &= 4(x^2 + 3) && \text{(add } 4(x^2 + 3) \text{ to each side)} \\ 0.5(y - 4) &= x^2 + 3 && \text{(divide each side by 4)} \\ 0.5(y - 4) - 3 &= x^2 && \text{(subtract 3 from each side)} \\ x &= \sqrt{0.5(y-4)-3} && \text{(take the square root of each side, and swap the sides for ease of reading)} \\ x &= \sqrt{0.5y - 5} \end{aligned}$$

3 (a) $2x > 11$

$x > \frac{11}{2}$ (divide both sides by 2)

$x > 5.5$

(b) $x + 3 > 15$

$x > 12$ (subtract 3 from both sides)

(c) $-3x < 7$

$-x < \frac{7}{3}$ (divide both sides by 3)

$x > -\frac{7}{3}$ (multiply both sides by –1 and so reverse the inequality)

(d) $7x + 11 > 2x + 5$

$5x > -6$ (subtract 2x and 11 from both sides)

$x > -\frac{6}{5}$ (divide both sides by 5)

(e) $2(x + 3) < x + 1$

$2x + 6 < x + 1$ (multiply out the brackets)

$x < -5$ (subtract x and 6 from both sides)

4 The gradient = | –1 |

If $y = 10 - x$, then $a = 10$ and $b = -1$ ($-1 \times x = -x$).

Therefore gradient = –1

5 $4y = 16x - 12$

Equation must be in the form $y = a + bx$

$y = 4x - 3$ (divide both sides by 4)

$y = -3 + 4x$ (rearrange the RHS)

Intercept = a = –3

Gradient = b = 4

Therefore the correct answer is A.

If you selected option D, you have obviously confused the intercept and the gradient. Remember that with an equation in the form $y = a + bx$, a = intercept (ie where the line of the graph crosses the y axis) and b = the slope or gradient of the line.

6 (a) Let C = total costs
C = total variable costs + total fixed costs
$C = 5q + 75$

(b) If q = 100, C = (5 × 100) + 75 = £575

(c) If q = 0, C = £75
If q = 100, C = £575

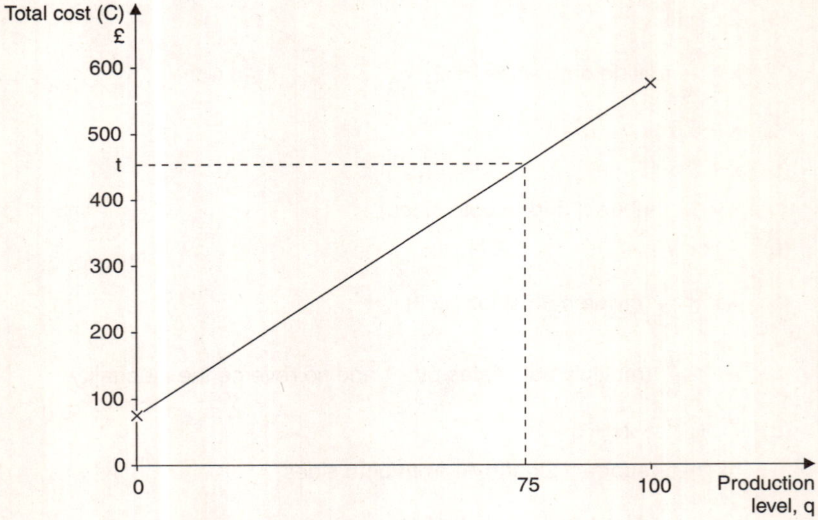

(d) From graph above, if q = 75, C = £450

7 $5x + 2y = 34$ (1)

$x + 3y = 25$ (2)

Multiply (2) × 5:

$5x + 15y = 125$ (3)

Subtract (1) from (3):

$13y = 91$

$y = 7$

Substitute into (2):

$x + 21 = 25$

$x = 25 - 21$

$x = 4$

The solution is x = 4, y = 7.

8 (a) $C = 25q - q^2$

If q = 15, $C = (25 \times 15) - 15^2 = 375 - 225 = £150$

(b)

q	*C*
0	0
5.0	100.00
10.0	150.00
12.5	156.25
15.0	150.00
20.0	100.00
25.0	0

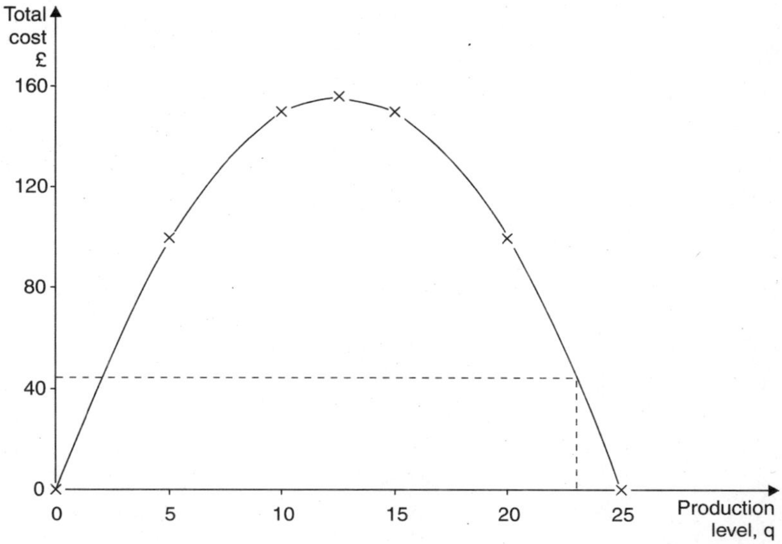

From the graph, if 23 units are produced the total cost is approximately £45.

Chapter 3 :

DATA PRESENTATION AND MEASUREMENTS OF LOCATION AND DISPERSION

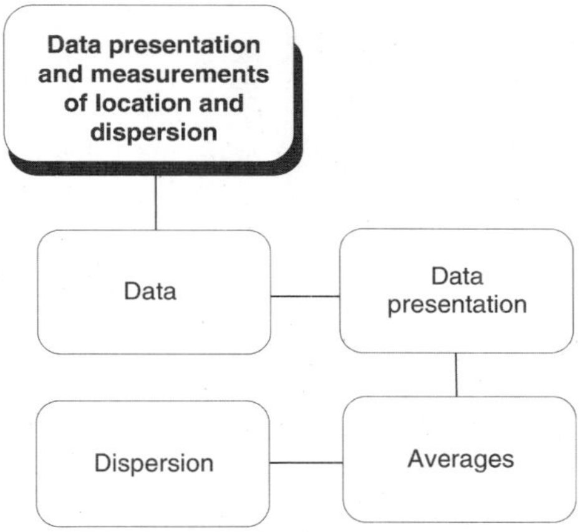

Introduction

The words 'quantitative methods' often strike terror into the hearts of students. They conjure up images of complicated mathematical formulae, scientific analysis of reams of computer output and the drawing of strange graphs and diagrams. Such images are wrong. Quantitative methods simply involves:

- **Collecting data**
- **Presenting the data in a useful form**
- **Inspecting the data**

A study of the subject will demonstrate that quantitative methods is nothing to be afraid of and that a knowledge of it is extremely advantageous in your working environment.

We will start our study of quantitative methods by looking at **data collection.**

We then consider how to **present** the data we have collected so that they can be of use. We begin by looking at how data can be presented in **tables** and **charts.** Such methods are helpful in presenting key data in a **concise** and **easy to understand way.**

Data that are a mass of numbers can usefully be summarised into a **frequency distribution. Histograms** and **ogives** are the **pictorial representation** of grouped and cumulative frequency distributions.

Sometimes you might need more information than that provided by diagrammatic representations of data. In such circumstances you may need to apply some sort of numerical analysis, for example you might wish to calculate a **measure of centrality** and a **measure of dispersion**.

An **average** is a representative figure that is used to give some impression of the size of all the items in the population. There are three main types of average.

- Arithmetic mean
- Mode
- Median

We will be looking at each of these averages in turn, their calculation, advantages and disadvantages and then we will move on to the second type of numerical measure, measures of dispersion.

Measures of dispersion give some idea of the **spread of a variable about its average**. The main measures we look at are the:

- range
- semi-interquartile range
- standard deviation.

Your objectives

In this chapter you will learn about the following:

- Data types
- Data presentation
- Averages
- Dispersion

1 DATA

Data
Data and information
Quantitative and qualitative data
Primary and secondary data
Discrete and continuous data

1.1 Data and information

Definition

> **Data** are the raw materials for data processing. **Information** is data that has been processed.

Examples of data

- The number of tourists who visit Hong Kong each year.
- The sales turnovers of all restaurants in Salisbury.
- The number of people (with black hair) who pass their driving test each year.

Information is sometimes referred to as processed data. The terms 'information' and 'data' are often used interchangeably. Let us consider the following situation in which data is **collected** and then **processed** in order to produce meaningful information.

EXAMPLE: DATA AND INFORMATION

Many companies providing a product or service like to research consumer opinion, and employ market research organisations to do so. A typical market research survey employs a number of researchers who request a sample of the public to answer questions relating to the product. Several hundred questionnaires may be completed. The questionnaires are input to a system. Once every questionnaire has been input, a number of processing operations are performed on the data. A report which summarises the results and discusses their significance is sent to the company that commissioned the survey.

Individually, a completed questionnaire would not tell the company very much, only the views of one consumer. In this case, the individual questionnaires are **data.** Once they have been processed, and analysed, the resulting report is **information**. The company will use it to inform its decisions regarding the product. If the report revealed that consumers disliked the product, the company would scrap or alter it.

The **quality of source data** affects the value of information. Information is worthless if the source data is flawed. If the researchers filled in questionnaires themselves, inventing the answers, then the conclusions drawn from the processed data would be wrong, and poor decisions would be made.

1.2 Quantitative and qualitative data

Definitions

> **Quantitative data** are data that can be measured. A **'variable'** is something which can be measured.
>
> **Qualitative data** cannot be measured, but have **attributes** (an attribute is something an object either has or does not have).

Examples of quantitative data include the following:

- The temperature on each day of January in Singapore. This can be **measured** in degrees Fahrenheit or Celsius.
- The time it takes you to swim 50 lengths. This can be **measured** in hours and minutes.

An example of **qualitative data** is whether someone is male or female. Whether you are male or female is an **attribute** because the sex of a person cannot be measured.

Quantitative and qualitative information

Just as data may be quantitative or qualitative, so too may information.

An example of **quantitative information** is 'The Chairman of the company has announced that the turnover for the year is **£4 million.**' You can see how this information is easily expressed in numerical terms.

An example of **qualitative information** is 'The standard of the books produced was **very high.**' This information cannot easily be expressed in terms of numbers, as the standard of something is usually described as being very high, quite low, or average and so on.

We have already seen how data can be classified as being quantitative or qualitative.

Classifying data

We shall now consider the ways in which data may be further classified as follows:

- Primary and secondary data
- Discrete and continuous data

1.3 Primary and secondary data

Definition

> Data may be **primary** (collected specifically for the purpose of a survey) or **secondary** (collected for some other purpose).

(a) **Primary data** are data collected especially for the purpose of whatever survey is being conducted. Raw data are primary data which have not been processed at all, and which are still just a list of numbers.

(b) **Secondary data** are data which have already been collected elsewhere, for some other purpose, but which can be used or adapted for the survey being conducted.

1.4 Discrete and continuous data

Quantitative data may be further classified as being **discrete** or **continuous.**

Definition

> **Discrete** data/variables can only take on a countable number of values. **Continuous** data/variables can take on any value.

(a) **Discrete data** are the number of goals scored by Arsenal against Chelsea in the FA Cup Final: Arsenal could score 0, 1, 2, 3 or even 4 goals (**discrete variables** = 0, 1, 2, 3, 4), but they cannot score 1½ or 2½ goals.

(b) **Continuous data** include the heights of all the members of your family, as these can take on any value: 1.542m, 1.639m and 1.492m for example. **Continuous variables** = 1.542, 1.639, 1.492.

The following diagram should help you to remember the ways in which data may be classified.

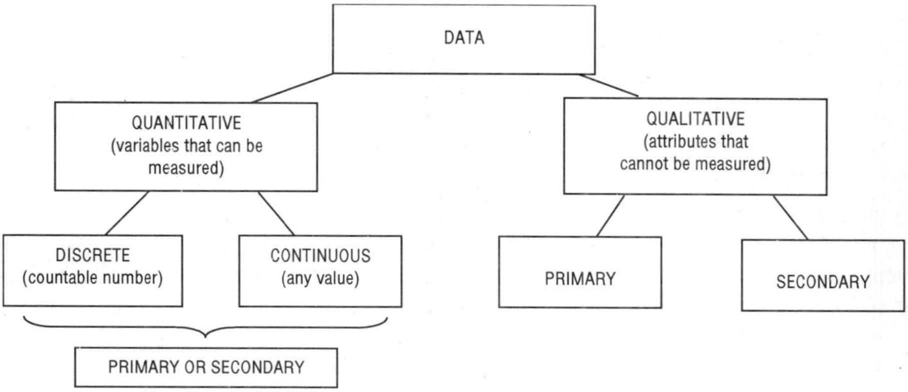

Activity 1 **(20 minutes)**

Quantitative and qualitative data

Look through the following list of surveys and decide whether each is collecting qualitative data or quantitative data. If you think the data is quantitative, indicate whether it is discrete or continuous.

(a) A survey of accountancy textbooks, to determine how many diagrams they contain.

(b) A survey of greetings cards on a newsagent's shelf, to determine whether or not each has a price sticker on it.

(c) A survey of the results in a cost accounting assessment, to determine what percentage of marks the students obtained.

(d) A survey of heights of telegraph poles in Papua New Guinea, to find out if there is any variation across the country.

(e) A survey of swimmers to find out how long they take to swim a kilometre.

2 DATA PRESENTATION

Data presentation
Pictograms
Tables
Charts
Frequency distributions
Histograms
Ogives
Scatter diagrams

2.1 Pictograms

A **pictogram** is the simplest form of diagram for information. A picture is used to represent a certain number of sales, services provided etc and the total for the period is then presented as the correct number of these pictures plus a proportion of the picture to make up the actual amount.

EXAMPLE: HOW IT WORKS

A gymnasium currently has 530 male members and 480 female members.

This could be represented in a pictogram.

Gymnasium – current membership

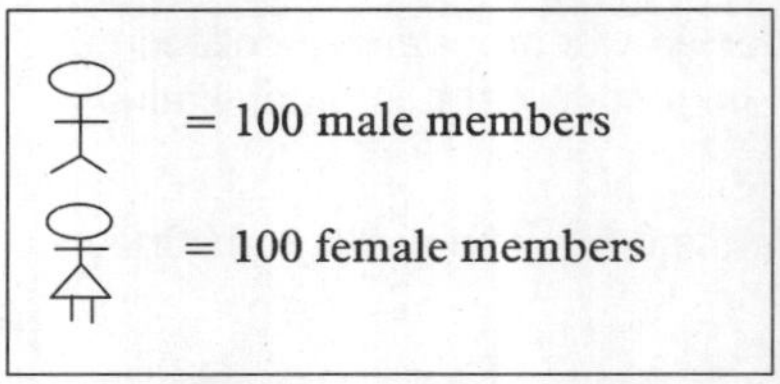

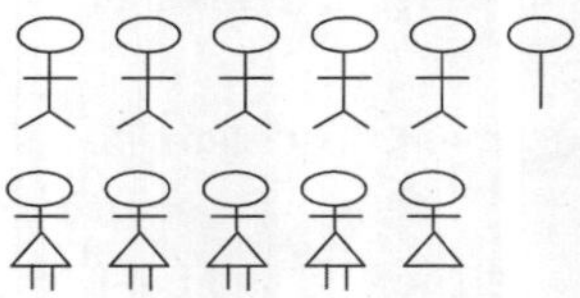

Note the following points:

- There is a title indicating clearly what the diagram is showing
- There is key showing what each picture means

A pictogram has an immediate visual impact but can only be used for very simple information, and it is never possible to determine the exact number that a part of one of the pictures represents.

2.2 Tables

Tables and tabulation

Tables are a simple way of presenting information about two variables.

Raw data (for example a list of results from a survey) need to be **summarised** and **analysed**, to give them meaning. One of the most basic ways is the preparation of a **table**.

Since a table is **two-dimensional**, it can only show **two variables**. To tabulate data, you need to recognise what the two dimensions should represent, prepare **rows** and **columns** accordingly with suitable **titles**, and then **insert the data** into the appropriate places in the table.

EXAMPLE: TABLES

The total number of employees in a certain trading company is 1,000. They are employed in three departments: production, administration and sales. 600 people are employed in the production department and 300 in administration. There are 110 males under 21 in employment, 110 females under 21, and 290 females aged 21 years and over. The remaining employees are males aged 21 and over.

In the production department there are 350 males aged 21 and over, 150 females aged 21 and over and 50 males under 21, whilst in the administration department there are 100 males aged 21 and over, 110 females aged 21 and over and 50 males aged under 21.

Draw up a table to show all the details of employment in the company and its departments and provide suitable secondary statistics to describe the distribution of people in departments.

SOLUTION

The basic table required has the following two dimensions:

- Departments
- Age/sex analysis

In this example we are going to show the percentage of the total workforce in each department.

Analysis of employees

	Department							
	Production		*Administration*		*Sales*		*Total*	
	No	%	*No*	%	*No*	%	*No*	%
Males 21 yrs +	350	58.4	100	33.3	40 **	40.0	490 *	49.0
Females 21 yrs +	150	25.0	110	36.7	30 **	30.0	290	29.0
Subtotals 21 yrs +	500	83.4	210	70.0	70	70.0	780	78.0
Males under 21	50	8.3	50	16.7	10 **	10.0	110	11.0
Females under 21	50 *	8.3	40 *	13.3	20 **	20.0	110	11.0
Subtotals under 21	100	16.6	90	30.0	30	30.0	220	22.0
Total	600	100.0	300	100.0	100	100.0	1,000	100.0

* Balancing figure to make up the column total

** Balancing figure then needed to make up the row total

Guidelines for tabulation

The example above illustrates certain guidelines which you should apply when presenting data in tabular form. These are as follows:

- The table should be given a **clear title**
- All columns should be **clearly labelled**
- Where appropriate, there should be **clear sub-totals**
- A **total column** may be presented; this would usually be the right-hand column
- A **total figure** is often advisable at the bottom of each column of figures
- Tables should not be packed with so much data that reading information is difficult
- Non-essential information should be eliminated
- Consider ordering columns/rows by order of importance/magnitude

2.3 Charts

Visual display

Charts often convey the meaning or significance of data more clearly than would a table.

Instead of presenting data in a table, it might be preferable to give a **visual display** in the form of a **chart**. The purpose of a chart is to convey the data in a way that will demonstrate its meaning more clearly than a table of data would. Charts are not always more appropriate than tables, and the most suitable way of presenting data will depend on the following.

(a) **What the data are intended to show.** Visual displays usually make one or two points quite forcefully, whereas tables usually give more detailed information.

(b) **Who is going to use the data**. Some individuals might understand visual displays more readily than tabulated data.

Bar charts

The **bar chart** is one of the most common methods of presenting data in a visual form. It is a chart in which quantities are shown in the form of bars.

There are three main types of bar chart: simple, component (including percentage component) and multiple (or compound).

Definition

> A **simple bar chart** is a chart consisting of one or more bars, in which the length of each bar indicates the magnitude of the corresponding data item.

EXAMPLE: A SIMPLE BAR CHART

A company's total sales for the years from 20X1 to 20X6 are as follows.

Year	*Sales*
	£'000
20X1	800
20X2	1,200
20X3	1,100
20X4	1,400
20X5	1,600
20X6	1,700

The data could be shown on a simple bar chart as follows:

Company sales

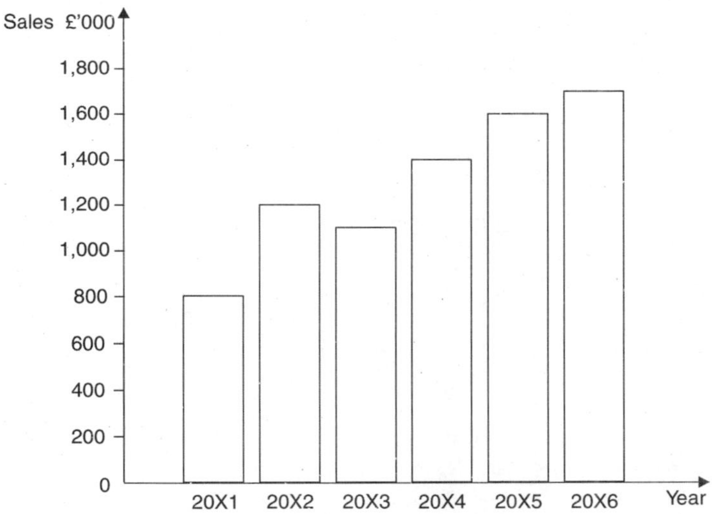

Each axis of the chart must be clearly labelled, and there must be a scale to indicate the magnitude of the data. Here, the y axis includes a scale for the amount of sales, and so readers of the bar chart can see not only that sales have been rising year by year (with 20X3 being an exception), but also what the actual sales have been each year.

Purposes of simple bar charts

Simple bar charts serve two purposes.

- The actual magnitude of each item is shown
- The lengths of bars on the chart allow magnitudes to be compared

EXAMPLE: A COMPONENT BAR CHART

Charbart plc's sales for the years from 20X7 to 20X9 are as follows.

	20X7	*20X8*	*20X9*
	£'000	*£'000*	*£'000*
Product A	1,000	1,200	1,700
Product B	900	1,000	1,000
Product C	500	600	700
Total	2,400	2,800	3,400

A component bar chart would show the following:

- How total sales have changed from year to year
- The components of each year's total

Chartbart plc sales 20X7-20X9

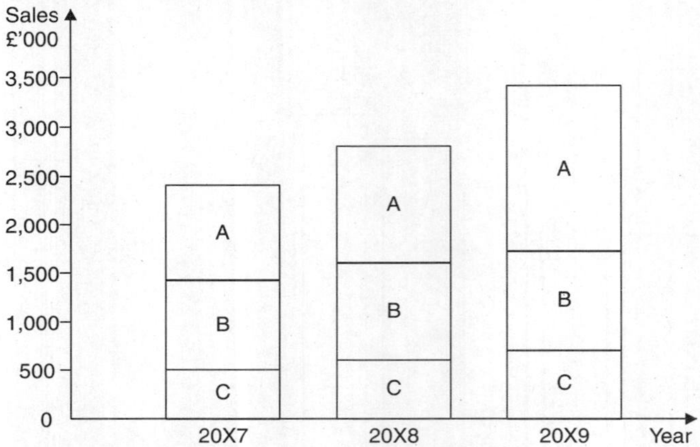

In this diagram the growth in sales is illustrated and the significance of growth in product A sales as the reason for the total sales growth is also fairly clear.

EXAMPLE: A PERCENTAGE COMPONENT BAR CHART

The information in the previous example of sales of Charbart plc could have been shown in a **percentage component bar chart** as follows.

Charbart plc sales analysis 20X7-20X9

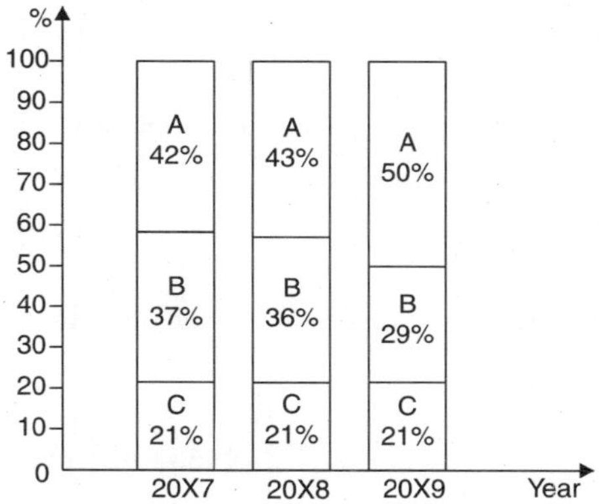

Working

	20X7		20X8		20X9	
	£'000	%	£'000	%	£'000	%
Product A	1,000	42	1,200	43	1,700	50
Product B	900	37	1,000	36	1,000	29
Product C	500	21	600	21	700	21
Total	2,400	100	2,800	100	3,400	100

This chart shows that sales of C have remained a steady proportion of total sales, but the proportion of A in total sales has gone up quite considerably, while the proportion of B has fallen correspondingly.

EXAMPLE: A MULTIPLE BAR CHART

The data on Charbart plc's sales could be shown in a multiple bar chart as follows.

Charbart plc sales analysis 20X7-X9

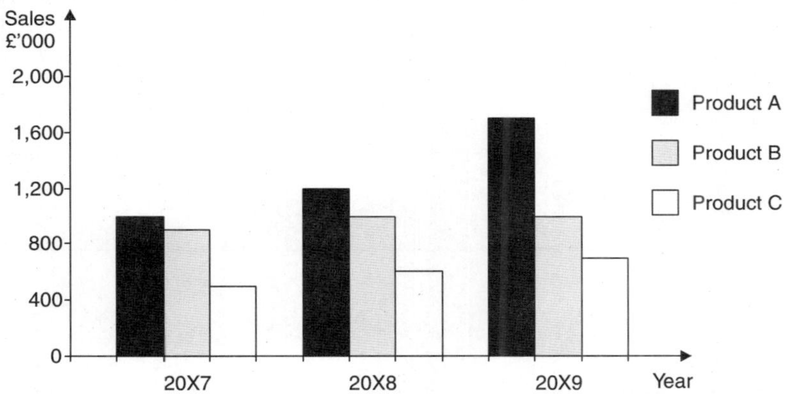

A multiple bar chart uses several bars for each total. In this multiple bar chart, the sales in each year are shown as three separate bars, one for each product, A, B and C.

Information presented by multiple bar charts

Multiple bar charts present similar information to component bar charts, except for the following:

(a) Multiple bar charts do not show the grand total whereas component bar charts do.

(b) Multiple bar charts illustrate the comparative magnitudes of the components more clearly than component bar charts.

Multiple bar charts are sometimes drawn with the bars horizontal instead of vertical.

Activity 2 **(15 minutes)**

Income for Canary Bank in 20X0, 20X1 and 20X2 is made up as follows.

	20X0	*20X1*	*20X2*
	£'000	£'000	£'000
Interest income	3,579	2,961	2,192
Commission income	857	893	917
Other income	62	59	70

Using the above data complete the following graphs.

(a) *A simple bar chart*

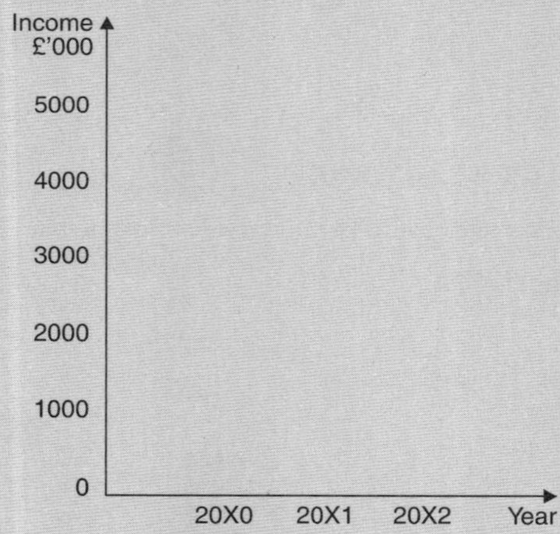

(b) *A multiple bar chart*

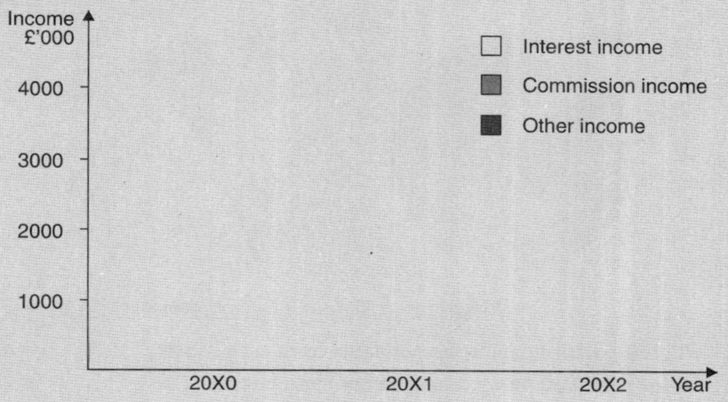

Pie charts

Definition

A **pie chart** is a chart which is used to show pictorially the relative size of component elements of a total.

It is called a pie chart because it is **circular**, and so has the **shape of a pie** in a round pie dish. The 'pie' is then cut into slices with each slice representing part of the total.

Pie charts have sectors of varying sizes, and you need to be able to draw sectors fairly accurately. To do this, you need a **protractor**. Working out sector sizes involves converting parts of the total into **equivalent degrees of a circle**. A complete 'pie' = 360°: the number of degrees in a circle = 100% of whatever you are showing. An element which is 50% of your total will therefore occupy a segment of 180°, and so on.

Using shading and colour

Two pie charts are shown as follows:

Breakdown of air and noise pollution complaints

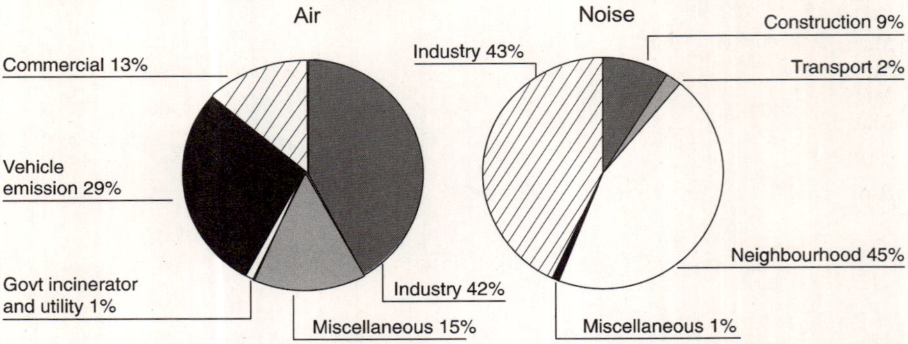

- **Shading** distinguishes the segments from each other
- **Colour** can also be used to distinguish segments

EXAMPLE: PIE CHARTS

The costs of materials at the Cardiff Factory and the Swansea Factory during January 20X0 were as follows.

	Cardiff factory		*Swansea factory*	
	£'000	%	£'000	%
Material W	70	35	50	20
Material A	30	15	125	50
Material L	90	45	50	20
Material E	10	5	25	10
	200	100	250	100

Show the costs for the factories in pie charts.

SOLUTION

To convert the components into degrees of a circle, we can use either the **percentage figures** or the **actual cost figures.**

Using the percentage figures

The total percentage is 100%, and the total number of degrees in a circle is 360°. To convert from one to the other, we multiply each percentage value by 360/100% = 3.6.

	Cardiff factory		*Swansea factory*	
	%	*Degrees*	%	*Degrees*
Material W	35	126	20	72
Material A	15	54	50	180
Material L	45	162	20	72
Material E	5	18	10	36
	100	360	100	360

Using the actual cost figures

	Cardiff factory		Swansea factory	
	£'000	*Degrees*	£'000	*Degrees*
Material W (70/200 × 360°)	70	126	50	72
Material A	30	54	125	180
Material L	90	162	50	72
Material E	10	18	25	36
	200	360	250	360

A pie chart could be drawn for each factory.

Cardiff factory

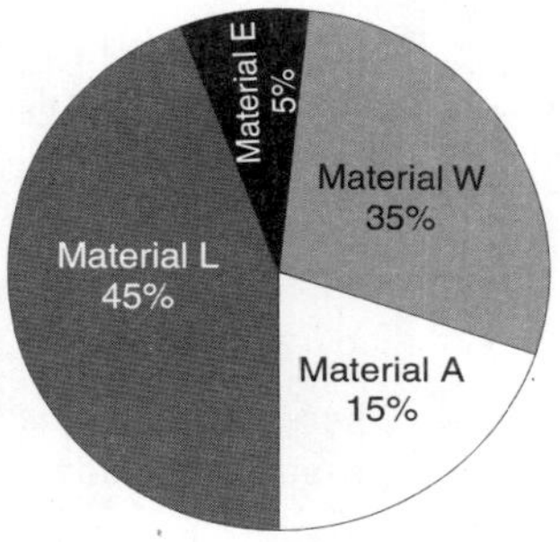

Swansea factory

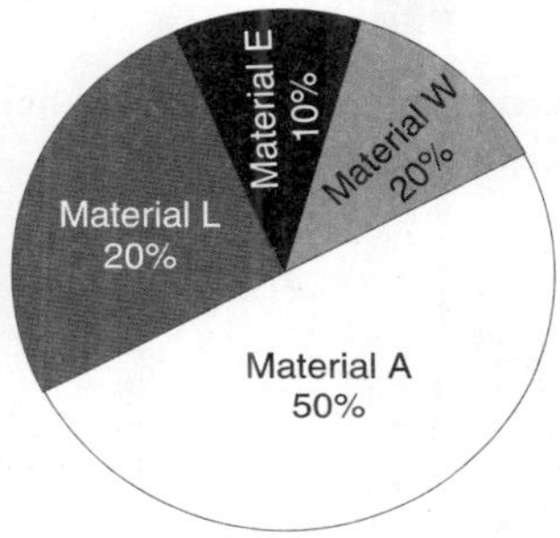

(a) If the pie chart is drawn manually, a protractor must be used to measure the degrees accurately to obtain the correct sector sizes.

(b) Using a computer makes the process much simpler, especially using a spreadsheet. You just draw up the data in a spreadsheet and click on the chart button to create a visual representation of what you want. Note that you can only use colour effectively if you have a colour printer!

Advantages of pie charts

- They give a simple pictorial display of the relative sizes of elements of a total
- They show clearly when one element is much bigger than others
- They can clearly show differences in the elements of two different totals

Disadvantages of pie charts

(a) They only show the relative sizes of elements. In the example of the two factories, for instance, the pie charts do not show that costs at the Swansea factory were £50,000 higher in total than at the Cardiff factory.

(b) They involve **calculating degrees of a circle** and drawing sectors accurately, and this can be time consuming unless computer software is used.

(c) It is often **difficult to compare sector sizes** easily. For example, suppose that the following two pie charts are used to show the elements of a company's sales.

2000

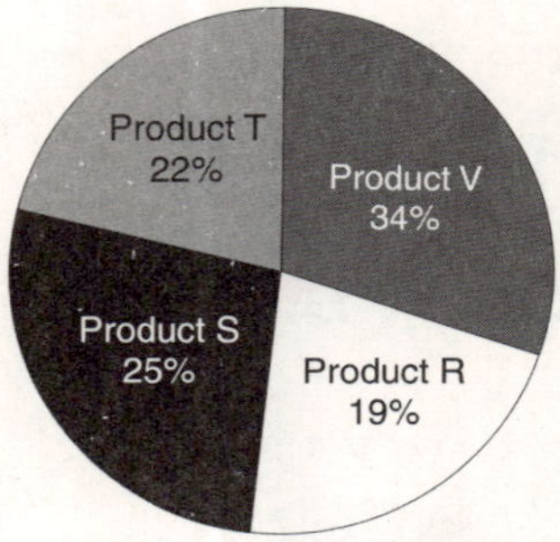

2001

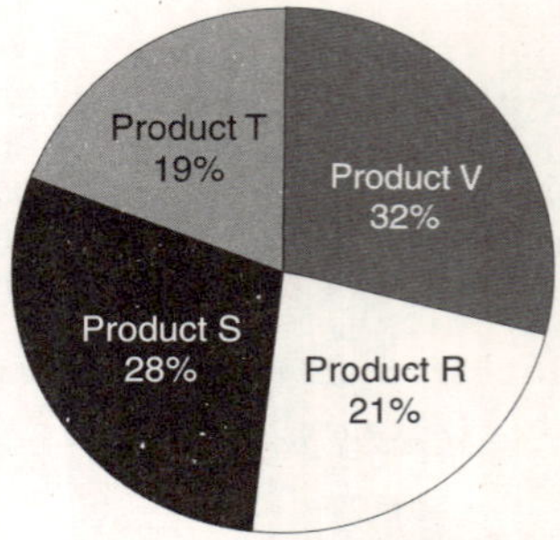

Without the percentage figures, it would not be easy to see how the distribution of sales had changed between 2000 and 2001.

Activity 3 **(25 minutes)**

The European division of Scent to You Ltd, a flower delivery service has just published its accounts for the year ended 30 June 20X0. The sales director made the following comments.

'Our total sales for the year were £1,751,000, of which £787,000 were made in the United Kingdom, £219,000 in Italy, £285,000 in France and £92,000 in Germany. Sales in Spain and Holland amounted to £189,000 and £34,000 respectively, while the rest of Europe collectively had sales of £145,000 in the twelve months to 30 June 20X0.'

Required

Present the above information in the form of a pie chart. Show all of your workings.

2.4 Frequency distributions

Introduction to frequency distributions

Frequency distributions are used if values of particular variables occur more than once. Frequently the data collected from a statistical survey or investigation is simply a mass of numbers.

65	69	70	71	70	68	69	67	70	68
72	71	69	74	70	73	71	67	69	70

The raw data above yields little information as it stands; imagine how much more difficult it would be if there were hundreds or even thousands of data items. The data could, of course, be arranged in **order size** (an **array**) and the lowest and highest data items, as well as typical items, could be identified.

EXAMPLE: FREQUENCY DISTRIBUTION

Many sets of data, however, contain a limited number of data values, even though there may be many occurrences of each value. It can therefore be useful to organise the data into what is known as a **frequency distribution** (or **frequency table**) which records the number of times each value occurs (the **frequency**). A frequency distribution for the data in Paragraph 2.4 (the output in units of 20 employees during one week) is as follows.

Output of employees in one week in units

Output Units	*Number of employees (frequency)*
65	1
66	0
67	2
68	2
69	4
70	5
71	3
72	1
73	1
74	1
	20

When the data are arranged in this way it is immediately obvious that 69 and 70 units are the most common volumes of output per employee per week.

Grouped frequency distributions

If there is a large set of data or if every (or nearly every) data item is different, it is often convenient to group frequencies together into **bands** or **classes**. For example, suppose that the output produced by another group of 20 employees during one week was as follows, in units.

1,087	850	1,084	792
924	1,226	1,012	1,205
1,265	1,028	1,230	1,182
1,086	1,130	989	1,155
1,134	1,166	1,129	1,160

Class intervals

The range of output from the lowest to the highest producer is 792 to 1,265, a **range** of 473 units. This range could be divided into classes of say, 100 units (the **class width** or **class interval**), and the number of employees producing output within each class could then be grouped into a single frequency, as follows.

Output Units	*Number of employees (frequency)*
700 – 799	1
800 – 899	1
900 – 999	2
1,000 – 1,099	5
1,100 – 1,199	7
1,200 – 1,299	4
	20

Note, however, that once items have been 'grouped' in this way their individual values are lost.

As well as being used for **discrete variables** (as above), grouped frequency distributions (or grouped frequency tables) can be used to present data for **continuous variables.**

EXAMPLE: A GROUPED FREQUENCY DISTRIBUTION FOR A CONTINUOUS VARIABLE

Suppose we wish to record the heights of 50 different individuals. The information might be presented as a grouped frequency distribution, as follows.

Height cm	*Number of individuals (frequency)*
Up to and including 154	1
Over 154, up to and including 163	3
Over 163, up to and including 172	8
Over 172, up to and including 181	16
Over 181, up to and including 190	18
Over 190	4
	50

Note the following points.

(a) It would be wrong to show the ranges as 0 – 154, 154 – 163, 163 – 172 and so on, because 154 cm and 163 cm would then be values in two classes, which is not permissible. Although each value should only be in one class, we have to make sure that each possible value can be included. Classes such as 154–162, 163–172 would not be suitable since a height of 162.5 cm would not belong in either class. Such classes could be used for discrete variables, however.

(b) **There is an open-ended class at each end of the range**. This is because heights up to 154 cm and over 190 cm are thought to be uncommon, so that a single 'open-ended' class is used to group all the frequencies together.

Guidelines for preparing grouped frequency distributions

To prepare a grouped frequency distribution, a decision must be made about how wide each class should be. You should observe the following guidelines if you are not told how many classes to use or what the class interval should be.

(a) The size of each class should be appropriate to the nature of the data being recorded, and the most appropriate class interval varies according to circumstances.

(b) The upper and lower limits of each class interval should be suitable 'round' numbers for class intervals which are in multiples of 5, 10, 100, 1,000 and so on. For example, if the class interval is 10, and data items range in value from 23 to 62 (discrete values), the class intervals should be 20–29, 30–39, 40–49, 50–59 and 60–69, rather than 23–32, 33–42, 43–52 and 53–62.

(c) With **continuous variables,** either the:

   (i) **upper limit** of a class should be '**up to and including ...**' and the **lower limit** of the next class should be '**over ...**'

   (ii) **upper limit** of a class should be '**less than...**', and the **lower limit** of the next class should be '**at least ...**'

Activity 4 **(15 minutes)**

Grouped frequency distributions

The commission earnings for May 20X0 of the assistants in a department store were as follows (in £).

60	35	53	47	25	44	55	58	47	71
63	67	57	44	61	48	50	56	61	42
43	38	41	39	61	51	27	56	57	50
55	68	55	50	25	48	44	43	49	73
53	35	36	41	45	71	56	40	69	52
36	47	66	52	32	46	44	32	52	58
49	41	45	45	48	36	46	42	52	33
31	36	40	66	53	58	60	52	66	51
51	44	59	53	51	57	35	45	46	54
46	54	51	39	64	43	54	47	60	45

Required

Prepare a grouped frequency distribution classifying the commission earnings into categories of £5 commencing with '£25 and under £30'

Cumulative frequency distributions

A cumulative frequency distribution (or cumulative frequency table) can be used to show the total number of times that a value above or below a certain amount occurs.

There are two possible cumulative frequency distributions for the grouped frequency distribution as given on page 67.

	Cumulative frequency		*Cumulative frequency*
≥ 700	20	< 800	1
≥ 800	19	< 900	2
≥ 900	18	<1,000	4
≥1,000	16	<1,100	9
≥1,100	11	<1,200	16
≥1,200	4	<1,300	20

(a) The symbol > means 'greater than' and ≥ means 'greater than or equal to'. The symbol < means 'less than' and ≤ means 'less than or equal to'. These symbols provide a convenient method of stating classes.

(b) The first cumulative frequency distribution shows that of the total of 20 employees, 19 produced 800 units or more, 18 produced 900 units or more, 16 produced 1,000 units or more and so on.

(c) The, second cumulative frequency distribution shows that, of the total of 20 employees, one produced under 800 units, two produced under 900 units, four produced under 1,000 units and so on.

Frequency distributions – a summary

Students often find frequency distributions tricky. The following summary might help to clarify the different types of frequency distribution we have covered in this section.

(a) **Frequency distribution**. Individual data items are arranged in a table showing the frequency each **individual** data item occurs.

(b) **Grouped frequency distribution – discrete variables**. Data items which are discrete variables, (eg the number of marks obtained in an examination) are divided into classes of say ten marks. The numbers of students (frequencies) scoring marks within each band are then grouped into a single frequency.

(c) **Grouped frequency distribution – continuous variables**. These are similar to the grouped frequency distributions for discrete variables (above.) However, as they are concerned with **continuous** variables note the following points.

   (i) There is an open-ended class at the end of the range.

   (ii) Class intervals must be carefully considered so that they capture all of the data once (and only once!).

(d) **Cumulative frequency distribution**. These distributions are used to show the number of times that a value above or below a certain amount occurs. Cumulative frequencies are obtained by adding the individual frequencies together.

2.5 Histograms

A **frequency distribution** can be represented pictorially by means of a **histogram**. The number of observations in a class is represented by the **area** covered by the bar, rather than by its height.

Histograms of frequency distributions with equal class intervals

If all the class intervals are the same, as in the frequency distribution given on page 67, **the bars of the histogram all have the same width and the heights will be proportional to the frequencies.** The histogram looks almost identical to a bar chart except that **the bars are joined together.** Because the bars are joined together, when presenting discrete data the data must be treated as continuous so that there are no gaps between class intervals. For example, for a cricketer's scores in various games the classes would have to be ≥ 0 but < 10, ≥ 10 but < 20 and so on, instead of 0–9, 10–19 and so on.

A histogram of the distribution from page 67 would be drawn as follows:

Histogram of weekly output

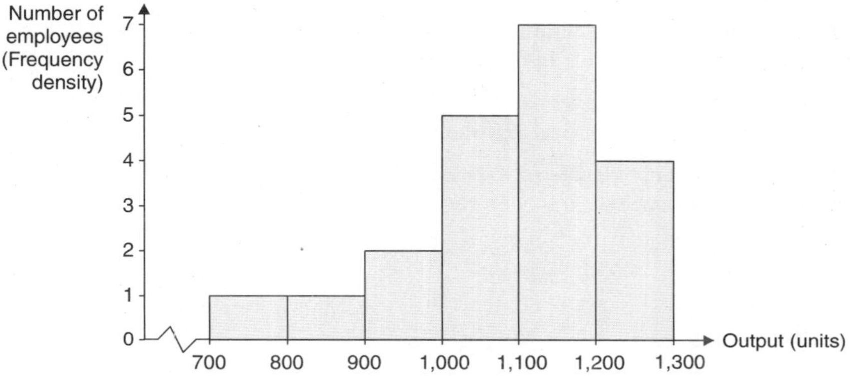

Note that the discrete data have been treated as continuous, the intervals being changed to >700 but ≤ 800, >800 but ≤ 900 and so on.

Histograms of frequency distributions with unequal class intervals

If a distribution has **unequal class intervals,** the **heights** of the bars have to be **adjusted** for the fact that the bars do not have the same width.

EXAMPLE: A HISTOGRAM WITH UNEQUAL CLASS INTERVALS

The weekly wages of employees of Salt Lake Company are as follows.

Wages per employee	*Number of employees*
Up to and including £60	4
> £60 ≤ £80	6
> £80 ≤ £90	6
> £90 ≤ £120	6
More than £120	3

The class intervals for wages per employee are not all the same, and range from £10 to £30.

SOLUTION

A histogram is drawn as follows:

(a) **The width of each bar on the chart must be proportionate to the corresponding class interval.** In other words, the bar representing wages of > £60 ≤ £80, a range of £20, will be twice as wide as the bar representing wages of > £80 ≤ £90, a range of only £10.

(b) **A standard width of bar must be selected.** This should be the size of class interval which occurs most frequently. In our example, class intervals £10, £20 and £30 each occur once. An interval of £20 will be selected as the standard width.

(c) **Open-ended classes must be closed off.** It is usual for the width of such classes to be the same as that of the adjoining class. In this example, the class 'up to and including £60' will become >£40 ≤ £60 and the class 'more than £120' will become >£120 ≤ £150.

(d) Each frequency is then multiplied by (standard class width ÷ actual class width) to obtain the height of the bar in the histogram.

(e) The height of bars no longer corresponds to **frequency** but rather to **frequency density** and hence the vertical axis should be labelled **frequency density**.

(f) Note that the data is considered to be **continuous** since the gap between, for example, £79.99 and £80.00 is very, very small.

Class interval	*Size of interval*	*Frequency*	*Adjustment*	*Height of bar*
> £40 ≤ £60	20	4	× 20/20	4
> £60 ≤ £80	20	6	× 20/20	6
> £80 ≤ £90	10	6	× 20/10	12
> £90 ≤ £120	30	6	× 20/30	4
> £120 ≤ £150	30	3	× 20/30	2

(a) The first two bars will be of normal height.

(b) The third bar will be twice as high as the class frequency (6) would suggest, to compensate for the fact that the class interval, £10, is only half the standard size.

(c) The fourth and fifth bars will be two-thirds as high as the class frequencies (6 and 3) would suggest, to compensate for the fact that the class interval, £30, is 150% of the standard size.

Histogram of weekly earnings: Salt Lake

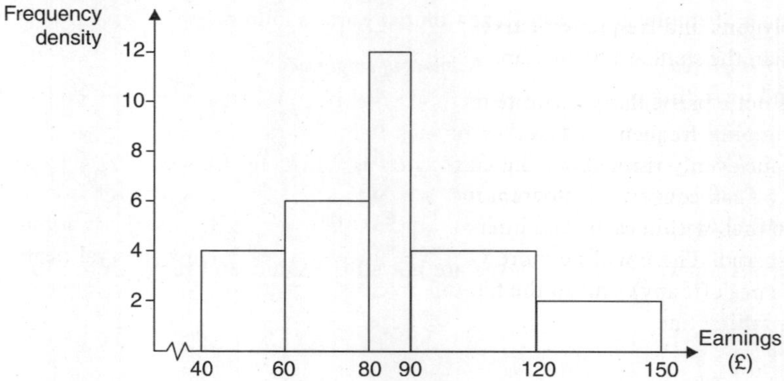

Activity 5 **(5 minutes)**

In a histogram in which one class interval is one-and-a-half times as wide as the remaining classes, the height to be plotted in relation to the frequency for that class is

A $\times 1.5$
B $\times 1.00$
C $\times 0.75$
D $\times 0.67$

Activity 6 **(20 minutes)**

The following grouped frequency distribution shows the performances of individual sales staff in one month.

Sales	*Number of sales staff*
Up to £10,000	1
> £10,000 ≤ £12,000	10
> £12,000 ≤ £14,000	12
> £14,000 ≤ £18,000	8
> £18,000 ≤ £22,000	4
> £22,000	1

Required

Draw a histogram from this information.

Frequency polygons

Frequency polygons and **frequency curves** are perhaps more accurate methods of data presentation than the standard histogram.

A histogram is not a particularly accurate method of presenting a frequency distribution because, in grouping frequencies together in a class interval, it is assumed that these frequencies occur evenly throughout the class interval, which is unlikely. To overcome this criticism, we can convert a histogram into a **frequency polygon**, which is drawn on the assumption that, within each class interval, the frequency of occurrence of data items is not evenly spread. There will be more values at the end of each class interval nearer the histogram's peak (if any), and so the flat top on a histogram bar should be converted into a rising or falling line.

Drawing a frequency polygon

A frequency polygon is drawn from a histogram, in the following way.

Step 1 Mark the mid-point of the top of each bar in the histogram.

Step 2 Join up all these points with straight lines.

Step 3 The ends of the diagram (the mid-points of the two end bars) should be joined to the base line at the mid-points of the next class intervals outside the range of observed data. These intervals should be taken to be of the same size as the last class intervals for observed data.

EXAMPLE: A FREQUENCY POLYGON

The following grouped frequency distribution relates to the number of occasions during the past 40 weeks that a particular cost has been a given amount.

Cost £	*Number of occasions*
> 800 ≤ 1,000	4
> 1,000 ≤ 1,200	10
> 1,200 ≤ 1,400	12
> 1,400 ≤ 1,600	10
> 1,600 ≤ 1,800	4
	40

Required

Prepare a frequency polygon.

SOLUTION

A histogram is first drawn, in the way described earlier. All classes are of the same width.

Histogram of frequency of particular costs

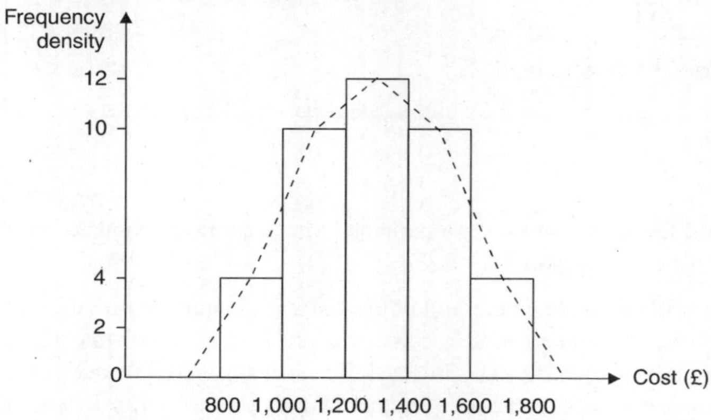

The mid-points of the class intervals outside the range of observed data are 700 and 1,900.

Frequency curves

Because a frequency polygon has straight lines between points, it too can be seen as an inaccurate way of presenting data. One method of obtaining greater accuracy would be to make the class intervals smaller. If the class intervals of a distribution were made small enough the frequency polygon would become very smooth. It would become a curve.

2.6 Ogives

Just as a grouped frequency distribution can be graphed as a histogram, a cumulative frequency distribution can be graphed as an ogive.

Definition

An **ogive** shows the cumulative number of items with a value less than or equal to, or alternatively greater than or equal to, a certain amount.

EXAMPLE

Consider the following frequency distribution.

Number of faulty units rejected on inspection	*Frequency*	*Cumulative frequency*
$> 0, \leq 1$	5	5
$> 1, \leq 2$	5	10
$> 2, \leq 3$	3	13
$> 3, \leq 4$	1	14
	14	

An ogive would be drawn as follows.

Ogive of rejected items

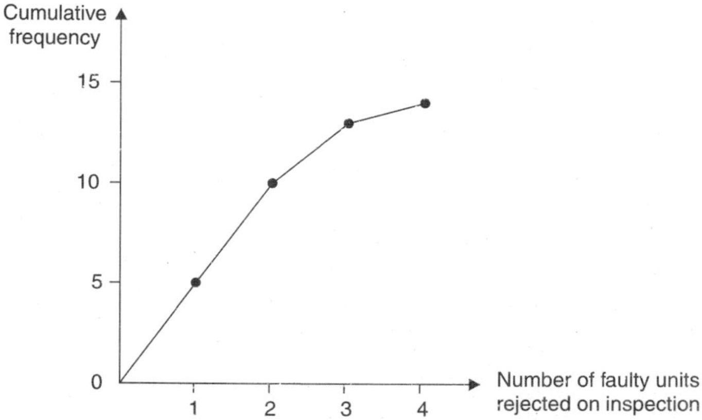

The ogive is drawn by plotting the cumulative frequencies on the graph, and joining them with straight lines. Although many ogives are more accurately curved lines, you can use straight lines to make them easier to draw. **An ogive drawn with straight lines may be referred to as a cumulative frequency polygon** (or **cumulative frequency diagram) whereas one drawn as a curve may be referred to as a cumulative frequency curve.**

For grouped frequency distributions, where we work up through values of the variable, the cumulative frequencies are plotted against the **upper limits** of the classes. For example, for the class 'over 2, up to and including 3', the cumulative frequency should be plotted against 3.

Activity 7 **(20 minutes)**

A grouped frequency distribution for the volume of output produced at a factory over a period of 40 weeks is as follows.

Output/units	*Number of times output achieved*
> 0 ≤ 200	4
> 200 ≤ 400	8
> 400 ≤ 600	12
> 600 ≤ 800	10
> 800 ≤ 1,000	6
	40

Required

Draw an appropriate ogive and estimate the number of weeks in which output was 550 units or less.

Downward-sloping ogives

We can also draw ogives to show the cumulative number of items with values greater than or equal to some given value.

EXAMPLE: DOWNWARD-SLOPING OGIVES

Output at a factory over a period of 80 weeks is shown by the following frequency distribution.

Output per week Units	*Number of times output achieved*
> 0 ≤ 100	10
> 100 ≤ 200	20
> 200 ≤ 300	25
> 300 ≤ 400	15
> 400 ≤ 500	10
	80

Required

Present this information in the form of a downward-sloping ogive.

SOLUTION

If we want to draw an ogive to show the number of weeks in which output **exceeded** a certain value, the cumulative total should begin at 80 and drop to 0. In drawing an ogive when we work down through values of the variable, the **descending cumulative frequency** should be plotted against the **lower limit** of each class interval.

Lower limit of interval	*Frequency*	*Cumulative ('more than') frequency*
0	10	80
100	20	70
200	25	50
300	15	25
400	10	10
500	0	0

Ogive of output achieved

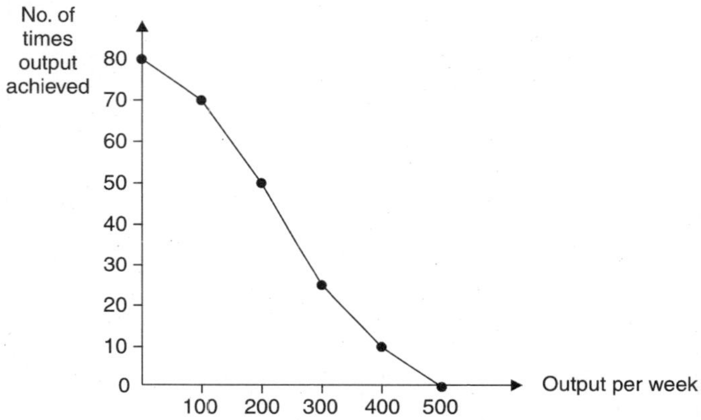

Make sure that you understand what this curve shows. For example, 350 on the x axis corresponds with about 18 on the y axis. This means that output of 350 units or more was achieved 18 times out of the 80 weeks.

2.7 Scatter diagrams

Scatter diagrams are graphs which are used to exhibit data, (rather than equations) in order to compare the way in which two variables vary with each other.

Constructing a scatter diagram

The x axis of a scatter diagram is used to represent the independent variable and the y axis represents the dependent variable.

To construct a scatter diagram or scattergraph, we must have several pairs of data, with each pair showing the value of one variable and the corresponding value of the other variable. Each pair is plotted on a graph. The resulting graph will show a number of pairs, scattered over the graph. The scattered points might or might not appear to follow a trend.

EXAMPLE: SCATTER DIAGRAM

The output at a factory each week for the last ten weeks, and the cost of that output, were as follows.

Week	*1*	*2*	*3*	*4*	*5*	*6*	*7*	*8*	*9*	*10*
Output (units)	10	12	10	8	9	11	7	12	9	14
Cost (£)	42	44	38	34	38	43	30	47	37	50

Required

Plot the data given on a scatter diagram.

SOLUTION

The data could be shown on a scatter diagram as follows.

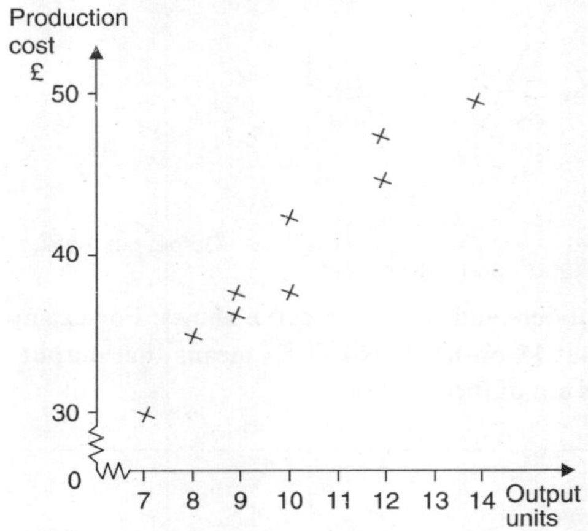

(a) The cost depends on the volume of output: volume is the independent variable and is shown on the x axis.

(b) You will notice from the graph that the plotted data, although scattered, lie approximately on a rising trend line, with higher total costs at higher output volumes. (The lower part of the axes have been omitted, so as not to waste space. The break in the axes is indicated by the jagged lines.)

The trend line

For the most part, scatter diagrams are used to try to identify **trend lines.**

If a trend can be seen in a scatter diagram, the next step is to try to draw a trend line.

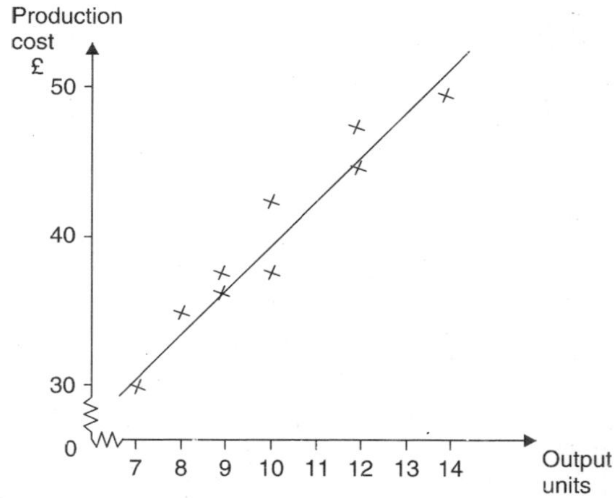

Using trend lines to make predictions

(a) In the previous example, we have drawn a trend line from the scatter diagram of output units and production cost. This trend line might turn out to be, say, $y = 10 + 3x$. We could then use this trend line to establish what we think costs ought to be, approximately if output were, say, 10 units or 15 units in any week. (These 'expected' costs could subsequently be compared with the actual costs, so that managers could judge whether actual costs were higher or lower than they ought to be.)

(b) If a scatter diagram is used to record sales over time, we could draw a trend line, and use this to forecast sales for next year.

Adding trend lines to scatter diagrams

The trend line could be a straight line, or a curved line. The simplest technique for drawing a trend line is to make a visual judgement about what the closest-fitting trend line seems to be, the 'line of best fit'.

Here is another example of a scatter diagram with a trend line added.

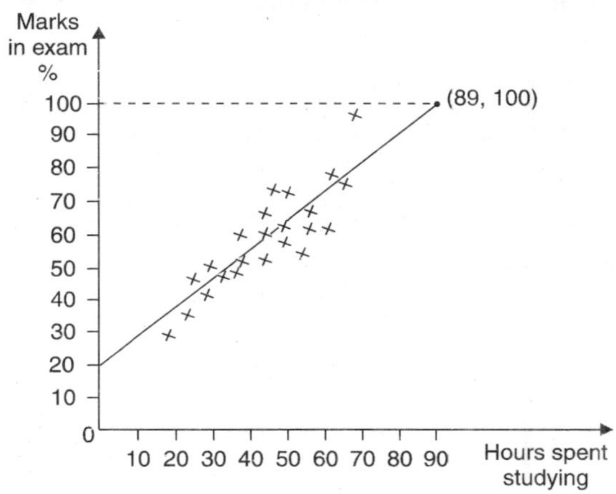

The equation of a straight line is given by y = a + bx, where a is the intercept on the y axis and b is the gradient.

The line passes through the point x = 0, y = 20, so a = 20. The line also passes through x = 89, y = 100, so:

$100 = 20 + (b \times 89)$

$$b = \frac{(100 - 20)}{89}$$

$$= 0.9$$

The line is y = 20 + 0.9x

Activity 8 **(20 minutes)**

The quantities of widgets produced by CND Ltd during the year ended 31 October 20X9 and the related costs were as follows.

Month	*Production Thousands*	*Factory cost £'000*
20X8		
November	7	45
December	10	59
20X9		
January	13	75
February	14	80
March	11	65
April	7	46
May	5	35
June	4	30
July	3	25
August	2	20
September	1	15
October	5	35

You may assume that the value of money remained stable throughout the year.

Required

(a) Draw a scatter diagram related to the data provided above and plot on it the line of best fit.

(b) Now answer the following questions.

(i) What would you expect the factory cost to have been if 12,000 widgets had been produced in a particular month?

(ii) What is your estimate of CND's monthly fixed cost?

3 AVERAGES

Averages
The arithmetic mean
The mode
The median

3.1 The arithmetic mean

Arithmetic mean of ungrouped data

The **arithmetic mean** is the best known type of average and is widely understood. It is used for further statistical analysis.

Arithmetic mean of ungrouped data $= \dfrac{\text{Sum of values of items}}{\text{Number of items}}$

The arithmetic mean of a variable x is shown as $\overline{x}$ ('x bar').

EXAMPLE: THE ARITHMETIC MEAN

The demand for a product on each of 20 days was as follows (in units).

3 12 7 17 3 14 9 6 11 10 1 4 19 7 15 6 9 12 12 8

The arithmetic mean of daily demand is $\overline{x}$.

$$\overline{x} = \frac{\text{Sum of demand}}{\text{Number of days}} = \frac{185}{20} = 9.25 \text{ units}$$

In this example, demand on any one day is never actually 9.25 units. The arithmetic mean is merely an **average representation** of demand on each of the 20 days.

Arithmetic mean of data in a frequency distribution

It is more likely in an assessment that you will be asked to calculate the arithmetic mean of a **frequency distribution**. In our previous example, the frequency distribution would be shown as follows.

Daily demand	*Frequency*	*Demand × frequency*
x	*f*	*fx*
1	1	1
3	2	6
4	1	4
6	2	12
7	2	14
8	1	8
9	2	18
10	1	10
11	1	11
12	3	36
14	1	14
15	1	15
17	1	17
19	1	19
	20	185

$$\bar{x} = \frac{185}{20} = 9.25$$

Sigma, Σ

Σ means 'the sum of' and is used as shorthand to mean 'the sum of a set of values'.

In the previous example:

(a) Σf would mean the sum of all the frequencies, which is 20

(b) Σfx would mean the sum of all the values of 'frequency multiplied by daily demand', that is, all 14 values of fx, so $\Sigma fx = 185$

Arithmetic mean of grouped data in class intervals

The **arithmetic mean of grouped data**, $\bar{x} = \frac{\Sigma fx}{n}$ or $\frac{\Sigma fx}{\Sigma f}$ where n is the number of values recorded, or the number of items measured.

You might also be asked to calculate (or at least approximate) the arithmetic mean of a frequency distribution, where the frequencies are shown in class intervals.

EXAMPLE: THE ARITHMETIC MEAN OF GROUPED DATA

Using the example given above, the frequency distribution might have been shown as follows.

Daily demand	*Frequency*
$> 0 \leq 5$	4
$> 5 \leq 10$	8
$>10 \leq 15$	6
$>15 \leq 20$	2
	20

There is, of course, an extra difficulty with finding the average now; as the data have been collected into classes, a **certain amount of detail has been lost** and the values of the variables to be used in the calculation of the mean are **not clearly specified.**

The mid-point of class intervals

To calculate the arithmetic mean of grouped data we therefore need to decide on **a value which best represents all of the values in a particular class interval.** This value is known as the **mid-point**.

The **mid-point** of each class interval is conventionally taken on the assumption that the frequencies occur **evenly** over the class interval range. In the example above, the variable is **discrete**, so the first class includes 1, 2, 3, 4 and 5, giving a mid-point of 3. With a **continuous** variable, the mid-points would have been 2.5, 7.5 and so on. Once the value of x has been decided, the mean is calculated using the formula for the arithmetic mean of grouped data.

Daily demand	*Mid-point* x	*Frequency* f	fx
$> 0 \leq 5$	3	4	12
$> 5 \leq 10$	8	8	64
$>10 \leq 15$	13	6	78
$>15 \leq 20$	18	2	36
		$\Sigma f = 20$	$\Sigma fx = 190$

Arithmetic mean $\bar{x} = \frac{\Sigma fx}{\Sigma f} = \frac{190}{20} = 9.5$ units

Because the assumption that frequencies occur evenly within each class interval is not quite correct in this example, our approximate mean of 9.5 is not exactly correct, and is in error by 0.25 (9.5 – 9.25). **As the frequencies become larger, the size of this approximating error should become smaller.**

EXAMPLE: THE ARITHMETIC MEAN OF COMBINED DATA

Suppose that the mean age of a group of five people is 27 and the mean age of another group of eight people is 32. How would we find the mean age of the whole group of 13 people?

Arithmetic mean $= \frac{\text{Sum of values of items}}{\text{Number of items}}$

The sum of the ages in the first group is $5 \times 27 = 135$
The sum of the ages in the second group is $8 \times 32 = 256$
The sum of all 13 ages is $135 + 256 = 391$

The mean age is therefore $\frac{391}{13} = 30.08$ years.

Activity 9 **(10 minutes)**

The mean weight of 10 units at 5 kgs, 10 units at 7 kgs and 20 units at X kgs is 8 kgs.

The value of X is [ ]

The advantages and disadvantages of the arithmetic mean

Advantages of the arithmetic mean

- It is easy to calculate
- It is widely understood
- It is representative of the whole set of data
- It is supported by mathematical theory and is suited to further statistical analysis

Disadvantages of the arithmetic mean

- **Its value may not correspond to any actual value.** For example, the 'average' family might have 2.3 children, but no family has exactly 2.3 children.
- **An arithmetic mean might be distorted by extremely high or low values.** For example, the mean of 3, 4, 4 and 6 is 4.25, but the mean of 3, 4, 4, 6 and 15 is 6.4. The high value, 15, distorts the average and in some circumstances the mean would be a misleading and inappropriate figure.

Activity 10 **(20 minutes)**

For the week ended 15 November, the wages earned by the 69 operators employed in the machine shop of Mermaid Ltd were as follows.

Wages	*Number of operatives*
under £60	3
£60 and under £70	11
£70 and under £80	16
£80 and under £90	15
£90 and under £100	10
£100 and under £110	8
Over £110	6
	69

Required

Calculate the arithmetic mean wage of the machine operators of Mermaid Ltd for the week ended 15 November.

3.2 The mode

The modal value

Definition

The **mode** or **modal value** is an average which means 'the most frequently occurring value'.

EXAMPLE: THE MODE

The daily demand for stock in a ten-day period is as follows.

Demand Units	*Number of days*
6	3
7	6
8	1
	10

The mode is 7 units, because it is the value which occurs most frequently.

The mode of a grouped frequency distribution

The **mode of a grouped frequency distribution** can be calculated from a histogram.

EXAMPLE: FINDING THE MODE FROM A HISTOGRAM

Consider the following grouped frequency distribution

Class interval			*Frequency*
0	and less than	10	0
10	and less than	20	50
20	and less than	30	150
30	and less than	40	100

(a) The modal class (the one with the highest frequency) is '20 and less than 30'. But how can we find a single value to represent the mode?

(b) What we need to do is draw a histogram of the frequency distribution.

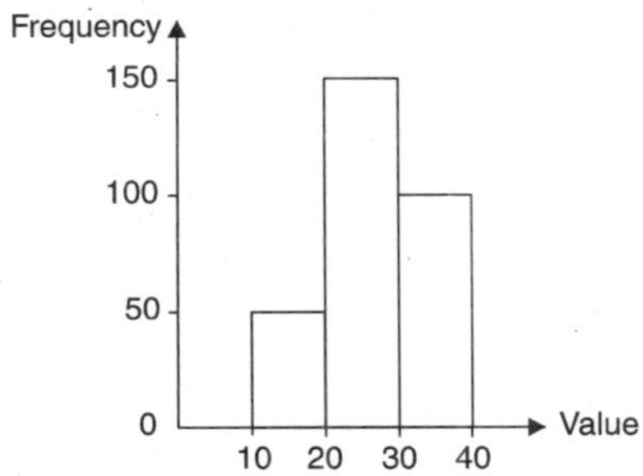

The modal class is always the class with the tallest bar. This may not be the class with the highest frequency if the classes do not all have the same width.

(c) We can estimate the mode graphically as follows.

Step 1 Join with a straight line the top left-hand corner of the bar for the modal class and the top left-hand corner of the next bar to the right.

Step 2 Join with a straight line the top right-hand corner of the bar for the modal class and the top right-hand corner of the next bar to the left.

(d) Where these two lines intersect, we find the **estimated modal value.** In this example it is approximately 26.7.

Histogram showing mode

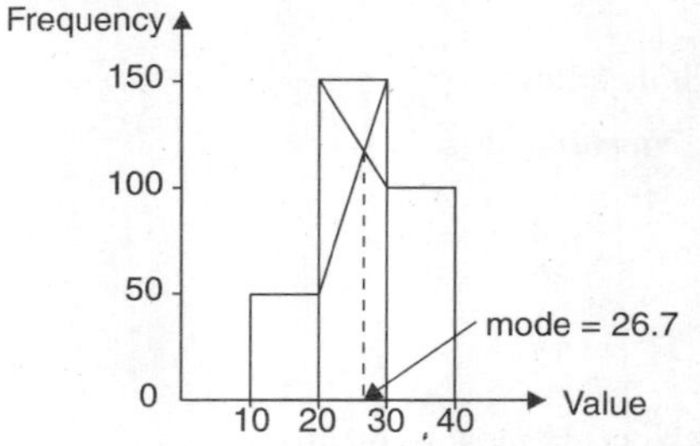

(e) We are assuming that the frequencies occur evenly within each class interval but this may not always be correct. It is unlikely that the 150 values in the modal class occur evenly. Hence **the mode in a grouped frequency distribution is only an estimate.**

The advantages and disadvantages of the mode

Advantages of the mode

- It is easy to find
- It is not influenced by a few extreme values
- It can be used for data which are not even numerical (unlike the mean and median)
- It can be the value of an actual item in the distribution

Disadvantages of the mode

- It may be unrepresentative; it takes no account of a high proportion of the data, only representing the most common value
- It does not take every value into account
- There can be two or more modes within a set of data
- If the modal class is only very slightly bigger than another class, just a few more items in this other class could mean a substantially different result, suggesting some instability in the measure

3.3 The median

The middle item of a distribution

The median of a set of ungrouped data is found by arranging the items in ascending or descending order of value, and selecting the item in the middle of the range. **A list of items in order of value is called an array.**

Definition

The **median** is the value of the middle member of an array. The middle item of an odd number of items is calculated as the $\frac{(n+1)}{2}^{th}$ item.

EXAMPLE: THE MEDIAN

(a) The median of the following nine values:

8 6 9 12 15 6 3 20 11

is found by taking the middle item (the fifth one) in the array:

3 6 6 8 9 11 12 15 20

The median is 9.

(b) Consider the following array.

1 2 2 2 3 5 6 7 8 11

The median is 4 because, with an even number of items, we have to take the arithmetic mean of the two middle ones (in this example, $(3 + 5)/2 = 4$).

Activity 11 **(5 minutes)**

The following times taken to produce a batch of 100 units of Product X have been noted.

21 mins,	17 mins,	24 mins,	11 mins,	37 mins,	27 mins
20 mins,	15 mins,	17 mins,	23 mins,	29 mins,	30 mins
24 mins,	18 mins,	17 mins,	21 mins,	24 mins,	20 mins

What is the median time?

Activity 12 **(10 minutes)**

The following scores are observed for the times taken to complete a task, in minutes.

12, 34, 14, 15, 21, 24, 9, 17, 11, 8

What is the median score?

A 14.00
B 14.10
C 14.50
D 14.60

Finding the median of an ungrouped frequency distribution

The median of an ungrouped frequency distribution is found in a similar way. Consider the following distribution.

Value x	*Frequency* f	*Cumulative frequency*
8	3	3
12	7	10
16	12	22
17	8	30
19	5	35
	35	

The median would be the $(35 + 1)/2 = 18^{th}$ item. The 18th item has a value of 16, as we can see from the cumulative frequencies in the right-hand column of the above table.

Finding the median of a grouped frequency distribution

The median of a grouped frequency distribution can be established from an ogive. Finding the median of a grouped frequency distribution from an ogive is best explained by means of an example.

EXAMPLE: THE MEDIAN FROM AN OGIVE

Construct an ogive of the following frequency distribution and hence establish the median.

Class £	*Frequency*	*Cumulative frequency*
$\geq 340, < 370$	17	17
$\geq 370, < 400$	9	26
$\geq 400, < 430$	9	35
$\geq 430, < 460$	3	38
$\geq 460, < 490$	2	40
	40	

SOLUTION

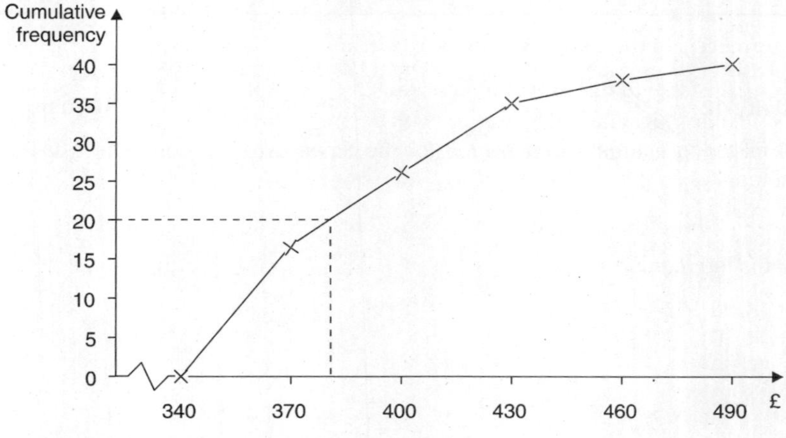

The median is at the $1/2 \times 40 = 20^{th}$ item. Reading off from the horizontal axis on the ogive, the value of the median is approximately £380.

Note that, **because we are assuming that the values are spread evenly within each class, the median calculated is only approximate.**

The advantages and disadvantages of the median

Advantages of the median

- It is easy to understand
- It is unaffected by extremely high or low values
- It can be the value of an actual item in the distribution

Disadvantages of the median

- It fails to reflect the full range of values
- It is unsuitable for further statistical analysis
- Arranging data into order of size can be tedious

4 DISPERSION

Dispersion
The range
Quartiles and the semi-interquartile range
The mean deviation

4.1 The range

Definition

> The **range** is the difference between the highest and lowest observations.

Main properties of the range as a measure of spread

- It is easy to find and to understand
- It is easily affected by one or two extreme values
- It gives no indication of spread between the extremes
- It is not suitable for further statistical analysis

Activity 13 **(5 minutes)**

Mean and range

Calculate the mean and the range of the following set of data.

4 8 7 3 5 16 24 5

Mean	Range

4.2 Quartiles and the semi-interquartile range

Quartiles

Definition

The **quartiles** and the **median** divide the population into four groups of equal size.

Quartiles are one means of identifying the range within which most of the values in the population occur.

- The **lower quartile** (Q_1) is the value below which 25% of the population fall
- The **upper quartile** (Q_3) is the value above which 25% of the population fall
- The **median** (Q_2) is the value of the middle member of an array

---

EXAMPLE: QUARTILES

If we had 11 data items:

- $Q_1 = 11 \times 1/4 = 2.75 = 3^{rd}$ item
- $Q_3 = 11 \times 3/4 = 8.25 = 9^{th}$ item
- $Q_2 = 11 \times 1/2 = 5.5 = 6^{th}$ item

The semi-interquartile range

Definition

The **semi-interquartile range** is half the difference between the upper and lower quartiles.

The lower and upper quartiles can be used to calculate a measure of spread called the **semi-interquartile range.**

The **semi-interquartile range** is half the difference between the lower and upper quartiles and is sometimes called the **quartile deviation,** $\frac{(Q_3 - Q_1)}{2}$.

For example, if the lower and upper quartiles of a frequency distribution were 6 and 11, the semi-interquartile range of the distribution would be (11 – 6)/2 = 2.5 units. This shows that the average distance of a quartile from the median is 2.5. The smaller the quartile deviation, the less dispersed is the distribution.

As with the range, the quartile deviation may be misleading as a measure of spread. If the majority of the data are towards the lower end of the range then the third quartile will be considerably further above the median than the first quartile is below it, and when the two distances from the median are averaged the difference is disguised. Therefore it is often better to quote the actual values of the two quartiles, rather than the quartile deviation.

The inter-quartile range

Definition

> The **inter-quartile range** is the difference between the values of the upper and lower quartiles ($Q_3 - Q_1$) and hence shows the range of values of the middle half of the population.

EXAMPLE: USING OGIVES TO FIND THE SEMI-INTERQUARTILE RANGE

Construct an ogive of the following frequency distribution and hence establish the semi-interquartile range.

Class £	*Frequency*	*Cumulative frequency*
≥ 340, < 370	17	17
≥ 370, < 400	9	26
≥ 400, < 430	9	35
≥ 430, < 460	3	38
≥ 460, < 490	2	40
	40	

SOLUTION

Establish which items are Q_1 and Q_3 (the lower and upper quartiles respectively).

Upper quartile (Q_3) = 3/4 × 40 = 30th value

Lower quartile (Q_1) = 1/4 × 40 = 10th value

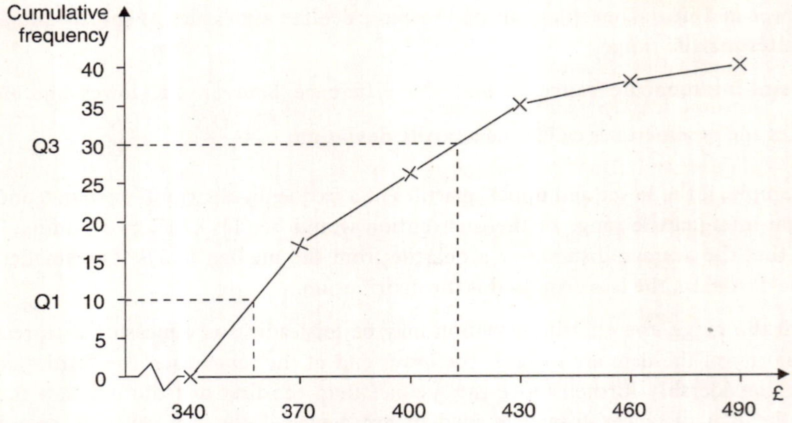

Reading off the values from the ogive, approximate values are as follows.

Q_3 (upper quartile) = £412

Q_1 (lower quartile) = £358

Semi-interquartile range $= \dfrac{Q_3 - Q_1}{2}$

$= \dfrac{£(412 - 358)}{2}$

$= \dfrac{£54}{2}$

$= £27$

4.3 The mean deviation

Measuring dispersion

Because it only uses the middle 50% of the population, the inter-quartile range is a useful measure of dispersion if there are **extreme values** in the distribution. If there are no extreme values which could potentially distort a measure of dispersion, however, it seems unreasonable to exclude 50% of the data. The mean deviation (the topic of this section), and the standard deviation (the topic of section 4) are often more useful measures.

Definition

> The **mean deviation** is a measure of the average amount by which the values in a distribution differ from the arithmetic mean.

Mean deviation $= \dfrac{\Sigma f|x - \bar{x}|}{n}$

Explaining the mean deviation formula

(a) $|x - \bar{x}|$ is the difference between each value (x) in the distribution and the arithmetic mean $\bar{x}$ of the distribution. When calculating the mean deviation for grouped data the deviations should be measured to the midpoint of each class: that is, x is the midpoint of the class interval. The vertical bars mean that all differences are taken as positive since the total of all of the differences, if this is not done, will always equal zero. Thus if x = 3 and $\bar{x}$ = 5, then $x - \bar{x} = -2$ but $|x - \bar{x}| = 2$.

(b) $f|x - \bar{x}|$ is the value in (a) above, multiplied by the frequency for the class.

(c) $\Sigma f|x - \bar{x}|$ is the sum of the results of all the calculations in (b) above.

(d) n (which equals Σf) is the number of items in the distribution.

EXAMPLE: THE MEAN DEVIATION

The hours of overtime worked in a particular quarter by the 60 employees of ABC Ltd are as follows.

Hours		*Frequency*
More than	*Not more than*	
0	10	3
10	20	6
20	30	11
30	40	15
40	50	12
50	60	7
60	70	6
		60

Required

Calculate the mean deviation of the frequency distribution shown above.

SOLUTION

Midpoint

x	*f*	*fx*	$\|x - \bar{x}\|$	$f\|x - \bar{x}\|$
5	3	15	32	96
15	6	90	22	132
25	11	275	12	132
35	15	525	2	30
45	12	540	8	96
55	7	385	18	126
65	6	390	28	168
	Σf = 60	Σfx = 2,220		780

Arithmetic mean $\bar{x} = \frac{\sum fx}{\sum f} = \frac{2{,}220}{60} = 37$

Mean deviation $= \frac{780}{60} = 13$ hours

Activity 14 **(20 minutes)**

Mean deviation

Complete the following table and then calculate the arithmetic mean and the mean deviation of the following frequency distribution (to one decimal place).

Value	*Frequency of occurrence*
5	4
15	6
25	8
35	20
45	6
55	6
	50

x	*f*	*fx*	$\lvert x-\bar{x} \rvert$	$f\lvert x-\bar{x} \rvert$
5				
15				
25				
35				
45				
55				

Arithmetic mean $\bar{x}$ = [——] = [ ]

Mean deviation = [——] = [ ]

Summary of the mean deviation

(a) It is a measure of dispersion which shows by how much, on average, each item in the distribution differs in value from the arithmetic mean of the distribution.

(b) Unlike quartiles, it uses all values in the distribution to measure the dispersion, but it is not greatly affected by a few extreme values because an average is taken.

(c) It is not, however, suitable for further statistical analysis.

Chapter roundup

- **Data** are the raw materials for data processing. **Information** is data that has been processed.
- **Quantitative data** are data that can be measured. A **'variable'** is something which can be measured.
- **Qualitative data** cannot be measured, but have **attributes** (an attribute is something an object either has or does not have).
- Data may be **primary** (collected specifically for the purpose of a survey) or **secondary** (collected for some other purpose).
- **Discrete** data/variables can only take on a countable number of values. **Continuous** data/variables can take on any value.
- **Tables** are a simple way of presenting information about two variables.
- **Charts** often convey the meaning or significance of data more clearly than would a table.
- There are three main **types of bar chart**: **simple**, **component** (including **percentage component**) and **multiple** (or **compound**).
- **Frequency distributions** are used if values of particular variables occur more than once.
- A **frequency distribution** can be represented pictorially by means of a **histogram**. The number of observations in a class is represented by the **area** covered by the bar, rather than by its height.
- **Frequency polygons** and **frequency curves** are perhaps more accurate methods of data presentation than the standard histogram.
- An **ogive** shows the cumulative number of items with a value less than or equal to, or alternatively greater than or equal to, a certain amount.
- **Scatter diagrams** are graphs which are used to exhibit data, (rather than equations) in order to compare the way in which two variables vary with each other.
- The **arithmetic mean** is the best known type of average and is widely understood. It is used for further statistical analysis.
- The **arithmetic mean of ungrouped data** = sum of items ÷ number of items.
- The **arithmetic mean of grouped data**, $\bar{x} = \frac{\sum fx}{n}$ or $\frac{\sum fx}{\sum f}$ where n is the number of values recorded, or the number of items measured.
- The **mode or modal value** is an average which means 'the most frequently occurring value'.
- The **mode of a grouped frequency distribution** can be calculated from a histogram.

- The **median** is the value of the middle member of an array. The middle item of an odd number of items is calculated as the $\frac{(n+1)^{th}}{2}$ item.
- The **median of a grouped frequency distribution** can be established from an ogive.
- The **range** is the difference between the highest and lowest observations.
- The **quartiles** and the **median** divide the population into four groups of equal size.
- The **semi-interquartile range** is half the difference between the upper and lower quartiles.
- The **inter-quartile range** is the difference between the upper and lower quartiles ($Q_3 - Q_1$) and hence shows the range of values of the middle half of the population.
- The **mean deviation** is a measure of the average amount by which the values in a distribution differ from the arithmetic mean.

Quick quiz

1 **Fill in the blanks** in the statements below using the words in the box.

Data can be either (1) .... (have variables) or (2) .... (have (3) ....). Variables can be either (4) .... (eg 0, 1, 2, 3) or (5) .... (eg 0.54, 0.612, 0.117). Data may also be classified as (6) .... (collected for a specific survey) or (7) .... (collected for some other purpose).

• Quantitative	• Continuous	• Attributes	• Primary
• Secondary	• Qualitative	• Discrete	

2 What are the two purposes served by simple bar charts?

3 When selecting a standard width of bar when calculating the heights of the bars in a histogram you would select the size of the class interval which occurs most frequently.

True ☐

False ☐

4 The steps involved in drawing a frequency polygon from a histogram are

Step 1 ....

Step 2 ....

Step 3 ....

5 A grouped frequency distribution can be drawn as a(n) histogram/ogive, whereas a cumulative frequency distribution can be graphed as a(n) ogive /histogram.

6 A scatter diagram has an x axis and a y axis which represent dependent and independent variables as follows.

x axis	?	independent variable
y axis		dependent variable

7 Insert the formulae in the box below into the correct position.

(a) The arithmetic mean of ungrouped data =

(b) The arithmetic mean of grouped data = or

- $\frac{\sum x}{n}$
- $\frac{\sum fx}{n}$
- $\frac{\sum fx}{\sum f}$

8 What is the name given to the average which means 'the most frequently occurring value'?

Arithmetic mean
Median
Mode

9 List four advantages of the arithmetic mean.

10 Calculate the mid-points for both discrete and continuous variables in the table below.

Class interval	*Mid-point (Discrete data)*	*Mid-point (Continuous data)*
25 < 30		
30 < 35		
35 < 40		
40 < 45		
45 < 50		
50 < 55		
55 < 60		
60 < 65		

11 (a) The mode of a grouped frequency distribution can be found from a(n) histogram/ogive.

(b) The median of a grouped frequency distribution can be found from a(n) histogram/ogive.

12 List four advantages of the mode.

13 List three disadvantages of the median.

14 What is the range?

15 Fill in the blanks in the statements below using the words in the box.

(a) .... quartile = Q_1 = value .... which 25% of the population fall.

(b) .... quartile = Q_3 = value .... which 25% of the population fall.

Upper	Above	Below	Lower

16 (a) The formula for the semi-interquartile range is ....

(b) The semi-interquartile range is also known as the ....

17 What are the main properties of the standard deviation?

Answers to quick quiz

1 (1) Quantitative (2) Qualitative (3) Attributes
(4) Discrete (5) Continuous (6) Primary
(7) Secondary

2
- The magnitude of each item is shown
- The lengths of bars on the chart allow magnitudes to be compared

3 True

4 ***Step 1*** Mark mid-points of each bar at the top

Step 2 Join all these points with straight lines

Step 3 Estimate the mid-points of the class intervals outside the range of observed data and join up with the mid-points of the two end bars

5 A grouped frequency distribution can be drawn as a **histogram**, whereas a cumulative frequency distribution can be graphed as an **ogive**.

6 x axis → independent variable
y axis → dependent variable

7 (a) $\frac{\Sigma x}{n}$

(b) $\frac{\Sigma fx}{n}$ or $\frac{\Sigma fx}{\Sigma f}$

8 Mode

9
- It is easy to calculate
- It is widely understood
- It is representative of the whole set of data
- It is suited to further statistical analysis

10

Class interval	*Mid-point (Discrete data)*	*Mid-point (Continuous data)*
25 < 30	27	27.5
30 < 35	32	32.5
35 < 40	37	37.5
40 < 45	42	42.5
45 < 50	47	47.5
50 < 55	52	52.5
55 < 60	57	57.5
60 < 65	62	62.5

11 (a) Histogram

(b) Ogive

12
- It is easy to find
- It is not influenced by a few extreme values
- It can be used for non-numerical data (unlike the mean and the median)
- It can be the value of an actual item in the distribution

13
- It fails to reflect the full range of values (unrepresentative)
- It is unsuitable for further statistical analysis
- Arranging data into order size can be tedious

14 The difference between the highest and lowest observations.

15 (a) **Lower** quartile = Q_1 = value **below** which 25% of the population fall.

(b) **Upper** quartile = Q_3 = value **above** which 25% of the population fall.

16 (a) $\frac{Q_3 - Q_1}{2}$

(b) Quartile deviation

17
- It is based on all values in the distribution
- It is suitable for further statistical analysis
- It is more difficult to understand than some other measures of dispersion

Answers to activities

1 (a) The number of diagrams in an accountancy text book is an example of **quantitative** data, because it can be measured. Because the number of diagrams can only be counted in whole number steps, the resulting data is **discrete.** You cannot for example have $42\frac{1}{2}$ diagrams, but you can have 42 or 43 diagrams.

(b) Whether or not a greetings card has a price sticker on it is not something that can be measured. This is therefore an example of **qualitative** data, as a greetings card either has a price sticker on it, or it does not have a price sticker on it.

(c) The results of a cost accounting assessment can be measured, and are therefore an example of **quantitative** data. The assessment results can only take on whole number values between 0% and 100%, and the data are therefore **discrete**. (It may be possible to score $62\frac{1}{2}$%, or $64\frac{1}{2}$%, but it is not possible to score 62.41%, so the variable is not continuous.)

(d) The heights of telegraph poles is an example of **quantitative** data as they can be measured. Since the telegraph poles may take on any height, the data is said to be **continuous.**

(e) The time taken to swim a kilometre may be measured and is therefore **quantitative** data. Because the time recorded can take on any value, in theory, the data is said to be **continuous.**

2 *Workings*

20X0	*20X1*	*20X2*
£'000	£'000	£'000
3,579	2,961	2,192
857	893	917
62	59	70
4,498	3,913	3,179

(a) *A simple bar chart*

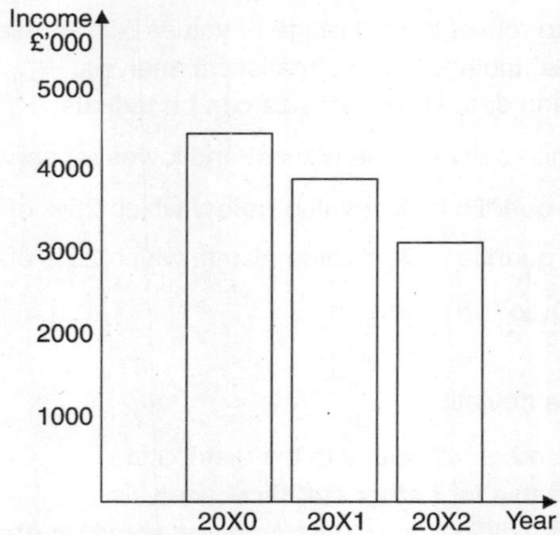

(b) *A multiple bar chart*

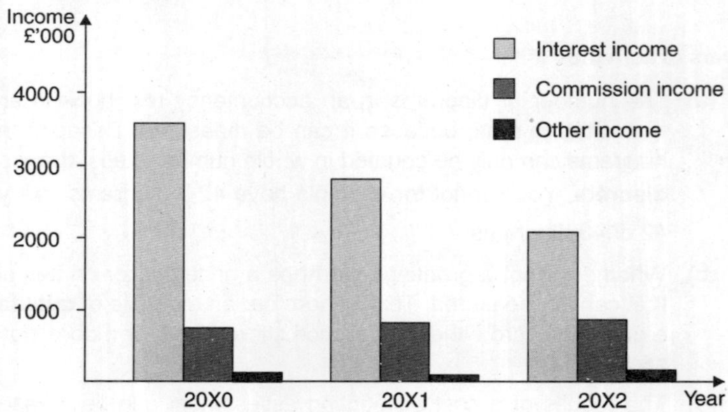

3 *Workings*

	Sales £'000		*Degrees*
United Kingdom	787	(787/1,751 × 360)	162
Italy	219		45
France	285		58
Germany	92		19
Spain	189		39
Rest of Europe	145		30
Holland	34		7
	1,751		360

Scent to You Ltd
Sales for the year ended 30 June 20X0

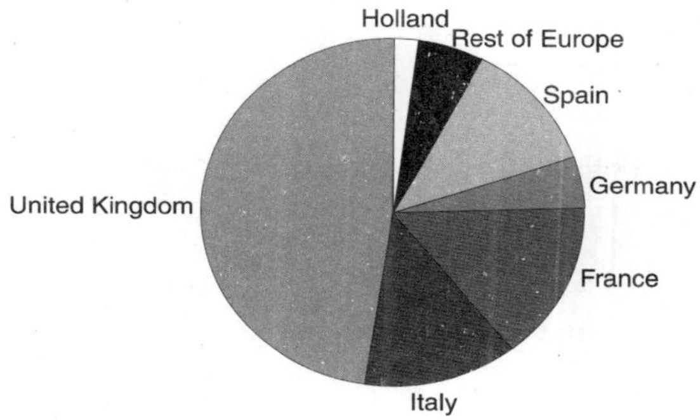

4 We are told what classes to use, so the first step is to identify the lowest and highest values in the data. The lowest value is £25 (in the first row) and the highest value is £73 (in the fourth row). This means that the class intervals must go up to '£70 and under £75'.

We can now set out the classes in a column, and then count the number of items in each class using tally marks.

Class interval	*Tally marks*	*Total*
£25 and less than £30	///	3
£30 and less than £35	////	4
£35 and less than £40	~~////~~ ~~////~~	10
£40 and less than £45	~~////~~ ~~////~~ ~~////~~	15
£45 and less than £50	~~////~~ ~~////~~ ~~////~~ ///	18
£50 and less than £55	~~////~~ ~~////~~ ~~////~~ ~~////~~	20
£55 and less than £60	~~////~~ ~~////~~ ///	13
£60 and less than £65	~~////~~ ///	8
£65 and less than £70	~~////~~ /	6
£70 and less than £75	///	3
	Total	100

5 If a distribution has unequal class intervals, the heights of the bars have to be adjusted for the fact that the bars do not have the same width. If the width of one bar is one and a half times the standard width, we must divide the frequency by one-and-a-half, ie multiply by 0.67 (1/1.5 = 2/3 = 0.67).

The correct answer is D.

6 This is a grouped frequency distribution for continuous variables.

Before drawing the histogram, we must decide on the following.

(a) A **standard class width**: £2,000 will be chosen.

(b) An **open-ended class width**. In this example, the open-ended class width will therefore be £2,000 for class 'up to £10,000' and £4,000 for the class '> £22,000'.

Class interval	*Size of interval* £	*Frequency*	*Adjustment*	*Height of bar*
Up to £10,000	2,000	1	× 2/2	1
> £10,000 ≤ £12,000	2,000	10	× 2/2	10
> £12,000 ≤ £14,000	2,000	12	× 2/2	12
> £14,000 ≤ £18,000	4,000	8	× 2/4	4
> £18,000 ≤ £22,000	4,000	4	× 2/4	2
> £22,000	4,000	1	× 2/4	½

Histogram of sales achieved by individual sales staff

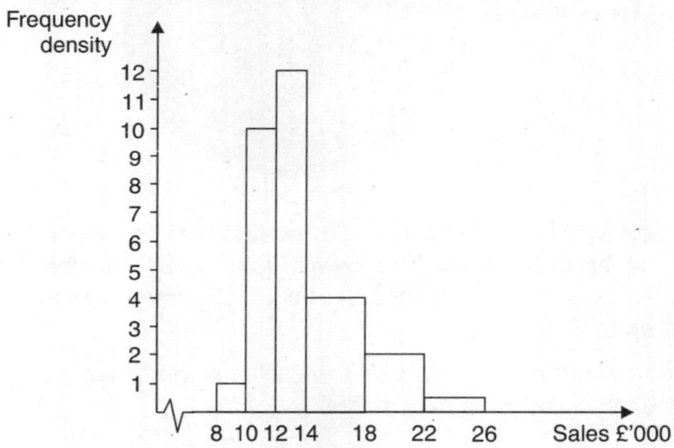

7

Upper limit of interval	*Frequency*	*Cumulative frequency*
200	4	4
400	8	12
600	12	24
800	10	34
1,000	6	40

Ogive of volume of output

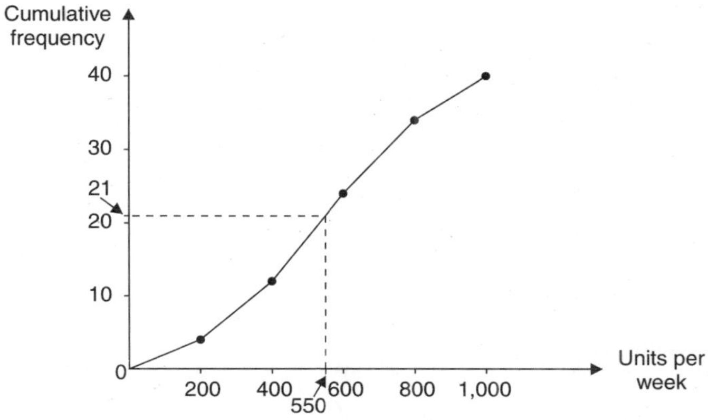

The dotted lines indicate that output of up to 550 units was achieved in 21 out of the 40 weeks.

8 Your answers to parts (b)(i) and (ii) may have been slightly different from those given here, but they should not have been very different, because the data points lay very nearly along a straight line.

(a) CND Ltd – Scatter diagram of production and factory costs, November 20X8-October 20X9

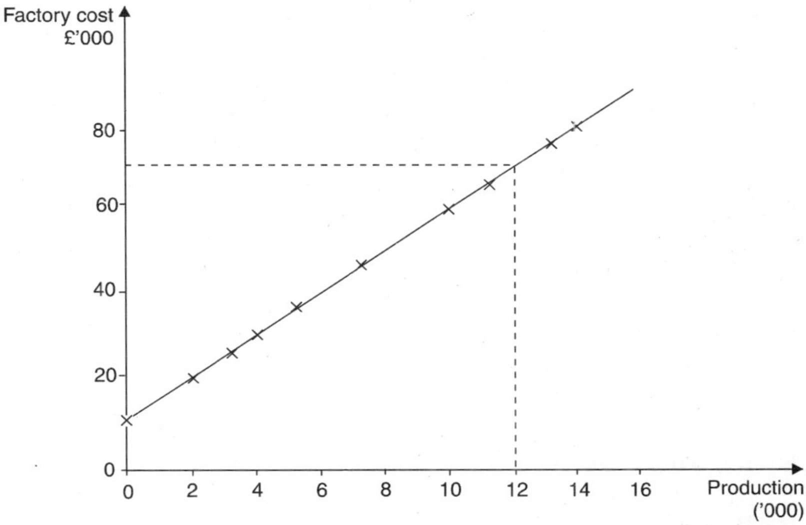

(b) (i) The estimated factory cost for a production of 12,000 widgets is £70,000.

(ii) The monthly fixed costs are indicated by the point where the line of best fit meets the vertical axis (costs at zero production). The fixed costs are estimated as £10,000 a month.

9 The value of X is 10

Workings

$$\text{Mean} = \frac{\text{Sum of values of items}}{\text{Number of items}}$$

Sum of first 10 units = 5 × 10 = 50 kgs

Sum of second 10 units = 7 × 10 = 70 kgs

Sum of third 20 units = 20 × X = 20X

Sum of all 40 units = 50 + 70 + 20X = 120 + 20X

$$\therefore \text{Arithmetic mean} = 8 = \frac{120+20X}{40}$$

$$\therefore 8 \times 40 = 120 + 20X$$

$$320 = 120 + 20X \text{ (subtract 120 from both sides)}$$

$$320 - 120 = 20X$$

$$200 = 20X$$

$$10 = X \text{ (divide both sides by 20)}$$

10 The mid-point of the range 'under £60' is assumed to be £55 and that of the range over £110 to be £115, since all other class intervals are £10. This is obviously an approximation which might result in a loss of accuracy, but there is no better alternative assumption to use. Because wages can vary in steps of 1p, they are virtually a continuous variable and hence the mid-points of the classes are halfway between their end points.

Mid-point of class x £	*Frequency* f	fx
55	3	165
65	11	715
75	16	1,200
85	15	1,275
95	10	950
105	8	840
115	6	690
	69	5,835

Arithmetic mean $= \frac{\Sigma fx}{\Sigma f} = \frac{5,835}{69} = £84.57$

11 The times can be arranged as follows.

11, 15, 17, 17, 17, 18, 20, 20, 21, 21, 23, 24, 24,

24, 27, 29 30, 37

There are eighteen items which is an even number, therefore the median is the arithmetic mean of the two middle items (ie ninth and tenth items) = 21 mins.

12 The first thing to do is to arrange the scores in order of magnitude.

8, 9, 11, 12, 14, 15, 17, 21, 24, 34

There are ten items, and so median is the arithmetic mean of the 5th and 6th items.

$= \frac{14+15}{2} = \frac{29}{2} = 14.50$

The correct answer is therefore C.

You could have eliminated options B and D straight away. Since there are ten items, and they are all whole numbers, the average of the 5th and 6th items is either going to be a whole number (14.00) or 'something and a half' (14.50).

13

Mean	Range
9	21

Workings

Mean, $\bar{x} = \frac{72}{8} = 9$

Range = 24 – 3 = 21

14

x	f	fx	$\lvert x-\bar{x}\rvert$	$f\lvert x-\bar{x}\rvert$
5	4	20	27.2	108.8
15	6	90	17.2	103.2
25	8	200	7.2	57.6
35	20	700	2.8	56.0
45	6	270	12.8	76.8
55	6	330	22.8	136.8
	50	1,610		539.2

Arithmetic mean $\bar{x} = \frac{1,610}{50} = 32.2$

Mean deviation $= \frac{539.2}{50} = 10.8$

Chapter 4 :
PROBABILITY

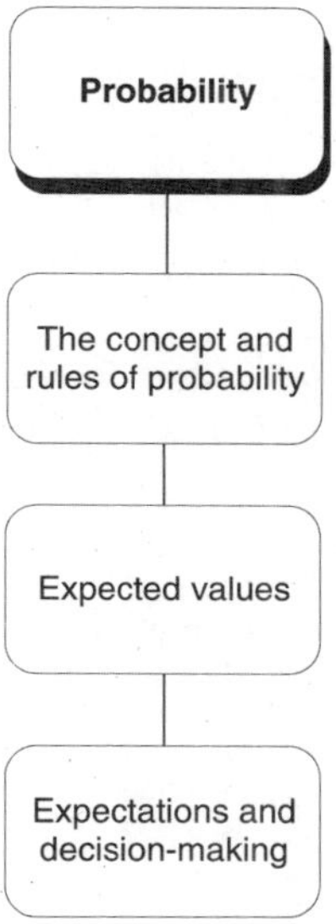

Introduction

'The likelihood of rain this afternoon is fifty per cent' warns the weather report from your radio alarm clock. 'There's no chance of you catching that bus' grunts the helpful soul as you puff up the hill. The headline on your newspaper screams 'Odds of Rainbow Party winning the election rise to one in four'.

'Likelihood' and **'chance'** are expressions used in our everyday lives to denote a **level of uncertainty**. **Probability,** a word which often strikes fear into the hearts of students, is simply the mathematical term used when we need to imply a degree of **uncertainty**.

An understanding of the concept of probability is vital if you are to take account of uncertainty.

This chapter will therefore explain various techniques for assessing probability and look at how it can be applied in business decision making.

Your objectives

In this chapter you will learn about the following:

- The concept and rules of probability
- Expected values
- Expectation and decision-making

1 THE CONCEPT AND RULES OF PROBABILITY

The concept and rules of probability
Introduction
Rules of probability

1.1 Introducing probability

Probability is a measure of **likelihood** and can be stated as a percentage, a ratio, or more usually as a number from 0 to 1.

Consider the following.

- Probability = 0 = impossibility
- Probability = 1 = certainty
- Probability = 1/2 = a 50% chance of something happening
- Probability = 1/4 = a 1 in 4 chance of something happening

Expressing probabilities

In statistics, **probabilities** are more commonly expressed as **proportions** than as **percentages.** Consider the following possible outcomes.

Possible outcome	*Probability as a percentage* %	*Probability as a proportion*
A	15.0	0.150
B	20.0	0.200
C	32.5	0.325
D	7.5	0.075
E	12.5	0.125
F	12.5	0.125
	100.0	1.000

It is useful to consider how probability can be quantified. A businessman might estimate that if the selling price of a product is raised by 20p, there would be a 90% probability that demand would fall by 30%, but how would he have reached his estimate of 90% probability?

Assessing probabilities

There are several ways of assessing probabilities.

- They may be measurable with **mathematical certainty.**
  - If a coin is tossed, there is a 0.5 probability that it will come down heads, and a 0.5 probability that it will come down tails.
  - If a die is thrown, there is a one-sixth probability that a 6 will turn up.
- They may be measurable from an analysis of **past experience.**
- Probabilities can be estimated from **research** or **surveys.**

It is important to note that probability is a measure of the likelihood of an event happening in the long run, or over a large number of times.

The rules of probability below will go through in detail how to calculate probabilities in various situations.

1.2 The rules of probability

Setting the scene

It is the year 2020 and examiners are extinct. A mighty but completely fair computer churns out examinations that are equally likely to be easy or difficult. There is no link between the number of questions on each paper, which is arrived at on a fair basis by the computer, and the standard of the paper. You are about to take five examinations.

Simple probability

It is vital that the first examination is easy as it covers a subject which you have tried, but unfortunately failed, to understand. What is the probability that it will be an easy examination?

Obviously (let us hope), the probability of an easy paper is 1/2 (or 50% or 0.5). This reveals a very important principle (which holds if each result is equally likely).

Formula

$$\textbf{Probability of achieving the desired result} = \frac{\text{Number of ways of achieving desired result}}{\text{Total number of possible outcomes}}$$

Let us apply the principle to our example.

Total number of possible outcomes = 'easy' or 'difficult' = 2
Total number of ways of achieving the desired result (which is 'easy') = 1
The probability of an easy examination, or P(easy examination) = 1/2

EXAMPLE: SIMPLE PROBABILITY

Suppose that a dice is rolled. What is the probability that it will show a six?

SOLUTION

$$\text{P(heads)} = \frac{\text{Number of ways of achieving desired result}}{\text{Total number of possible outcomes}}$$

$$= \frac{1}{6} \text{ or } 16.7\% \text{ or } 0.167$$

Venn diagrams

A Venn diagram is a pictorial method of showing probability. We can show all the possible outcomes (E) and the outcome we are interested in (A).

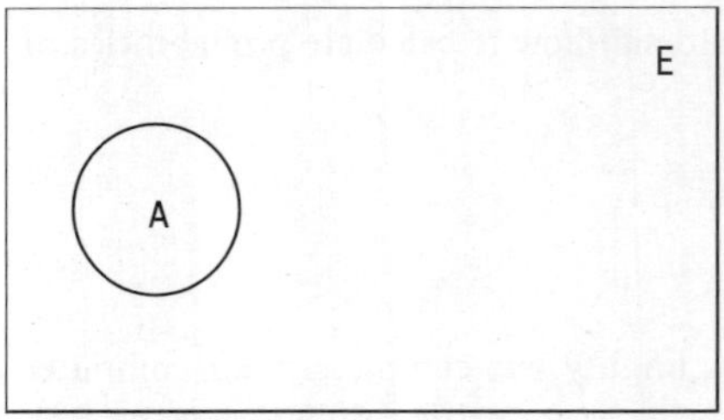

Complementary outcomes

You are desperate to pass more of the examinations than your sworn enemy but, unlike you, he is more likely to pass the first examination if it is difficult. (He is very strange!) What is the probability of the first examination being more suited to your enemy's requirements?

We know that the probability of certainty is one. The certainty in this scenario is that the examination will be easy or difficult.

P(easy or difficult examination)	=	1
From page 117, P(easy examination)	=	1/2
P(not easy examination)	=	P(difficult examination)
	=	1 – P(easy examination)
	=	1 – 1/2
	=	1/2

Formula

$P(\bar{A}) = 1 - P(A)$, where $\bar{A}$ is 'not A'.

Venn diagram: complementary outcomes

The probability of **not** A is shown by the shaded region.

EXAMPLE: COMPLEMENTARY OUTCOMES

If there is a 25 per cent chance of the Rainbow Party winning the next general election, use the law of complementary events to calculate the probability of the Rainbow Party *not* winning the next election.

SOLUTION

P(winning) = 25% = 1/4
P(not winning) = 1 – P(winning) = 1 –1/4 = 3/4

The simple addition or OR law

The **simple addition law** for two mutually exclusive events, A and B, is as follows.

$P(A \text{ or } B) = P(A \cup B) = P(A) + P(B)$

The time pressure in the second examination is enormous. The computer will produce a paper which will have between five and nine questions. You know that, easy or difficult, the examination must have six questions at the most for you to have any hope of passing it.

What is the probability of the computer producing an examination with six or fewer questions? In other words, what is the probability of an examination with five *or* six questions?

Don't panic. Let us start by using the basic principle.

$$P(5 \text{ questions}) = \frac{\text{Total number of ways of achieving a five question examination}}{\text{Total number of possible outcomes } (= 5, 6, 7, 8 \text{ or } 9 \text{ questions})}$$

$$= \frac{1}{5}$$

Likewise $P(6 \text{ questions}) = \frac{1}{5}$

Either five questions or six questions would be acceptable, so the probability of you passing the examination must be greater than if just five questions or just six questions (but not both) were acceptable. We therefore add the two probabilities together so that the probability of passing the examination has increased.

$$\text{So } P(5 \text{ or } 6 \text{ questions}) = P(5 \text{ questions}) + P(6 \text{ questions})$$

$$= \frac{1}{5} + \frac{1}{5} = \frac{2}{5}$$

Mutually exclusive outcomes are outcomes where the occurrence of one of the outcomes excludes the possibility of any of the others happening.

In the example the outcomes are **mutually exclusive** because it is impossible to have five questions *and* six questions in the same examination.

Venn diagram: Mutually exclusive outcomes

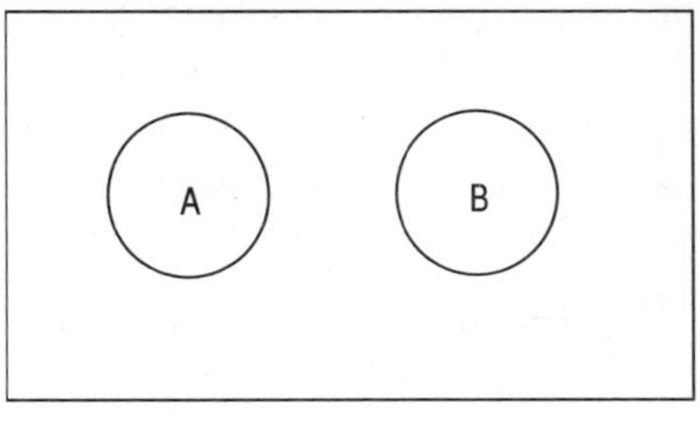

EXAMPLE: MUTUALLY EXCLUSIVE OUTCOMES

The delivery of an item of raw material from a supplier may take up to six weeks from the time the order is placed. The probabilities of various delivery times are as follows.

Delivery time	*Probability*
≤ 1 week	0.10
$> 1, \leq 2$ weeks	0.25
$> 2, \leq 3$ weeks	0.20
$> 3, \leq 4$ weeks	0.20
$> 4, \leq 5$ weeks	0.15
$> 5, \leq 6$ weeks	0.10
	1.00

Required

Calculate the probability that a delivery will take the following times.

(a) Two weeks or less
(b) More than three weeks

SOLUTION

(a) $P(\leq 1 \text{ or } > 1, \leq 2 \text{ weeks}) = P(\leq 1 \text{ week}) + P(>1, \leq 2 \text{ weeks})$
$= 0.10 + 0.25$
$= 0.35$

(b) $P(> 3, \leq 6 \text{ weeks}) = P(> 3, \leq 4 \text{ weeks}) + P(> 4, \leq 5 \text{ weeks}) + P(> 5, \leq 6 \text{ weeks})$
$= 0.20 + 0.15 + 0.10$
$= 0.45$

The simple multiplication or AND law

The **simple multiplication law** for two independent events, A and B, is as follows.

$P(A \text{ and } B) = P(A \cap B) = P(A)P(B)$

Note: P(A and B) = 0 when A and B have mutually exclusive outcomes.

You still have three examinations to sit: astrophysics, geography of the moon and computer art. Stupidly, you forgot to revise for the astrophysics examination, which will have between 15 and 20 questions. You think that you may scrape through this paper if it is easy *and* if there are only 15 questions.

What is the probability that the paper the computer produces will exactly match your needs? Do not forget that there is no link between the standard of the examination and the number of questions, ie they are **independent** events.

The best way to approach this question is diagrammatically, showing all the possible outcomes.

	Number of questions					
Type of paper	*15*	*16*	*17*	*18*	*19*	*20*
Easy (E)	E and 15*	E and 16	E and 17	E and 18	E and 19	E and 20
Difficult (D)	D and 15	D and 16	D and 17	D and 18	D and 19	D and 20

The diagram shows us that, of the twelve possible outcomes, there is only one 'desired result' (which is asterisked). We can therefore calculate the probability as follows.

P(easy paper *and* 15 questions) = 1/12.

The answer can be found more easily as follows.

P(easy paper *and* 15 questions) = P(easy paper) × P(15 questions) = 1/2 × 1/6 = 1/12.

The number of questions has no effect on, nor is it affected by whether it is an easy or difficult paper.

Definition

> **Independent events** are events where the outcome of one event in no way affects the outcome of the other events.

EXAMPLE: INDEPENDENT EVENTS

A die is thrown and a coin is tossed simultaneously. What is the probability of throwing a 5 and getting heads on the coin?

SOLUTION

The probability of throwing a 5 on a die is 1/6
The probability of a tossed coin coming up heads is 1/2
The probability of throwing a 5 and getting heads on a coin is 1/2 × 1/6 = 1/12

The general rule of addition

The **general rule of addition** for two events, A and B, which are not mutually exclusive, is as follows.

P(A or B) = P $(A \cup B)$ = P(A) + P(B) – P(A and B)

The three examinations you still have to sit are placed face down in a line in front of you at the final examination sitting. There is an easy astrophysics paper, a difficult geography of the moon paper and a difficult computer art paper. Without turning over any of the papers you are told to choose one of them. What is the probability that the first paper that you select is difficult *or* is the geography of the moon paper?

Let us think about this carefully.

There are two difficult papers, so P(difficult) = 2/3

There is one geography of the moon paper, so P(geography of the moon) = 1/3

If we use the OR law and add the two probabilities then we will have double counted the difficult geography of the moon paper. It is included in the set of difficult papers *and* in the set of geography of the moon papers. In other words, we are *not* faced with mutually exclusive outcomes because the occurrence of a geography of the moon paper does not exclude the possibility of the occurrence of a difficult paper. We therefore need to take account of this **double counting.**

P(difficult paper or geography of the moon paper) = P(difficult paper) + P(geography of the moon paper) – P(difficult paper and geography of the moon paper).

Using the AND law, P(difficult paper or geography of the moon paper) = 2/3 + 1/3 – (1/3) = 2/3.

Since it is *not* impossible to have an examination which is difficult *and* about the geography of the moon, these two events are not mutually exclusive.

Venn diagram: General rule of addition

We can show how to calculate $P(A \cup B)$ from three diagrams.

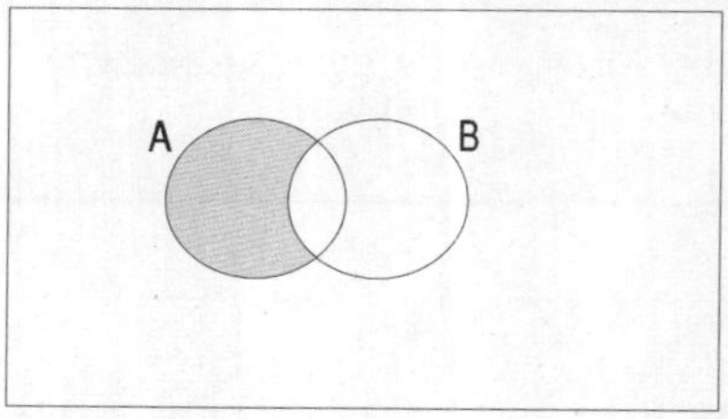

The shaded area is the probability of A and **not** B = $P(A) - P(A \cap B)$

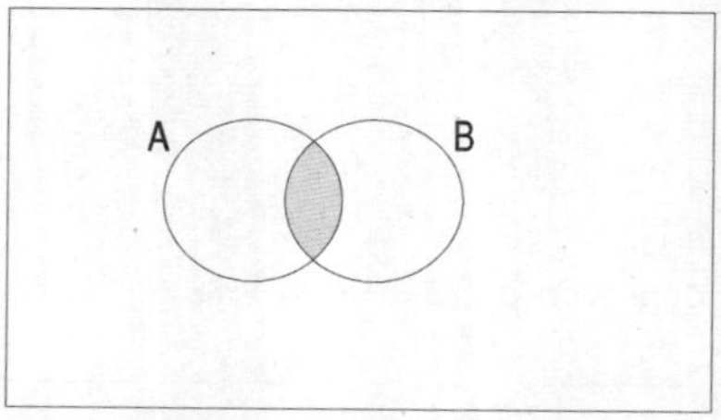

The shaded area is the probability of A **and** B = $P(A \cap B)$

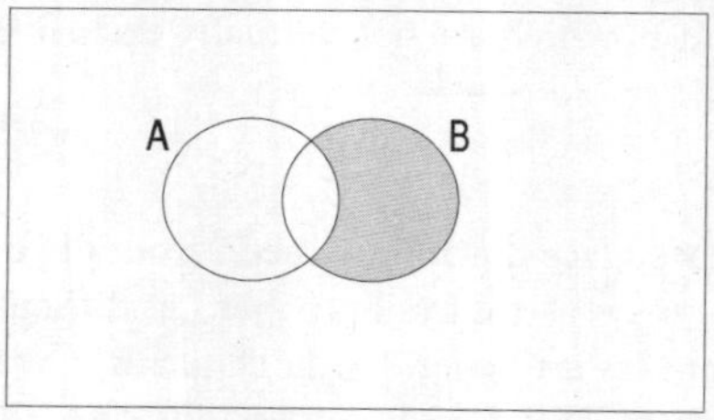

The shaded area is the probability of B and **not** A = $P(B) - (A \cap B)$

If we add these three sections together we get the formula for the probability of A **or** B = $P(A) + P(B) - P(A \cap B)$

Activity 1 **(5 minutes)**

General rule of addition

If one card is drawn from a normal pack of 52 playing cards, what is the probability of getting an ace or a spade?

Probability

Ace	*Spade*	*Ace of spades*	*Ace or spade*

The general rule of multiplication

The **general rule of multiplication** for two dependent events, A and B is as follows.

$$\begin{aligned} P(\text{A and B}) &= P(A \cap B)\, P(A) \times P(B/A) \\ &= P(B) \times P(A/B) \end{aligned}$$

Computer art is your last examination. Understandably you are very tired and you are uncertain whether you will be able to stay awake. You believe that there is a 70% chance of your falling asleep if it becomes too hot and stuffy in the examination hall. It is well known that the air conditioning system serving the examination hall was installed in the last millennium and is therefore extremely unreliable. There is a 1 in 4 chance of it breaking down during the examination, thereby causing the temperature in the hall to rise. What is the likelihood that you will drop off?

The scenario above has led us to face what is known as **conditional probability**. We can rephrase the information provided as 'the probability that you will fall asleep, given that it is too hot and stuffy, is equal to 70%' and we can write this as follows.

P(fall asleep/too hot and stuffy) = 70%.

Definition

Dependent or **conditional** events are events where the outcome of one event depends on the outcome of the others.

Whether you fall asleep is **conditional** upon whether the hall becomes too hot and stuffy. The events are not, therefore, independent and so we cannot use the simple multiplication law. So:

P(it becomes too hot and stuffy and you fall asleep)

= P(too hot and stuffy) × P(fall asleep/too hot and stuffy)
= 25% × 70% = 0.25 × 0.7 = 0.175 = 17½%

Note. When A and B are independent events, then P(B/A) = P(B) since, by definition, the occurrence of B (and therefore P(B)) does not depend upon the occurrence of A. Similarly P(A/B) = P(A).

EXAMPLE: CONDITIONAL PROBABILITY

The board of directors of Shuttem Ltd has warned that there is a 60% probability that a factory will be closed down unless its workforce improves its productivity. The factory's manager has estimated that the probability of success in agreeing a productivity deal with the workforce is only 30%.

Required

Determine the likelihood that the factory will be closed.

SOLUTION

If outcome A is the shutdown of the factory and outcome B is the failure to improve productivity:

$$\begin{aligned} P(A \text{ and } B) &= P(B) \times P(A/B) \\ &= 0.7 \times 0.6 \\ &= 0.42 \end{aligned}$$

Contingency tables can be useful for dealing with **conditional probability.**

EXAMPLE: CONTINGENCY TABLES

A cosmetics company has developed a new anti-dandruff shampoo which is being tested on volunteers. Seventy per cent of the volunteers have used the shampoo whereas others have used a normal shampoo, believing it to be the new anti-dandruff shampoo. Two-sevenths of those using the new shampoo showed no improvement whereas one-third of those using the normal shampoo had less dandruff.

Required

A volunteer shows no improvement. What is the probability that he used the normal shampoo?

SOLUTION

The problem is solved by drawing a contingency table, showing 'improvement' and 'no improvement', volunteers using normal shampoo and volunteers using the new shampoo.

Let us suppose that there were 1,000 volunteers (we could use any number). We could depict the results of the test on the 1,000 volunteers as follows.

	New shampoo	*Normal shampoo*	*Total*
Improvement	***500	****100	600
No improvement	**200	200	400
	*700	***300	1,000

* 70% × 1,000   ** $\frac{2}{7} \times 700$

*** Balancing figure   **** $\frac{1}{3} \times 300$

We can now calculate P(shows no improvement)

$$\text{P(shows no improvement)} = \frac{400}{1,000}$$

$$\text{P(used normal shampoo/shows no improvement)} = \frac{200}{400} = \frac{1}{2}$$

Other probabilities are just as easy to calculate.

$$\text{P(shows improvement/used new shampoo)} = \frac{500}{700} = \frac{5}{7}$$

$$\text{P(used new shampoo/shows improvement)} = \frac{500}{600} = \frac{5}{6}$$

Activity 2 **(15 minutes)**

Independent events

The independent probabilities that the three sections of a college will encounter one computer error in a week are respectively 0.1, 0.2 and 0.3. There is never more than one computer error encountered by any one section in a week. Calculate the probability that there will be the following number of errors encountered by the college next week.

(a) At least one computer error

(b) One and only one computer error

Activity 3 **(10 minutes)**

General rule of addition

In a student survey, 60% of the students are male and 75% are full-time students. The probability that a student chosen at random is either female or full-time is:

A 0.85

B 0.30

C 0.40

D 1.00

We have now introduced the basic rules and concepts of probability.

2 EXPECTED VALUES

Expected values
How to calculate
Expected values and single events
The expected value equation

We are now going to move on to look at expected values. At the end of this session, if you have understood it, you should be able to apply it to numerous everyday situations – even TV game shows such as 'Deal or No Deal'.

An **expected value** (or **EV**) is a weighted average value, based on probabilities. The expected value for a single event can offer a helpful guide for management decisions.

2.1 How to calculate expected values

If the probability of an outcome of an event is p, then the expected number of times that this outcome will occur in n events (the expected value) is equal to n × p.

For example, suppose that the probability that a transistor is defective is 0.02. How many defectives would we expect to find in a batch of 4,000 transistors?

EV = 4,000 × 0.02
= 80 defectives

EXAMPLE: EXPECTED VALUES

The daily sales of Product T may be as follows.

Units	*Probability*
1,000	0.2
2,000	0.3
3,000	0.4
4,000	0.1
	1.0

Required

Calculate the expected daily sales.

SOLUTION

The EV of daily sales may be calculated by multiplying each possible outcome (volume of daily sales) by the probability that this outcome will occur.

Units	*Probability*		*Expected value* Units
1,000	0.2		200
2,000	0.3		600
3,000	0.4		1,200
4,000	0.1		400
		EV of daily sales	2,400

In the long run the expected value should be approximately the actual average, if the event occurs many times over. In the example above, we do not expect sales on any one day to equal 2,400 units, but in the long run, over a large number of days, average sales should equal 2,400 units a day.

2.2 Expected values and single events

The point made in the preceding paragraph is an important one. An **expected value** can be calculated when the **event will only occur once or twice**, but it will not be a true long-run average of what will actually happen, because there is no long-run.

EXAMPLE: EXPECTED VALUES AND SINGLE EVENTS

Suppose, for example, that a businessman is trying to decide whether to invest in a project. He estimates that there are three possible outcomes.

Outcome	*Profit/(loss)* £	*Probability*
Success	10,000	0.2
Moderate success	2,000	0.7
Failure	(4,000)	0.1

The expected value of profit may be calculated as follows.

Profit/(loss) £	*Probability*	*Expected value* £
10,000	0.2	2,000
2,000	0.7	1,400
(4,000)	0.1	(400)
	Expected value of profit	3,000

In this example, the project is a one-off event, and as far as we are aware, it will not be repeated. The actual profit or loss will be £10,000, £2,000 or £(4,000), and the average value of £3,000 will not actually happen. There is no long-run average of a single event.

Nevertheless, the expected value can be used to help the manager decide whether or not to invest in the project.

Activity 4 **(20 minutes)**

Expected values

A company manufactures and sells product D. The selling price of the product is £6 per unit, and estimates of demand and variable costs of sales are as follows.

Probability	*Demand*	*Probability*	*Variable cost per unit*
	Units		£
0.3	5,000	0.1	3.00
0.6	6,000	0.3	3.50
0.1	8,000	0.5	4.00
		0.1	4.50

The unit variable costs do not depend on the volume of sales.

Fixed costs will be £10,000.

Required

Calculate the expected profit.

2.3 The expected value equation

The expected value is summarised in equation form as follows.

$E(x) = \sum xP(x)$

This is read as 'the expected value of a particular outcome "x" is equal to the sum of the products of each value of x and the corresponding probability of that value of x occurring'.

3 EXPECTATION AND DECISION-MAKING

Expectation and decision-making
Decision-making
Pay off tables
Limitations of expected values
Risk and uncertainty

3.1 Decision-making

The concepts of probability and expected value are vital in **business decision-making.** The expected values for single events can offer a helpful guide for management decisions.

- A project with a positive expected value (EV) should be accepted
- A project with a negative expected value (EV) should be rejected

Another decision rule involving expected values that you are likely to come across is the choice of an option or alternative which has the **highest EV of profit** (or the **lowest EV of cost**).

Choosing the option with the highest EV of profit is a decision rule that has both merits and drawbacks, as the following simple example will show.

EXAMPLE: THE EXPECTED VALUE CRITERION

Suppose that there are two mutually exclusive projects with the following possible profits.

Project A		*Project B*	
Probability	*Profit*	*Probability*	*Profit/(loss)*
	£		£
0.8	5,000	0.1	(2,000)
0.2	6,000	0.2	5,000
		0.6	7,000
		0.1	8,000

Required

Determine which project should be chosen.

SOLUTION

The EV of profit for each project is as follows.

		£
(a)	Project A $(0.8 \times 5{,}000) + (0.2 \times 6{,}000)$	= 5,200
(b)	Project B $(0.1 \times (2{,}000)) + (0.2 \times 5{,}000) + (0.6 \times 7{,}000) + (0.1 \times 8{,}000)$	= 5,800

Project B has a higher EV of profit. This means that on the balance of probabilities, it could offer a better return than A, and so is arguably a better choice.

On the other hand, the minimum return from project A would be £5,000 whereas with B there is a 0.1 chance of a loss of £2,000. So project A might be a safer choice.

Activity 5 **(10 minutes)**

Expected values

A company is deciding whether to invest in a project. There are three possible outcomes of the investment:

Outcome	*Profit/(Loss)*
	£'000
Optimistic	19.2
Most likely	12.5
Pessimistic	(6.7)

There is a 30% chance of the optimistic outcome, and a 60% chance of the most likely outcome arising. The expected value of profit from the project is

A £7,500
B £12,590
C £13,930
D £25,000

3.2 Payoff tables

Decisions have to be taken about a wide variety of matters (capital investment, controls on production, project scheduling and so on) and under a wide variety of conditions from **virtual certainty** to **complete uncertainty**.

There are, however, certain common factors in many business decisions.

(a) When a decision has to be made, there will be a range of possible **actions.**

(b) Each action will have certain **consequences**, or **payoffs** (for example, profits, costs, time).

(c) The payoff from any given action will depend on the **circumstances** (for example, high demand or low demand), which may or may not be known when the decision is taken. Frequently each circumstance will be assigned a probability of occurrence. The circumstances are *not* dependent on the action taken.

For a decision with these elements, a **payoff table** can be prepared.

A payoff table is simply a table with **rows for circumstances** and **columns for actions** (or *vice versa*), and the payoffs in the cells of the table.

For example, a decision on the level of advertising expenditure to be undertaken given different states of the economy, would have payoffs in £'000 of profit after advertising expenditure as follows.

			Actions: expenditure	
		High	*Medium*	*Low*
Circumstances:	Boom	+50	+30	+15
the state of the	Stable	+20	+25	+5
economy	Recession	0	–10	–35

EXAMPLE: PAYOFF TABLE

A cinema has to decide how many programmes to print for a premiere of a film. From previous experience of similar events, it is expected that the probability of sales will be as follows.

Number of programmes demanded	*Probability of demand*
250	0.1
500	0.2
750	0.4
1,000	0.1
1,250	0.2

The best print quotation received is £2,000 plus 20 pence per copy. Advertising revenue from advertisements placed in the programme totals £2,500. Programmes are sold for £2 each. Unsold programmes are worthless.

Required

(a) Construct a payoff table.
(b) Find the most profitable number of programmes to print.

SOLUTION

(a) *Actions: print levels*

		250	*500*	*750*	*1,000*	*1,250*
	250 (p = 0.1)	950	900	850	800	750
Circumstances:	500 (p = 0.2)	950	1,400	1,350	1,300	1,250
demand levels	750 (p = 0.4)	950	1,400	1,850	1,800	1,750
	1,000 (p = 0.1)	950	1,400	1,850	2,300	2,250
	1,250 (p = 0.2)	950	1,400	1,850	2,300	2,750

These figures are calculated as the profit under each set of circumstances. For example, if the cinema produces 1,000 programmes and 1,000 are demanded, the profit is calculated as follows.

Total revenue = Advertising revenue + sale of programmes
= £2,500 + £(1,000 × 2)
= £4,500

Total costs = £2,000 + £(0.20 × 1,000)
= £2,000 + £200
= £2,200

Profit = Total revenue – total costs = £4,500 – £2,200 = £2,300

Similarly, if the cinema produces 750 programmes, but only 500 are demanded, the profit is calculated as follows.

Total revenue = £2,500 + £(500 × 2)
= £2,500 + £1,000 = £3,500

Total costs = £2,000 + £(0.20 × 750)
= £2,000 + £150
= £2,150

Profit = Total revenue – total costs = £3,500 – £2,150 = £1,350

Note that whatever the print level, the maximum profit that can be earned is determined by the demand. This means that when 250 programmes are printed, the profit is £950 when demand is 250. Profit is also £950 when demand is 500, 750, 1,000 or 1,250.

(b) The expected profits from each of the possible print levels are as follows.

Print 250

Expected profit = £((950 × 0.1) + (950 × 0.2) + (950 × 0.4) + (950 × 0.1) + (950 × 0.2)) = £950

Print 500

Expected profit = £((900 × 0.1) + (1,400 × (0.2 + 0.4 + 0.1 + 0.2))) = £1,350

Print 750

Expected profit = £((850 × 0.1) + (1,350 × 0.2) + (1,850 × 0.7)) = £1,650

Print 1,000

Expected profit = £((800 × 0.1) + (1,300 × 0.2) + (1,800 × 0.4) + (2,300 × 0.3)) = £1,750

Print 1,250

Expected profit = £((750 × 0.1) + (1,250 × 0.2) + (1,750 × 0.4) + (2,250 × 0.1) + (2,750 × 0.2)) = £1,800

1,250 programmes should therefore be printed in order to **maximise expected profit.**

Remember E(x) = Expected value = Probability × Payoff

Activity 6 **(10 minutes)**

Payoff tables

In a restaurant there is a 30% chance of five apple pies being ordered a day and a 70% chance of ten being ordered. Each apple pie sells for £2. It costs £1 to make an apple pie. Using a payoff table, decide how many apple pies the restaurant should prepare each day, bearing in mind that unsold apple pies must be thrown away at the end of each day.

3.3 Limitations of expected values

Evaluating decisions by using expected values has a number of limitations.

(a) The **probabilities** used when calculating expected values are likely to be estimates. They may therefore be **unreliable** or **inaccurate.**

(b) Expected values are **long-term averages** and may not be suitable for use in situations involving **one-off decisions**. They may therefore be useful as a **guide** to decision making.

(c) Expected values do not consider the **attitudes to risk of** the people involved in the decision-making process. They do not, therefore, take into account all of the factors involved in the decision.

(d) The time value of money may not be taken into account: £100 now is worth more than £100 in ten years' time.

3.4 Risk and uncertainty

Probability is used to help to calculate **risk** in decision-making.

Risk involves situations or events which may or may not occur, but whose probability of occurrence can be calculated statistically and the frequency predicted.

Uncertainty involves situations or events whose outcome cannot be predicted with statistical confidence.

Chapter roundup

- Probability is a measure of **likelihood** and can be stated as a percentage, a ratio, or more usually as a number from 0 to 1.
- The **simple addition law** for two mutually exclusive events, A and B is as follows.

  P(A or B) = P(A) + P(B)
- **Mutually exclusive outcomes** are outcomes where the occurrence of one of the outcomes excludes the possibility of any of the others happening.
- The **simple multiplication law** for two independent events A and B, is as follows.

  P(A and B) = P(A) P(B)
- **Independent events** are events where the outcome of one event in no way affects the outcome of the other events.
- The **general rule of addition** for two events, A and B, which are not mutually exclusive, is as follows.

  P(A or B) = P(A) + P(B) – P(A and B)
- The **general rule of multiplication** for two dependent events, A and B, is as follows.

  $$\begin{aligned} P(A \text{ and } B) &= P(A) \times P(B/A) \\ &= P(B) \times P(A/B) \end{aligned}$$
- **Dependent** or **conditional** events are events where the outcome of one event depends on the outcome of the others.
- **Contingency tables** can be useful for dealing with **conditional probability**.
- An **expected value (**or **EV)** is a weighted average, based on probabilities. The expected value for a single event can offer a helpful guide for management decisions: **a project with a positive EV should be accepted** and a **project with a negative EV should be rejected**.
- **Probability and expectation should be seen as an aid to decision-making**.
- A payoff table is simply a table with **rows for circumstances** and **columns for actions** (or *vice versa*), and the payoffs in the cells of the table.
- Probability is used to help to calculate **risk** in decision making.

Quick quiz

1 Complete the following equations

(a) $P(\overline{x}) = 1 -$ ....

(b) Simple addition/OR law

P(A or B or C) = ...

where A, B and C are ....

(c) Simple multiplication/AND law

P(A and B) = ...

where A and B are ....

(d) General rule of addition

P(A or B) = ...

where A and B are ....

(e) General rule of multiplication

P(A and B) = ...

where A and B are ....

2

1	Mutually exclusive outcomes
2	Independent events
3	Conditional events

A	The occurrence of one of the outcomes excludes the possibility of any of the others happening	1	2	3
B	Events where the outcome of one event depends on the outcome of the others	1	2	3
C	Events where the outcome of one event in no way affects the outcome of the other events	1	2	3

3 An analysis of 480 working days in a factory shows that on 360 days there were no machine breakdowns. Assuming that this pattern will continue, what is the probability that there will be a machine breakdown on a particular day?

A 0%
B 25%
C 35%
D 75%

4 A production director is responsible for overseeing the operations of three factories – North, South and West. He visits one factory per week. He visits the West factory as often as he visits the North factory, but he visits the South factory twice as often as he visits the West factory.

What is the probability that in any one week he will visit the North factory?

A 0.17
B 0.20
C 0.25
D 0.33

5 What is an expected value?

6 Expected values can be used to help managers decide whether or not to invest in a project. Generally, a project with a .... EV should be rejected, and one with a .... EV should be ....

Answers to quick quiz

1 (a) 1 – P(X)

(b)	P(A) + P(B) + P(C)	Mutually exclusive outcomes
(c)	P(A) × P(B)	Independent events
(d)	P(A) + P(B) – P(A and B)	Not mutually exclusive outcomes
(e)	P(A) × P(B/A) = P(B) × P(A/B)	Dependent events

2 A = 1
B = 3
C = 2

3 B The data tells us that there was a machine breakdown on 120 days (480 – 360) out of a total of 480.

P(machine breakdown) = 120/480 × 100%
= 25%

You should have been able to eliminate option A immediately since a probability of 0% = impossibility.

If you selected option C, you calculated the probability of a machine breakdown as 120 out of a possible 365 days instead of 480 days.

If you selected option D, you incorrectly calculated the probability that there was **not** a machine breakdown on any particular day.

4

Factory	*Ratio of visits*
North	1
South	2
West	1
	4

Pr(visiting North factory) = 1/4 = 0.25

If you didn't select the correct option, make sure that you are clear about how the correct answer has been arrived at. Remember to look at the **ratio** of visits since no actual numbers of visits are given.

5 A weighted average value based on probabilities.

6 Generally, a project with a negative EV should be rejected, and one with a positive EV should be accepted.

Answers to activities

1 Probability

Ace	Spade	Ace of spades	Ace or spade
$\frac{4}{52}$	$\frac{13}{52}$	$\frac{1}{52}$	$\frac{4}{13}$

Working

$$P(\text{ace or spade}) = \frac{4}{52}+\frac{13}{52}-\frac{1}{52}=\frac{16}{52}=\frac{4}{13}$$

2 (a) The probability of at least one computer error is 1 minus the probability of no error. The probability of no error is $0.9 \times 0.8 \times 0.7 = 0.504$.

(Since the probability of an error is 0.1, 0.2 and 0.3 in each section, the probability of no error in each section must be 0.9, 0.8 and 0.7 respectively.)

The probability of at least one error is $1 - 0.504 = 0.496$.

(b) Y = yes, N = no

		Section 1	*Section 2*	*Section 3*
(i)	Error?	Y	N	N
(ii)	Error?	N	Y	N
(iii)	Error?	N	N	Y

		Probabilities
(i)	$0.1 \times 0.8 \times 0.7 =$	0.056
(ii)	$0.9 \times 0.2 \times 0.7 =$	0.126
(iii)	$0.9 \times 0.8 \times 0.3 =$	0.216
	Total	0.398

The probability of only one error only is 0.398.

3 P(male) = 60% = 0.6

P(female) = 1 – 0.6 = 0.4

P(full-time student) = 75% = 0.75

We need to use the general rule of addition to avoid double counting.

∴ P(female or full-time student) = P(female) + P(full-time student) – P(female *and* full-time student)

$= 0.4 + 0.75 - (0.4 \times 0.75)$
$= 1.15 - 0.3$
$= 0.85$

The correct answer is A.

You should have been able to eliminate options C and D immediately. 0.4 is the probability that the candidate is female and 1.00 is the probability that something will definitely happen – neither of these options are likely to correspond to the probability that the candidate is either female or a full-time student.

4 The EV of demand is as follows:

Demand Units	*Probability*	*Expected value* Units
5,000	0.3	1,500
6,000	0.6	3,600
8,000	0.1	800
	EV of demand	5,900

The EV of the variable cost per unit is as follows:

Variable costs £	*Probability*	*Expected value* £
3.00	0.1	0.30
3.50	0.3	1.05
4.00	0.5	2.00
4.50	0.1	0.45
	EV of unit variable costs	3.80

		£
Sales	5,900 units × £6.00	35,400
Less: variable costs	5,900 units × £3.80	22,420
Contribution		12,980
Less: fixed costs		10,000
Expected profit		2,980

5 B Since the probabilities must total 100%, the probability of the pessimistic outcome = 100% – 60% – 30% = 10%.

Outcome	*Profit/(Loss)* £	*Probability*	*Expected value* £
Optimistic	19,200	0.3	5,760
Most likely	12,500	0.6	7,500
Pessimistic	(6,700)	0.1	(670)
		1.0	12,590

If you selected option A, you calculated the expected value of the most likely outcome instead of the entire project.

If you selected option C, you forgot to treat the 6,700 as a loss, ie as a negative value.

If you selected option D, you forgot to take into account the probabilities of the various outcomes arising.

6

		Prepared Five	*Prepared* Ten
Demand	Five (P = 0.3)	5	0
	Ten (P = 0.7)	5	10

Prepare five, profit = (£5 × 0.3) + (£5 × 0.7) = £5

Prepare ten, profit = (£0 × 0.3) + (£10 × 0.7) = £7

Ten pies should be prepared.

Chapter 5 :

FREQUENCY DISTRIBUTIONS, THE NORMAL CURVE AND SAMPLING

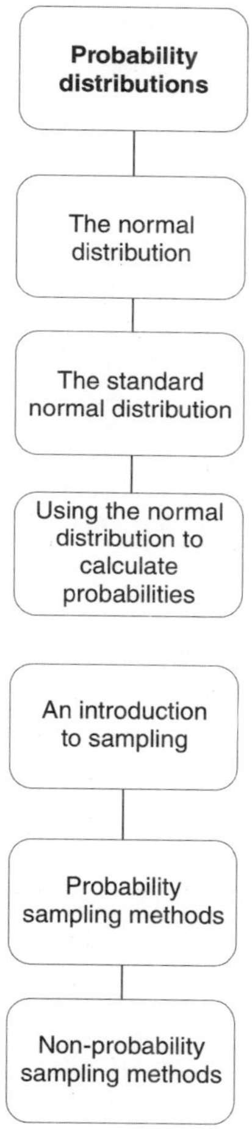

Introduction

This chapter will build on many of the statistical topics already covered. A frequency distribution of continuous data can be drawn as a symmetrical bell-shaped curve called the **normal distribution**. This can be linked with the calculation of probabilities and is a useful business decision-making tool.

The second half of the chapter then looks at sampling. Every ten years the UK government collects information on every individual living in the UK. This information is then used in numerous ways, including planning. When information is collected on the whole population it is called a census.

The time and cost of collecting information on every member of a population is huge. For this reason individuals, corporations and governments may choose to collect information on just part of the population. This process is called sampling and is the subject of this chapter.

Your objectives

In this chapter you will learn about the following:

- Probability distributions
- The normal distribution
- Using the normal distribution to calculate probabilities
- An introduction to sampling
- Probability sampling methods
- Non-probability sampling methods

1 PROBABILITY DISTRIBUTIONS

Probability distribution
Converting frequency distributions
Graphing probability distributions

1.1 Converting frequency distributions into probability distributions

If we convert the frequencies in a frequency distribution table into proportions, we get a **probability distribution**.

Marks out of 10 (statistics test)	*Number of students (frequency distribution)*	*Proportion or probability (probability distribution)*
0	0	0.00
1	0	0.00
2	1	0.02*
3	2	0.04
4	4	0.08
5	10	0.20
6	15	0.30
7	10	0.20
8	6	0.12
9	2	0.04
10	0	0.00
	50	1.00

* 1/50 = 0.02

Definition

> A **probability distribution** is an analysis of the proportion of times each particular value occurs in a set of items.

1.2 Graphing probability distributions

A graph of the probability distribution would be the same as the graph of the frequency distribution, but with the **vertical axis marked in proportions** rather than in numbers.

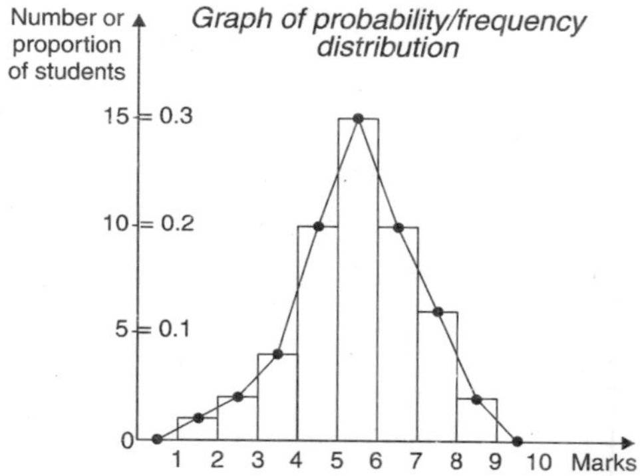

(a) The area under the curve in the frequency distribution represents the total number of students whose marks have been recorded, 50 people.

(b) **The area under the curve in a probability distribution is 100%, or 1** (the total of all the probabilities).

Having covered probability distributions we now turn to the normal distribution.

2 THE NORMAL DISTRIBUTION

The normal distribution
Graphing
Properties
Importance

Definition

> The **normal distribution** is a probability distribution which usually applies to **continuous variables**, such as distance and time.

Introduction

In calculating P(x), x can be any value, and does not have to be a whole number.

The normal distribution can also apply to **discrete variables** which can take **many possible values**. For example, the volume of sales, in units, of a product might be any whole number in the range 100 – 5,000 units. There are so many possibilities within this range that the variable is for all practical purposes **continuous**.

2.1 Graphing the normal distribution

The normal distribution can be drawn as a graph, and it would be a **bell-shaped curve.**

Normal distribution

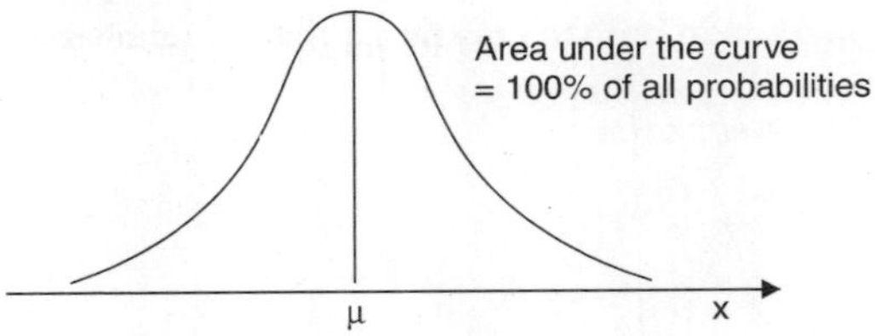

2.2 Properties of the normal distribution

Properties of the normal distribution are as follows:

- It is symmetrical and bell-shaped
- It has a mean, μ (pronounced mew)
- The area under the curve totals exactly 1
- The area to the left of μ = area to the right of μ = 0.5

2.3 Importance of the normal distribution

The normal distribution is important because in the practical application of statistics, it has been found that **many probability distributions are close enough to a normal distribution** to be treated as one without any significant loss of accuracy. This means that the normal distribution can be used as a tool in business decision-making involving probabilities.

3 THE STANDARD NORMAL DISTRIBUTION

The standard normal distribution
Introduction
Normal distribution table

3.1 Introduction

For any normal distribution, the **dispersion** around the mean (μ) of the frequency of occurrences can be measured exactly in terms of the **standard deviation** (σ) (a concept we covered in Chapter 3).

The **standard** normal distribution has a mean (μ) of 0 and a standard deviation (σ) of 1.

(a) The entire frequency curve represents all the possible outcomes and their frequencies of occurrence. Since the normal curve is **symmetrical**, 50% of occurrences have a value greater than the mean value (μ), and 50% of occurrences have a value less than the mean value (μ).

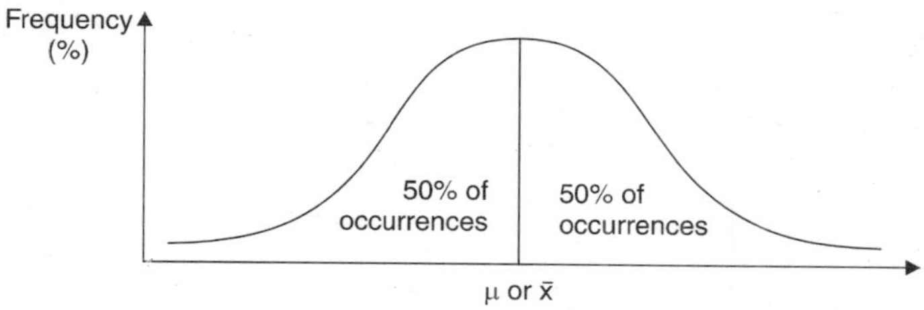

(b) About 68% of frequencies have a value within one standard deviation either side of the mean.

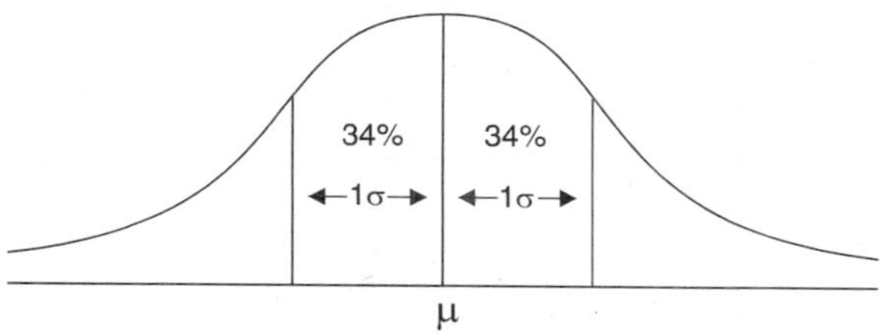

(c) 95% of the frequencies in a normal distribution occur in the range ± 1.96 standard deviations from the mean.

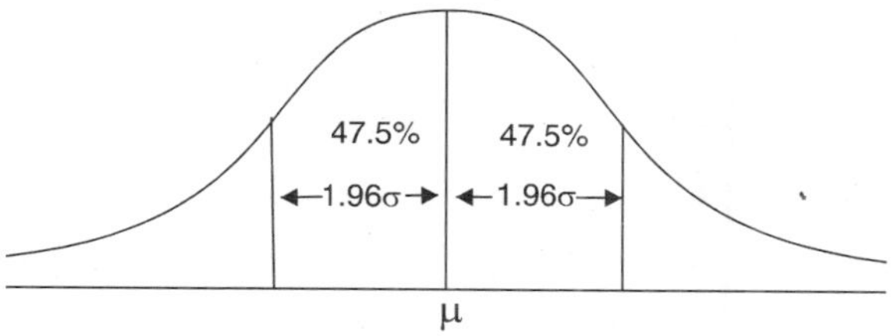

You will not need to remember these precise figures as a **normal distribution table** can be used to find the relevant proportions and this will be given to you in the exam.

3.2 Normal distribution tables

Although there is an infinite number of normal distributions, depending on values of the mean μ and the standard deviation σ, **the relative dispersion of frequencies around the mean, measured as proportions of the total population, is exactly the same for all normal distributions**. In other words, whatever the normal distribution, 47.5% of outcomes will always be in the range between the mean and 1.96 standard deviations below the mean, 49.5% of outcomes will always be in the range between the mean and 2.58 standard deviations below the mean and so on.

A **normal distribution table**, shown at the end of this text, gives the proportion of the total between the mean and a point above or below the mean for any multiple of the standard deviation.

EXAMPLE: NORMAL DISTRIBUTION TABLES

What is the probability that a randomly picked item will be in the shaded area of the diagram below?

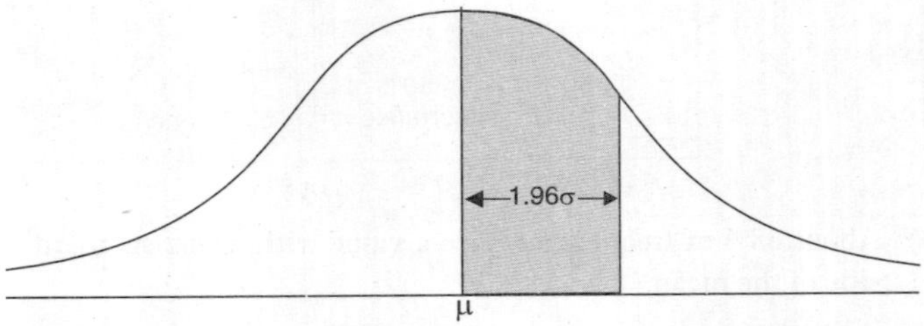

Look up 1.96 in the normal distribution table and you will obtain the value .475. This means there is a 47.5% probability that the item will be in the shaded area.
Since the normal distribution is symmetrical 1.96σ below the mean will also correspond to an area of 47.5%.

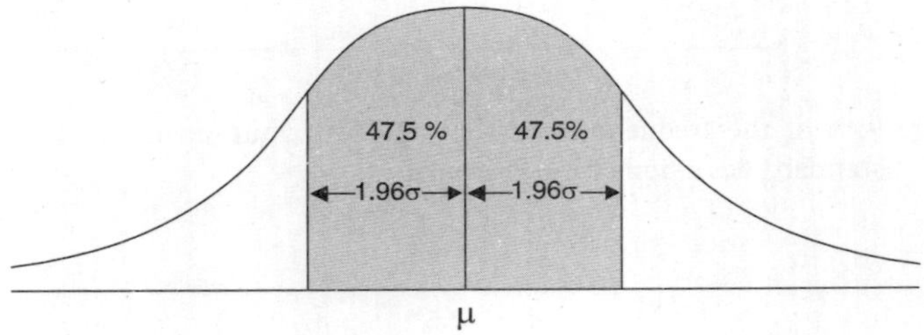

The total shaded area = 47.5% × 2 = 95%

In Paragraph 3.1(c) we said that 95% of the frequencies in a normal distribution lie in the range ± 1.96 standard deviations from the mean but we did not say what this figure was based on. It was of course based on the corresponding value in the normal distribution tables (when z = 1.96) as shown above.

We can also show that 99% of the frequencies occur in the range ± 2.58 standard deviation from the mean.

Using the normal distribution table, a z score of 2.58 corresponds to an area of 0.4949 (or 49.5%). Remember, the normal distribution is symmetrical.

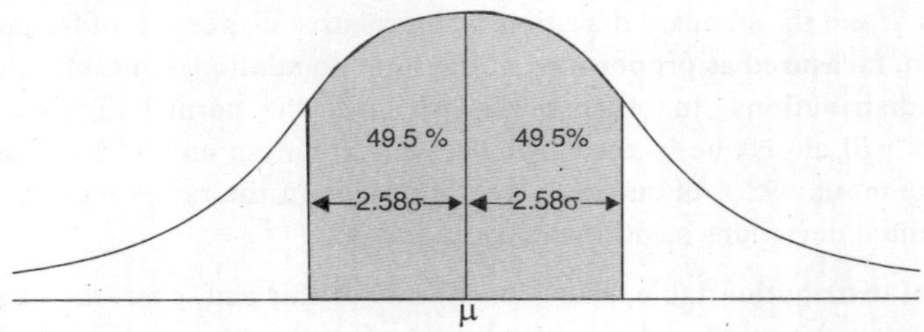

49.5% × 2 = 99%

If		
	mean, $\mu + 2.58\sigma$	= 49.5% and
	mean, $\mu - 2.58\sigma$	= 49.5%
	Range = mean $\pm 2.58\sigma$	= 99.0%

Therefore, 99% of frequencies occur in the range mean (μ) $\pm$ 2.58 standard deviations (σ), as proved by using normal distribution tables.

Activity 1 **(10 minutes)**

Prove that approximately 68% of frequencies have a value within one standard deviation either side of the mean, μ.

4 USING THE NORMAL DISTRIBUTION TO CALCULATE PROBABILITIES

Using the normal distribution to calculate probabilities
Introduction
Calculating Z
Extended example

4.1 Introduction

The normal distribution can be used to calculate probabilities. Sketching a graph of a normal distribution curve often helps in normal distribution problems.

$$z = \frac{x - \mu}{\sigma}$$

where z = the number of standard deviations above or below the mean (z score)
x = the value of the variable under consideration
μ = the mean
σ = the standard deviation.

In order to calculate probabilities, we need to **convert** a normal distribution (x) with a mean μ and standard deviation σ to the standard normal distribution (z) before using the table to find the probability figure.

EXAMPLE: CALCULATING Z

Calculate the following z scores and identify the corresponding proportions using normal distribution tables.

(a) $x = 100, \mu = 200, \sigma = 50$
(b) $x = 1{,}000, \mu = 1{,}200, \sigma = 200$
(c) $x = 25, \mu = 30, \sigma = 6$

SOLUTION

(a) $z = \frac{x - \mu}{\sigma}$

$= \frac{100 - 200}{50}$

$= 2$

A z score of 2 corresponds to a proportion of 0.4772 or 47.72%.

(b) $z = \frac{x - \mu}{\sigma}$

$= \frac{1{,}000 - 1{,}200}{200}$

$= 1$

A z score of 1 corresponds to a proportion of 0.3413 or 34.13%.

(c) $z = \frac{x - \mu}{\sigma}$

$= \frac{25 - 30}{6}$

$= 0.8333$

0.8333 corresponds to a proportion of 0.2967 or 29.67.

EXAMPLE: USING THE NORMAL DISTRIBUTION TO CALCULATE PROBABILITIES

A frequency distribution is normal, with a mean of 100 and a standard deviation of 10.

Required

Calculate the proportion of the total frequencies which will be

(a) above 80
(b) above 90
(c) above 100
(d) above 115
(e) below 85
(f) below 95
(g) below 108
(h) in the range 80 – 110
(i) in the range 90 – 95

SOLUTION

(a) If the value (x) is **below** the mean (μ), the total proportion is 0.5 plus proportion between the value and the mean (area (a)).

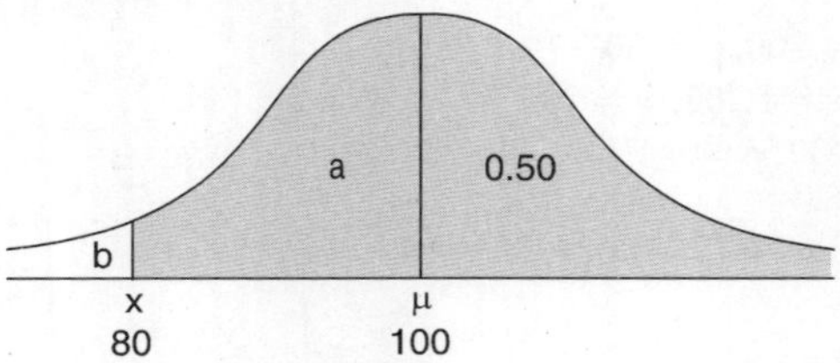

The proportion of the total frequencies which will be above 80 is calculated as follows:

$$\frac{80-100}{10} = 2 \text{ standard deviations } \textbf{below} \text{ the mean.}$$

From the tables, where z = 2 the proportion is 0.4772.

The proportion of frequencies above 80 is 0.5 + 0.4772 = 0.9772.

(b) The proportion of the total frequencies which will be above 90 is calculated as follows:

$$\frac{90-100}{10} = 1 \text{ standard deviation } \textbf{below} \text{ the mean.}$$

From the tables, when z = 1, the proportion is 0.3413.

The proportion of frequencies above 90 is 0.5 + 0.3413 = 0.8413.

(c) 100 is the mean. The proportion above this is 0.5. (The normal curve is symmetrical and 50% of occurrences have a value greater than the mean, and 50% of occurrences have a value less than the mean.)

(d) If the value is **above** the mean, the proportion (b) is 0.5 minus the proportion between the value and the mean (area (a)).

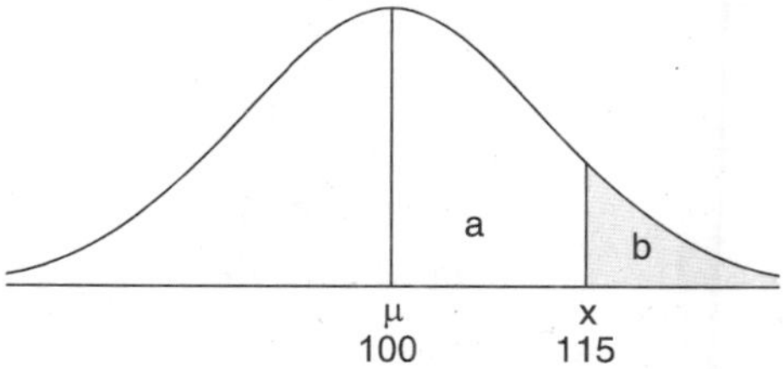

The proportion of the total frequencies which will be above 115 is calculated as follows:

$$\frac{115-100}{10} = 1.5 \text{ standard deviations } \textbf{above} \text{ the mean.}$$

From the tables, where z = 1.5, the proportion is 0.4332.

The proportion of frequencies above 115 is therefore 0.5 – 0.4332 = 0.0668.

(e) If the value is **below** the mean, the proportion (b) is 0.5 minus the proportion between the value and the mean (area (a)).

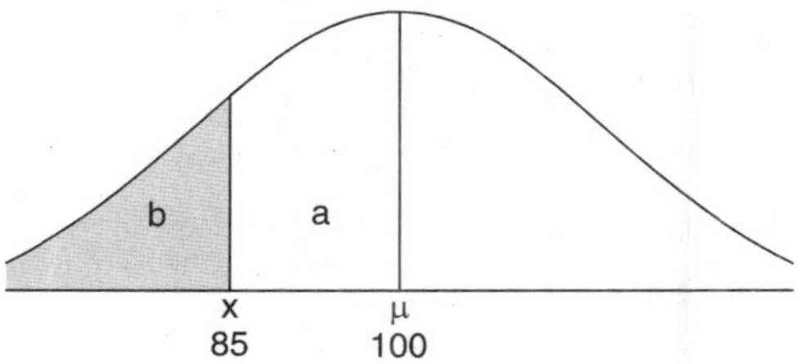

The proportion of the total frequencies which will be below 85 is calculated as follows:

$$\frac{85-100}{10} = 1.5 \text{ standard deviations } \textbf{below} \text{ the mean.}$$

The proportion of frequencies below 85 is therefore the same as the proportion above 115 = 0.0668.

(f) The proportion of the total frequencies which will be below 95 is calculated as follows:

$\frac{95-100}{10}$ = 0.5 standard deviations **below** the mean.

When z = 0.5, the proportion from the tables is 0.1915. The proportion of frequencies below 95 is therefore 0.5 – 0.1915 = 0.3085.

(g) If the value is **above** the mean, the proportion required is 0.5 plus the proportion between the value and the mean (area (a)).

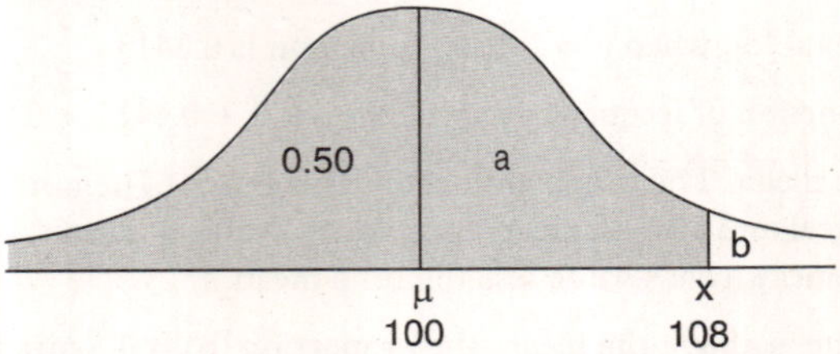

The proportion of the total frequencies which will be below 108 is calculated as follows.

$\frac{108-100}{10}$ = 0.8 standard deviations **above** the mean.

From the tables for z = 0.8 the proportion is 0.2881.

The proportion of frequencies below 108 is 0.5 + 0.2881 = 0.7881.

(h) The proportion of the total frequencies which will be in the range 80–110 is calculated as follows. The range 80 to 110 may be divided into two parts:

(i) 80 to 100 (the mean)
(ii) 100 to 110

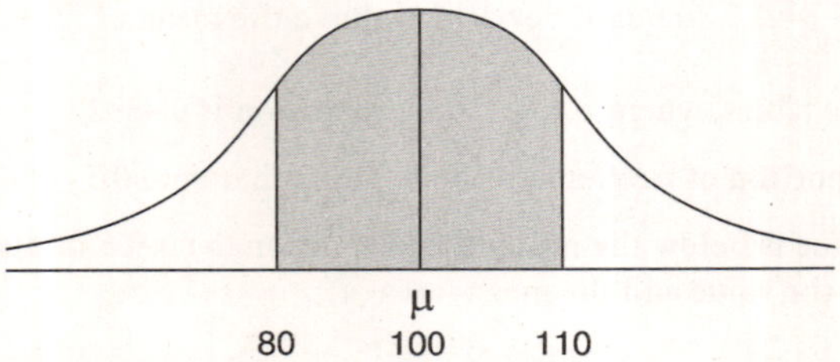

The proportion in the range 80 to 100 is (2 standard deviations) 0.4772.

The proportion in the range 100 to 110 is (1 standard deviation) 0.3413.

The proportion in the total range 80 to 110 is 0.4772 + 0.3413 = 0.8185.

(i) The range 90 to 95 may be analysed as

(i) the proportion above 90 and below the mean
(ii) minus the proportion above 95 and below the mean.

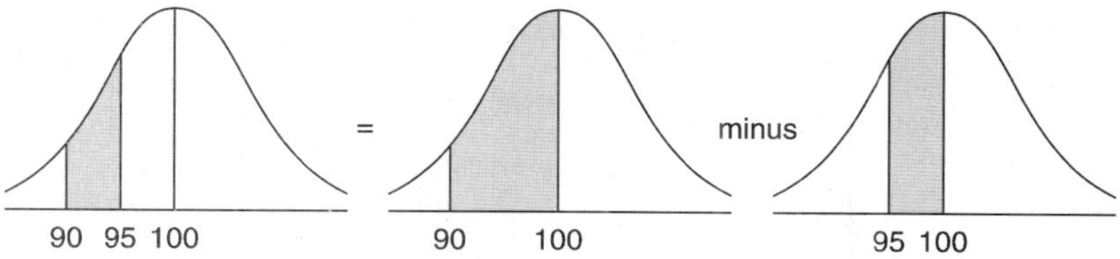

Proportion above 90 and below the mean (1 standard deviation)	0.3413
Proportion above 95 and below the mean (0.5 standard deviations)	0.1915
Proportion between 90 and 95	0.1498

Activity 2 **(15 minutes)**

Normal distribution and proportions

The salaries of employees in an industry are normally distributed, with a mean of £14,000 and a standard deviation of £2,700.

Required

(a) Calculate the proportion of employees who earn less than £12,000.

(b) Calculate the proportion of employees who earn between £11,000 and £19,000.

Activity 3 **(15 minutes)**

Normal distribution

The specification for the width of a widget is a minimum of 42mm and a maximum of 46.2mm. A normally distributed batch of widgets is produced with a mean of 45mm and a variance of 4mm.

Required

(a) Calculate the percentage of parts that are too small.

(b) Calculate the percentage of parts that are too big.

5 AN INTRODUCTION TO SAMPLING

5.1 Samples and populations

Data are often collected from a **sample** rather than from a population. If the whole population is examined, the survey is called a **census**.

In many situations, it will not be practical to carry out a survey which considers every item of the **population**. For example, if a poll is taken to try to predict the results of an election, it would not be possible to ask all eligible voters how they are going to vote. To ask the whole population would take far too long and cost too much money.

In such situations where it is not possible to survey the whole population, a **sample** is selected. The results obtained from the sample are used to estimate the results of the whole population.

5.2 Census

In situations where the whole population is examined, the survey is called a **census**. This situation is quite rare, which means that the investigator must chose a **sample**.

Disadvantages of a census

- The high cost of a census may exceed the value of the results obtained.
- It might be out-of-date by the time you complete it.

Advantages of a sample

(a) It can be shown mathematically that once a certain sample size has been reached, very little accuracy is gained by examining more items. The larger the size of the sample, however, the more accurate the results.

(b) It is possible to ask more questions with a sample.

5.3 The choice of a sample

One of the most important requirements of sample data is that they should be **complete**. That is, the data should **cover all areas** of the population to be examined. If this requirement is not met, then the sample will be **biased**.

5.4 Sampling methods

Sampling methods are categorised as follows:

- **Probability** sampling methods
- **Non-probability** sampling methods

6 PROBABILITY SAMPLING METHODS

Probability sampling methods
Random sampling
Stratified random sampling
Systematic sampling
Multistage sampling
Cluster sampling

A **probability sampling method** is a sampling method in which there is a known chance of each member of the population appearing in the sample.

6.1 Random sampling

Definition

> A **simple random sample** is a sample selected in such a way that every item in the population has an equal chance of being included.

If a sample is selected using random sampling, it will be free from bias (since every item will have an equal chance of being selected). Once the sample has been selected, valid inferences about the population being sampled can be made.

For example, if you wanted to take a random sample of library books, it would not be good enough to pick them off the shelves, even if you picked them at random. This is because the books which were out on loan would stand no chance of being chosen. You would either have to make sure that all the books were on the shelves before taking your sample, or find some other way of sampling (for example, using the library index cards).

A random sample is not necessarily a perfect sample. For example, you might pick what you believe to be a completely random selection of library books, and find that every one of them is a detective thriller. It is a remote possibility, but it could happen. The only way to eliminate the possibility altogether is to take **100% survey (a census)** of the books, which, unless it is a tiny library, is impractical.

Sampling frames

If random sampling is used then it is necessary to construct a **sampling frame**.

Random sampling requires the construction of a **sampling frame**. A sampling frame is a numbered list of all items in a population.

Once a numbered list of all items in the population has been made, it is easy to select a random sample, simply by generating a list of random numbers.

For instance, if you wanted to select a random sample of children from a school, it would be useful to have a list of names:

0 J Adams
1 R Brown
2 S Brown
...

Now the numbers 0, 1, 2 and so on can be used to select the random sample. It is normal to start the numbering at 0, so that when 0 appears in a list of random numbers it can be used.

Sometimes it is not possible to draw up a sampling frame. For example, if you wanted to take a random sample of Americans, it would take too long to list all Americans.

Characteristics of sampling frames

A sampling frame should have the following characteristics:

- **Completeness.** Are all members of the population included on the list?
- **Accuracy.** Is the information correct?
- **Adequacy.** Does it cover the entire population?
- **Up-to-dateness.** Is the list up-to-date?
- **Convenience.** Is the sampling frame readily accessible?
- **Non-duplication.** Does each member of the population appear on the list only once?

Readily available sampling frames

Two **readily available sampling frames** for the human population of Great Britain are the **council tax register** (list of dwellings) and the **electoral register** (list of individuals).

Random number tables

Assuming that a sampling frame can be drawn up, then a random sample can be picked from it by one of the following methods:

- The lottery method (picking numbered pieces of paper out of a box)
- The use of random number tables

Using random number tables

Set out below is part of a typical random number table:

93716	16894	98953	73231
32886	59780	09958	18065
92052	06831	19640	99413
39510	35905	85244	35159
27699	06494	03152	19121
92962	61773	22109	78508
10274	12202	94205	50380
75867	20717	82037	10268
85783	47619	87481	37220

You should note the following points:

(a) The sample is found by selecting groups of random numbers with the number of digits depending on the total population size, as follows:

Total population size	*Number of random digits*
1 – 10	1
1 – 100	2
1 – 1,000	3

The items selected for the sample are those corresponding to the random numbers selected.

(b) The starting point on the table should be selected at random. After that, however, numbers must be selected in a consistent manner. In other words, you should use the table row by row or column by column. By jumping around the table from place to place, personal bias may be introduced.

(c) In many practical situations it is more convenient to use a computer to generate a list of random numbers, especially when a large sample is required.

EXAMPLE: RANDOM NUMBER TABLES

An investigator wishes to select a random sample from a population of 800 people, who have been numbered 000, 001, ...799. As there are three digits in 799 the random numbers will be selected in groups of three. Working along the first line of the table given earlier, the first few groups are as follows:

937 161 689 498 953 732

Numbers over 799 are discarded. The first four people in the sample will therefore be those numbered 161, 689, 498 and 732.

Drawbacks of random sampling

(a) Selected items are subject to the full range of variation inherent in the population.

(b) An unrepresentative sample may result.

(c) An adequate sampling frame might not exist.

(d) The numbering of the population might be laborious.

(e) It might be difficult to obtain the data if the selected items cover a wide area.

(f) It might be costly to obtain the data if the selected items cover a wide area.

6.2 Stratified random sampling

A variation on the random sampling method is **stratified random sampling.**

Definition

> **Stratified random sampling** is a method of sampling which involves dividing the population into strata or categories. Random samples are then taken from each stratum or category.

In many situations, stratified sampling is the best method of choosing a sample. Stratified sampling is best demonstrated by means of an example.

EXAMPLE STRATIFIED SAMPLING

The number of cost and management accountants in each type of work in a particular country are as follows:

Partnerships	500
Public companies	500
Private companies	700
Public practice	800
	2,500

If a sample of 20 was required the sample would be made up as follows:

		Sample
Partnerships	$\frac{500}{2{,}500} \times 20$	4
Public companies	$\frac{500}{2{,}500} \times 20$	4
Private companies	$\frac{700}{2{,}500} \times 20$	6
Public practice	$\frac{800}{2{,}500} \times 20$	6
		20

Advantages and disadvantages of stratification

Advantages	Disadvantages
The sample selected will be representative since it guarantees that every important category will have elements in the final sample.	The main disadvantage of stratification is that it requires prior knowledge of each item in the population; sampling frames do not always contain such information.
The structure of the sample will reflect that of the population if the same proportion of individuals is chosen from each stratum.	
Each stratum is represented by a randomly chosen sample and therefore inferences can be made about each stratum.	
Precision is increased. Sampling takes place within strata and, because the range of variation is less in each stratum than in the population as a whole and variation between strata does not enter as a chance effect, higher precision is obtainable.	

6.3 Systematic sampling

Definition

> **Systematic sampling** is a sampling method which works by selecting every n^{th} item after a random start.

If it were decided to select a sample of 20 from a population of 800, then every 40th (800 ÷ 20) item after a random start in the first 40 should be selected. The starting point could be found using the lottery method or random number tables. If (say) 23 was chosen, then the sample would include the 23rd, 63rd, 103rd, 143rd ... 783rd items. The gap of 40 is known as the **sampling interval**.

Advantages and disadvantages of systematic sampling

Advantages	Disadvantages
It is easy to use.	It is possible that a biased sample might be chosen if there is a regular pattern to the population which coincides with the sampling method.
It is cheap.	It is not completely random since some samples have a zero chance of being selected.

6.4 Multistage sampling

Definition

> **Multistage sampling** is a probability sampling method which involves dividing the population into a number of sub-populations and then selecting a small sample of these sub-populations at random.
>
> Each sub-population is then divided further, and then a small sample is again selected at random. This process is repeated as many times as is necessary.

EXAMPLE: MULTISTAGE SAMPLING

A survey of spending habits is being planned to cover the whole of Britain. It is obviously **impractical to draw up a sampling frame**, so **random sampling is not possible**. Multistage sampling is to be used instead.

The country is divided into a number of areas and a small sample of these is selected at random. Each of the areas selected is subdivided into smaller units and again, a smaller number of these is selected at random. This process is repeated as many times as necessary and, finally, a random sample of the relevant people living in each of the smallest units is taken. A fair approximation to a random sample can be obtained.

Thus, we might choose a random sample of eight areas, and from each of these areas select a random sample of five towns. From each town, a random sample of 200 people might be selected so that the total sample size is $8 \times 5 \times 200 = 8{,}000$ people.

Advantages and disadvantages of multistage sampling

Advantages	Disadvantages
Fewer investigators are needed.	There is the **possibility of bias** if, for example, only a small number of regions are selected.
It is not so costly to obtain a sample.	The method is **not truly random** as once the final sampling areas have been selected the rest of the population cannot be in the sample. If the population is heterogeneous, the areas chosen should reflect the **full range of the diversity**. Otherwise, choosing some areas and excluding others (even if it is done randomly) will result in a biased sample.

6.5 Cluster sampling

Definition

Cluster sampling is a non-random sampling method that involves selecting one definable subsection of the population as the sample, that subsection taken to be representative of the population in question.

For example, the pupils of one school might be taken as a cluster sample of all children at school in one county.

Advantages and disadvantages of cluster sampling

Advantages	Disadvantages
It is a good alternative to multistage sampling if a satisfactory sampling frame does not exist.	The potential for considerable bias.
It is inexpensive to operate.	

Activity 4 **(10 minutes)**

Sampling methods

Sampling methods are frequently used for the collection of data. Five commonly used types of samples are (A) simple random, (B) stratified random, (C) systematic, (D) cluster and (E) quota. State which of these sample types is being described in the following situations:

(a) One school in an area is selected at random and then all pupils in that school are surveyed.

Type of sample is ☐

(b) The local authority has a list of all pupils in the area and the sample is selected in such a way that all pupils have an equal probability of selection.

Type of sample is ☐

(c) An interviewer surveys pupils emerging from every school in the area, attempting to question them randomly but in line with specified numbers of boys and girls in the various age groups.

Type of sample is ☐

(d) The local authority has a list of all pupils in the selected area, categorised according to their gender and age. The sample selected is chosen randomly from the various categories, in proportion to their sizes.

Type of sample is ☐

(e) The local authority has a list of all pupils in the selected area. The first pupil is selected randomly from the list and then every 100th pupil thereafter is selected for the survey.

Type of sample is ☐

Activity 5 **(5 minutes)**

Systemic sampling

Which of the following are disadvantages of systematic sampling? Tick as appropriate.

☐ The sample chosen might be biased

☐ Some samples have a zero chance of being selected so sampling method is not completely random

☐ Prior knowledge of each item in the population is required

7 NON-PROBABILITY SAMPLING METHODS

Non-probability sampling methods
Quota sampling
Advantages and disadvantages of quota sampling

A **non-probability sampling method** is a sampling method in which the chance of each member of the population appearing in the sample is not known, for example, **quota sampling.**

7.1 Quota sampling

Definition

> In **quota sampling**, randomness is forfeited in the interests of cheapness and administrative simplicity. Investigators are told to interview all the people they meet, up to a certain quota.

EXAMPLE: QUOTA SAMPLING

Consider the figures above, but with the following additional information relating to the sex of the cost and management accountants.

	Male	*Female*
Partnerships	300	200
Public companies	400	100
Private companies	300	400
Public practice	300	500

An investigator's quotas might be as follows.

	Male	*Female*	*Total*
Partnerships	30	20	50
Public companies	40	10	50
Private companies	30	40	70
Public practice	30	50	80
			250

Using quota sampling, the investigator would interview the first 30 male cost and management accountants in partnerships that he met, the first 20 female cost and management accountants in partnerships that he met and so on.

7.2 Advantages and disadvantages of quota sampling

Advantages	Disadvantages
It is cheap and administratively easy.	An interviewer in a shopping centre may fill his quota by only meeting people who can go shopping during the week.
A much larger sample can be studied, and hence more information can be gained at a faster speed for a given outlay than when compared with a fully randomised sampling method.	The non-random nature of the method rules out any valid estimate of the sampling error (a concept you will meet later in your studies) in estimates derived from the sample.
Although a fairly detailed knowledge of the characteristics of a population is required, no sampling frame is necessary because the interviewer questions every person he meets up to the quota.	
It may be the only possible approach in certain situations, such as television audience research.	
Given suitable, trained and properly briefed field workers, quota sampling yields enough accurate information for many forms of commercial market research.	

Note. Once data have been collected they need to be **presented** and **analysed**. It is important to remember that if data have not been collected properly, no amount of careful presentation or analysis can remedy this.

Chapter roundup

- If we convert the frequencies in a frequency distribution table into proportions, we get a **probability distribution**.
- The **normal distribution** is a probability distribution which usually applies to **continuous variables**, such as distance and time.
- Properties of the normal distribution are as follows:
  - It is symmetrical
  - It has a mean, μ (pronounced mew)
  - The area under the curve totals exactly 1
  - The area to the left of μ = area to right of μ
  - It is a bell shaped curve
- Distances above or below the mean of a normal distribution are expressed in numbers of **standard deviations, z**.

  $$z = \frac{x - \mu}{\sigma}$$

  Where z = the number of standard deviations above or below the mean
  x = the value of the variable under consideration
  μ = the mean
  σ = the standard deviation
- The normal distribution can be used to calculate probabilities. Sketching a graph of a normal distribution curve often helps in normal distribution problems.
- Data are often collected from a **sample** rather than from a population. If the whole population is examined, the survey is called a **census**.
- A **probability sampling method** is a sampling method in which there is a known chance of each member of the population appearing in the sample.

  Probability sampling methods

  - Random
  - Stratified random
  - Systematic
  - Multistage
  - Cluster
- Random sampling requires the construction of a **sampling frame**. A sampling frame is a numbered list of all items in a population.
- A **non-probability sampling method** is a sampling method in which the chance of each member of the population appearing in the sample is not known, for example, **quota sampling**.

Quick quiz

1 The normal distribution is a type of .... distribution.

2 The area under the curve of a normal distribution = ... which represents ....% of all probabilities.

3 The mean of a normal distribution = σ

True ☐

False ☐

4 Use the following symbols to create a formula for calculating the 'z score':

x	μ	z	σ

5 What proportions/percentages do the following z scores represent?

(a) 1.45
(b) 2.93
(c) 0.955

6 What are the corresponding z scores for the following proportions/ percentages?

(a) 0.4382
(b) 0.4750
(c) 0.4747

7 The essence of systematic sampling is that

A Each element of the population has an equal chance of being chosen

B Members of various strata are selected by the interviewers up to predetermined limits

C Every nth item of the population is selected

D Every element of one definable sub-section of the population is selected

Answers to quick quiz

1 Probability

2 1, 100%

3 False. The mean of a normal distribution = μ

4 $z = \frac{x-\mu}{\sigma}$

5 (a) 0.4265 = 42.65%

(b) 0.4983 = 49.83%

(c) 0.3302 = 33.02% (Take average of 0.95 and 0.96 = (0.3289 + 0.3315) ÷ 2 = 0.3302.)

6 (a) 1.54
(b) 1.96
(c) 1.955

7 C

Answers to activities

1 One standard deviation corresponds to z = 1

If z = 1, we can look this value up in normal distribution tables to get a value (area) of 0.3413. One standard deviation above the mean can be shown on a graph as follows:

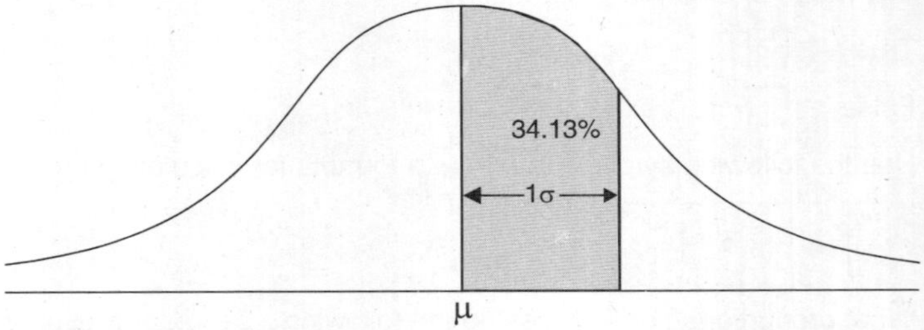

The normal distribution is symmetrical, and we must therefore show the area corresponding to one standard deviation below the mean on the graph also.

2 (a)

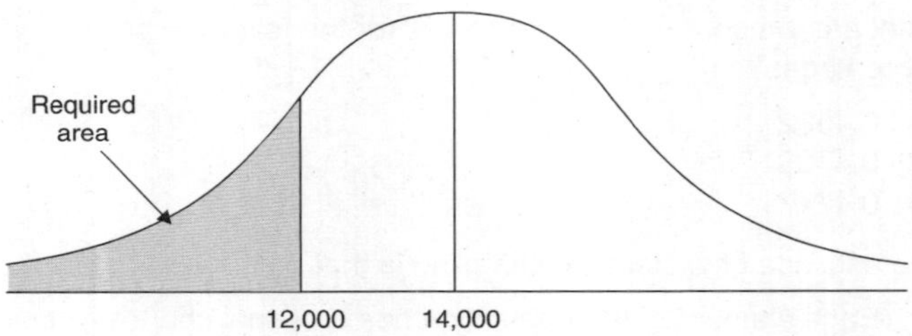

$$z = \frac{12{,}000 - 14{,}000}{2{,}700}$$
$$= -0.74$$

From normal distribution tables, the proportion of salaries between £12,000 and £14,000 is 0.2704 (from tables). The proportion of salaries less than £12,000 is therefore 0.5 – 0.2704 = 0.2296.

(b)

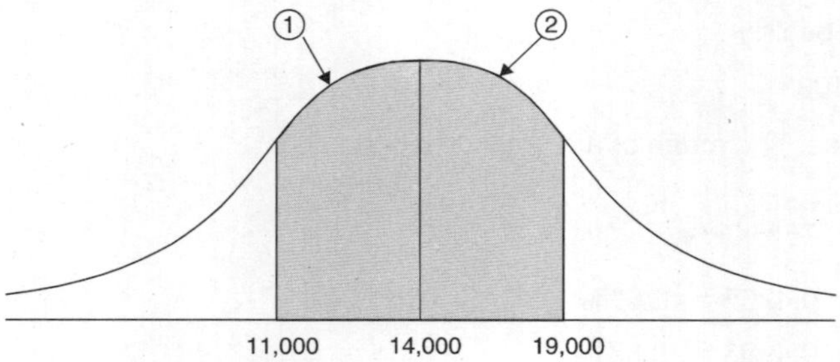

(1) $z = \frac{11{,}000 - 14{,}000}{2{,}700}$

$= 1.11$

(2) $z = \frac{19{,}000 - 14{,}000}{2{,}700}$

$= 1.85$

The proportion with earnings between £11,000 and £14,000 is 0.3665 (from tables where z = 1.11).

The proportion with earnings between £14,000 and £19,000 is 0.4678 (from tables where z = 1.85).

The required proportion is therefore 0.3665 + 0.4678 = 0.8343.

Note that the normal distribution is, in fact, a way of calculating probabilities. In this question, for example, the **probability** that an employee earns less than £12,000 (part (a)) is 0.2296 (or 22.96%) and the probability that an employee earns between £11,000 and £19,000 is 0.8343 (or 83.43%).

3 (a)

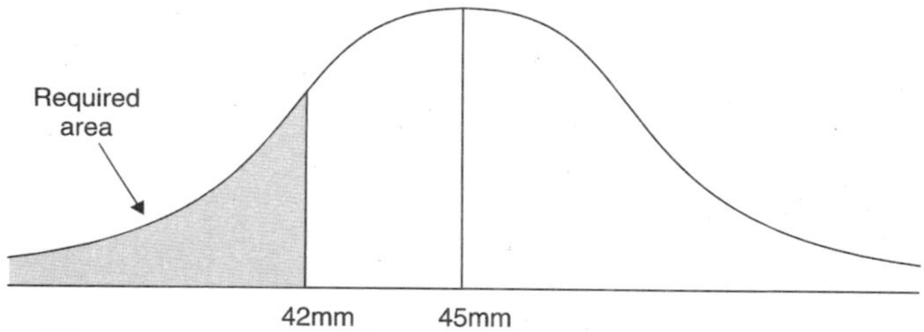

$\sigma = \sqrt{4} = 2$

$z = \dfrac{42-45}{2} = -1.5$

Proportion of widgets between 42mm and 45mm = 0.4332.
Proportion of widgets smaller than 42mm = 0.5 – 0.4332 = 0.0668
= 6.68%

(b)

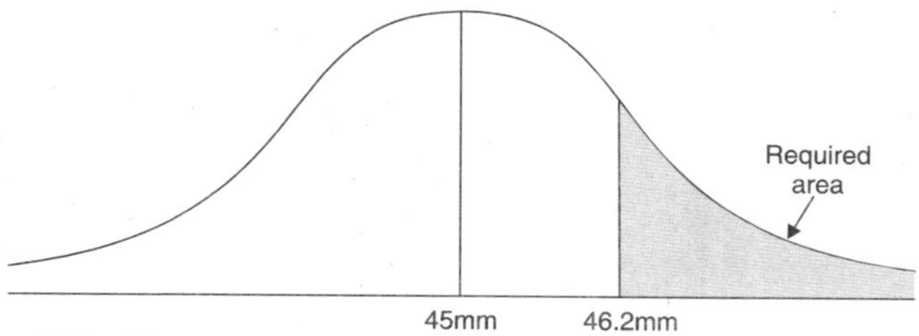

$z = \dfrac{46.2-45}{2} = 0.6$

Proportion of widgets between 45mm and 46.2mm = 0.2257.
Proportion of widgets bigger than 46.2mm = 0.5 – 0.2257 = 0.2743
= 27.43%

4

(a) D

(b) A

(c) E

(d) B

(e) C

5

- [x] The sample chosen might be biased
- [x] Some samples have a zero chance of being selected so sampling method is not completely random
- [ ] Prior knowledge of each item in the population is required

Chapter 6 :
DECISION-MAKING

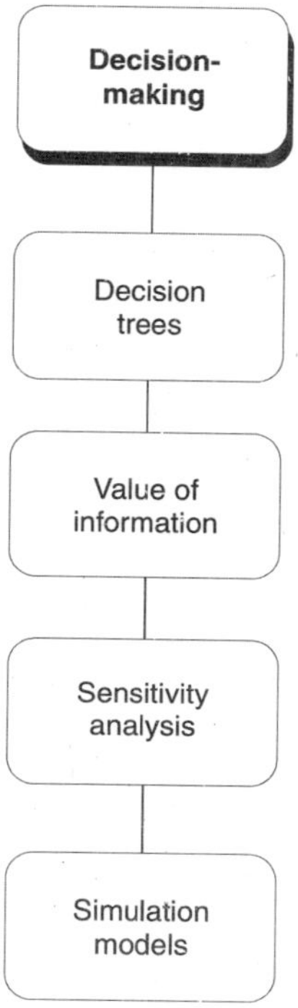

Introduction

In any business decisions are being continuously made. How much do we charge for our products? Should we enter a new market? Which machine should we buy? are just some of the typical questions faced.

Businesses will have to make choices. Some of these will be made quickly and with little thought. This chapter introduces some techniques that people in business can use to help them make choices.

Your objectives

In this chapter you will learn about the following:

- Decision trees
- The value of information
- Sensitivity analysis
- Simulation models

1 DECISION TREES

Decision trees
Constructing a decision tree
Evaluating the decision
Sensitivity analysis and decision trees

Decision trees are diagrams which illustrate the choices and possible outcomes of a decision.

Definition

> A **decision tree** is a pictorial method of showing a sequence of interrelated decisions and their expected outcomes. Decision trees can incorporate both the probabilities of, and values of, expected outcomes, and are used in decision-making.

A probability problem such as 'what is the probability of throwing a six with one throw of a die?' is fairly straightforward and can be solved using the basic principles of probability.

More complex probability questions, although solvable using the basic principles, require a clear logical approach to ensure that all possible choices and outcomes of a decision are taken into consideration. **Decision trees** are a useful means of interpreting such probability problems.

Exactly how does the use of a decision tree permit a clear and logical approach?

- All the possible **choices** that can be made are shown as **branches** on the tree.
- All the possible **outcomes** of each choice are shown as **subsidiary branches** on the tree.

1.1 Constructing a decision tree

There are two stages in preparing a decision tree:

- Drawing the tree itself to show all the choices and outcomes
- Putting in the numbers (the probabilities, outcome values and EVs)

Every **decision tree starts** from a **decision point** with the **decision options** that are currently being considered.

(a) It helps to identify the **decision point**, and any subsequent decision points in the tree, with a symbol. Here, we shall use a **square shape**.

(b) There should be a **line**, or **branch**, for each **option** or **alternative**.

It is conventional to draw decision trees from left to right, and so a decision tree will start as follows:

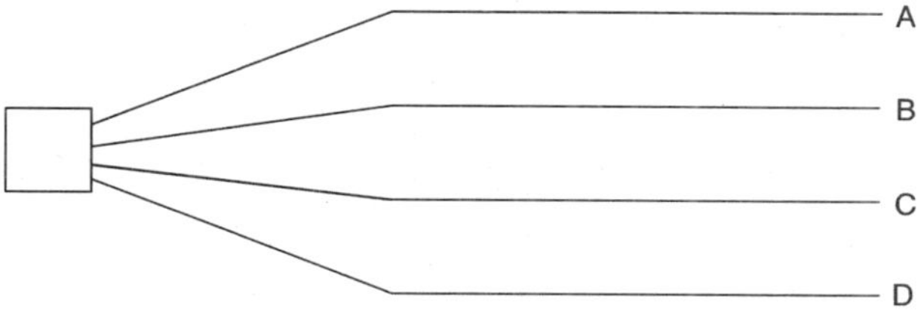

The **square** is the **decision point**, and A, B, C and D represent **four alternatives** from which a choice must be made (such as buy a new machine with cash, hire a machine, continue to use existing machine, raise a loan to buy a machine).

If the outcome from any choice is certain, the branch of the decision tree for that alternative is complete.

If the outcome of a particular choice is uncertain, the various possible outcomes must be shown.

We show the various possible outcomes on a decision tree by inserting an **outcome point** on the **branch** of the tree. Each possible outcome is then shown as a **subsidiary branch,** coming out from the outcome point. The probability of each outcome occurring should be written on to the branch of the tree which represents that outcome.

To distinguish decision points from outcome points, **a circle will be used as the symbol for an outcome point**.

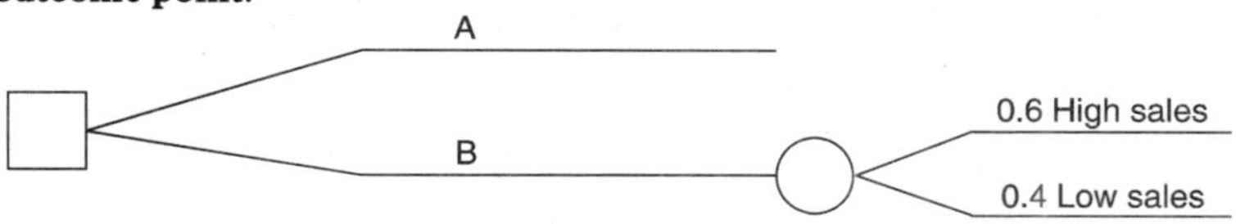

In the example above, there are two choices facing the decision-maker, A and B. The outcome if A is chosen is known with certainty, but if B is chosen, there are two possible outcomes, high sales (0.6 probability) or low sales (0.4 probability).

When several outcomes are possible, it is usually simpler to show two or more stages of outcome points on the decision tree.

EXAMPLE: SEVERAL POSSIBLE OUTCOMES

A company can choose to launch a new product XYZ or not. If the product is launched, expected sales and expected unit costs might be as follows:

Sales		*Unit costs*	
Units	*Probability*	*£*	*Probability*
10,000	0.8	6	0.7
15,000	0.2	8	0.3

(a) The decision tree could be drawn as follows:

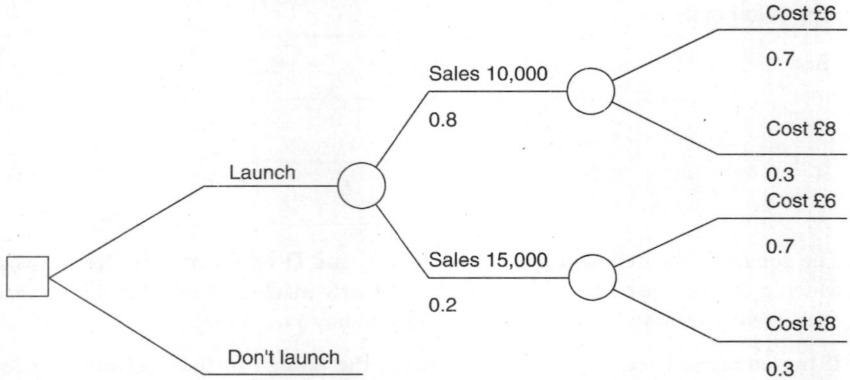

(b) The layout shown above will usually be easier to use than the alternative way of drawing the tree, which is as follows:

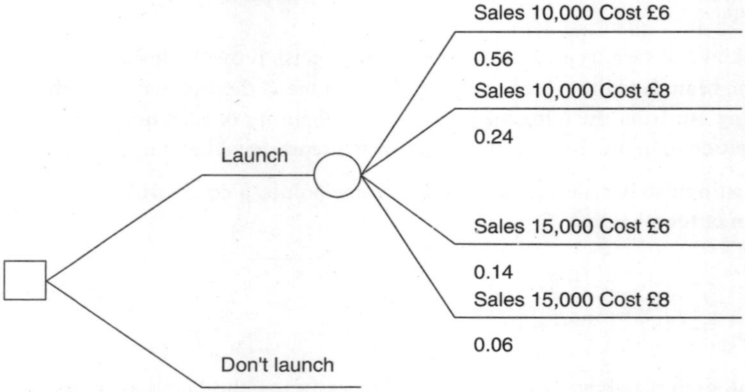

Sometimes, a **decision taken now** will lead to **other decisions to be taken in the future**. When this situation arises, the decision tree can be drawn as a **two-stage tree**, as follows:

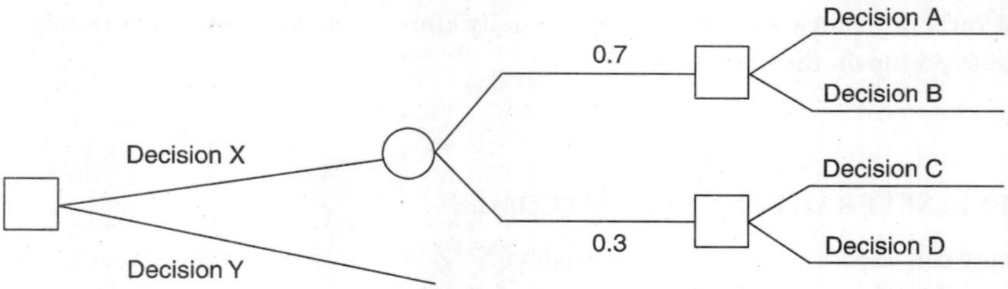

In this tree, either a choice between A and B or else a choice between C and D will be made, depending on the outcome which occurs after choosing X.

The decision tree should be in **chronological order** from **left to right**. When there are two-stage decision trees, the first decision in time should be drawn on the left.

EXAMPLE: A DECISION TREE

Beethoven has a new wonder product, the vylin, of which it expects great things. At the moment the company has two courses of action open to it, to test market the product or abandon it.

If the company test markets it, the cost will be £100,000 and the market response could be positive or negative with probabilities of 0.60 and 0.40.

If the response is positive the company could either abandon the product or market it full scale.

If it markets the vylin full scale, the outcome might be low, medium or high demand, and the respective net gains/(losses) would be (200), 200 or 1,000 in units of £1,000 (the result could range from a net loss of £200,000 to a gain of £1,000,000). These outcomes have probabilities of 0.20, 0.50 and 0.30 respectively.

If the result of the test marketing is negative and the company goes ahead and markets the product, estimated losses would be £600,000.

If, at any point, the company abandons the product, there would be a net gain of £50,000 from the sale of scrap. All the financial values have been discounted to the present.

Required

(a) Draw a decision tree.
(b) Include figures for cost, loss or profit on the appropriate branches of the tree.

SOLUTION

The starting point for the tree is to **establish what decision has to be made now**. What are the options?

(a) To test market
(b) To abandon

The outcome of the 'abandon' option is known with certainty. There are two possible outcomes of the option to test market, positive response and negative response.

Depending on the outcome of the test marketing, another decision will then be made, to abandon the product or to go ahead.

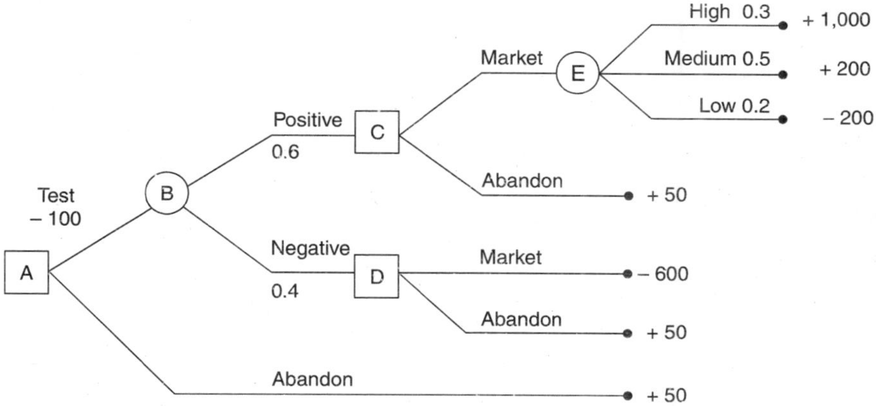

The next part of this chapter relies on the concept of Expected Values (EV) which was covered in Chapter 3. If you have not already read Chapter 3 then please do so now.

1.2 Evaluating the decision with a decision tree

Rollback analysis evaluates the EV of each decision option. You have to work from right to left and calculate EVs at each outcome point.

The Expected Value (EV) of each decision option can be evaluated, using the decision tree to help with keeping the logic properly sorted out. The basic rules are as follows:

(a) We start on the **right hand side** of the tree and **work back** towards the left-hand side and the current decision under consideration. This is sometimes known as the '**rollback technique**' or '**rollback analysis**'.

(b) Working from **right to left**, we calculate the **EV of revenue, cost, contribution or profit** at each outcome point on the tree.

In the above example, the right-hand-most outcome point is point E, and the EV is as follows:

	Profit	*Probability*	
	x	*p*	*px*
	£'000		*£'000*
High	1,000	0.3	300
Medium	200	0.5	100
Low	(200)	0.2	(40)
		EV	360

This is the EV of the decision to market the product if the test shows positive response. It may help you to write the EV on the decision tree itself, at the appropriate outcome point (point E).

(a) **At decision point C,** the **choice** is as follows:

(i) Market, EV = + 360 (the EV at point E)
(ii) Abandon, value = + 50

The choice would be to market the product, and so the EV at decision point C is +360.

(b) **At decision point D,** the **choice** is as follows:

(i) Market, value = – 600
(ii) Abandon, value = +50

The choice would be to abandon, and so the EV at decision point D is +50.

The second stage decisions have therefore been made. If the original decision is to test market, the company will market the product if the test shows positive customer response, and will abandon the product if the test results are negative.

The evaluation of the decision tree is completed as follows:

(a) **Calculate the EV at outcome point B.**

$$
\begin{aligned}
& 0.6 \times 360 \quad \text{(EV at C)} \\
+ \; & 0.4 \times 50 \quad \text{(EV at D)} \\
= \; & 216 + 20 = 236.
\end{aligned}
$$

(b) **Compare the options at point A**, which are as follows:

(i) Test: EV = EV at B minus test marketing cost = 236 – 100 = 136
(ii) Abandon: Value = 50

The choice would be to test market the product, because it has a **higher EV of profit**.

Activity 1 **(10 minutes)**

Simple decision tree

Consider the following diagram.

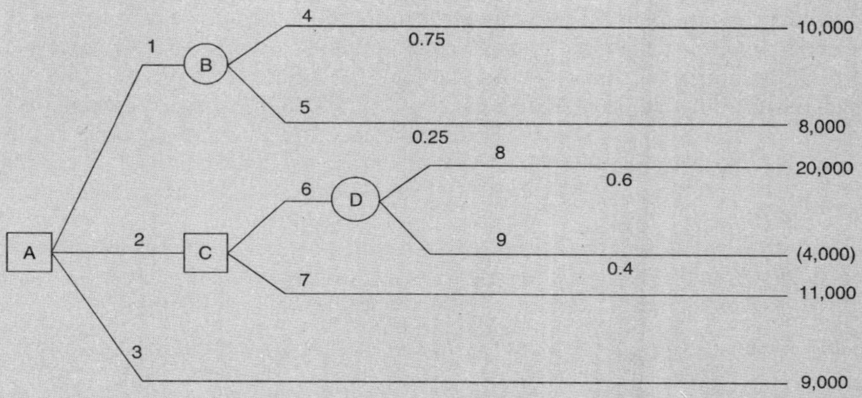

If a decision-maker wished to maximise the value of the outcome, which options should be selected?

A Option 2 and option 7
B Option 3
C Option 1 and option 4
D Option 2, option 6 and option 8

Evaluating decisions by using **decision trees has a number of limitations.**

(a) The time value of money may not be taken into account.

(b) Decision trees are not very suitable for use in complex situations.

(c) The outcome with the highest EV may have the greatest risks attached to it. Managers may be reluctant to take risks which may lead to losses.

(d) The probabilities associated with different branches of the 'tree' are likely to be estimates, and possibly unreliable or inaccurate.

Activity 2 **(30 minutes)**

More complex decision tree

A software company has just won a contract worth £80,000 if it delivers a successful product on time, but only £40,000 if it is late. It faces the problem now of whether to produce the work in-house or to sub-contract it. To sub-contract the work would cost £50,000, but the local sub-contractor is so fast and reliable as to make it certain that successful software is produced on time.

If the work is produced in-house the cost would be only £20,000 but, based on past experience, would have only a 90% chance of being successful. In the event of the software *not* being successful, there would be insufficient time to rewrite the whole package internally, but there would still be the options of either a 'late rejection' of the contract (at a further cost of £10,000) or of 'late sub-contracting' the work on the same terms as before. With this late start the local sub-contractor is estimated to have only a 50/50 chance of producing the work on time or of producing it late. In this case the sub-contractor still has to be paid £50,000, regardless of whether he meets the deadline or not.

Required

(a) Draw a decision tree for the software company, using squares for decision points and circles for outcome (chance) points, including all relevant data on the diagram.

(b) Calculate expected values as appropriate and recommend a course of action to the software company with reasons.

1.3 Sensitivity analysis and decision trees

Look again at **Activity 2: More complex decision tree**. By how much can the probability of success fall before the optimal EV decision changes?

Suppose the probability of success = p (and so the probability of failure = 1 – p). At decision **point A** we want to find the point where **EV (sub-contract) = EV (in-house).**

$$30 = (80 \times p) + (10 \times (1 - p)) - 20$$
$$30 = 80p + 10 - 10p - 20$$
$$40 = 70p$$
$$p = 0.57$$

Since the probability of success can drop to 57% from 90% before we change our decision, we would probably consider the decision insensitive to this factor.

So far we have assumed that we have probabilities with certainty. This is called perfect information. In the next section we will look at the value of knowing it.

2 THE VALUE OF INFORMATION

Value of information
The value of perfect information
Perfect information and decision trees
The value of imperfect information

Perfect information is guaranteed to predict the future with 100% accuracy. **Imperfect information** is better than no information at all but could be wrong in its prediction of the future.

Definition

Perfect information removes all doubt and uncertainty from a decision, and enables managers to make decisions with complete confidence that they have selected the optimum course of action.

2.1 The value of perfect information

The **value of perfect information** is the difference between the EV of profit with perfect information and the EV of profit without perfect information.

Step 1 If we **do not have perfect information** and we must choose between two or more decision options, we would **select** the decision option which offers the **highest EV** of profit. This option will not be the best decision under all circumstances. There will be some probability that what was really the best option will not have been selected, given the way actual events turn out.

Step 2 With **perfect information,** the **best decision option will always be selected.** Just what the profits from the decision will be must depend on the future circumstances which are predicted by the information; nevertheless, the EV of profit with perfect information should be higher than the EV of profit without the information.

Step 3 The **value of perfect information** is **the difference between these two EVs.**

EXAMPLE: THE VALUE OF PERFECT INFORMATION

The management of Ivor Ore must choose whether to go ahead with either of two mutually exclusive projects, A and B. The expected profits are as follows:

	Profit if there is strong demand	*Profit/(loss) if there is weak demand*
Option A	£4,000	£(1,000)
Option B	£1,500	£500
Probability of demand	0.3	0.7

Required

(a) Ascertain what the decision would be, based on expected values, if no information about demand were available.

(b) Calculate the value of perfect information about demand.

SOLUTION

Step 1 If there were **no information** to help with the decision, the project with the higher EV of profit would be selected.

Probability	*Project A*		*Project B*	
	Profit	*EV*	*Profit*	*EV*
	£	£	£	£
0.3	4,000	1,200	1,500	450
0.7	(1,000)	(700)	500	350
		500		800

Project B would be selected.

This is clearly the better option if demand turns out to be weak. However, if demand were to turn out to be strong, project A would be more profitable. There is a 30% chance that this could happen.

Step 2 **Perfect information** will indicate for certain whether demand will be weak or strong. If demand is forecast 'weak', project B would be selected. If demand is forecast as 'strong', project A would be selected, and perfect information would improve the profit from £1,500, which would have been earned by selecting B, to £4,000.

Forecast demand	*Probability*	*Project chosen*	*Profit*	*EV of profit*
			£	£
Weak	0.7	B	500	350
Strong	0.3	A	4,000	1,200
EV of profit with perfect information				1,550

Step 3

	£
EV of profit without perfect information (that is, if project B is always chosen)	800
EV of profit with perfect information	1,550
Value of perfect information	750

Provided that the information does not cost more than £750 to collect, it would be worth having.

Activity 3 **(10 minutes)**

Decision based on EV of profit

Watt Lovell must decide at what level to market a new product, the urk. The urk can be sold nationally, within a single sales region (where demand is likely to be relatively strong) or within a single area. The decision is complicated by uncertainty about the general strength of consumer demand for the product, and the following conditional profit table has been constructed.

			Demand	
		Weak	*Moderate*	*Strong*
		£	£	£
Market	nationally (A)	(4,000)	2,000	10,000
	in one region (B)	0	3,500	4,000
	in one area (C)	1,000	1,500	2,000
Probability		0.3	0.5	0.2

Option B should be selected, based on EVs of profit. *True or false?*

Activity 4 **(10 minutes)**

Using the information in your answer to the question above (Decision based on EV of profit), fill in the blank in the sentence below.

The value of information about the state of demand is £.......... .

2.2 Perfect information and decision trees

When the option exists to obtain information, the decision can be shown, like any other decision, in the form of a decision tree, as follows. We will suppose, for illustration, that the cost of obtaining perfect information is £400.

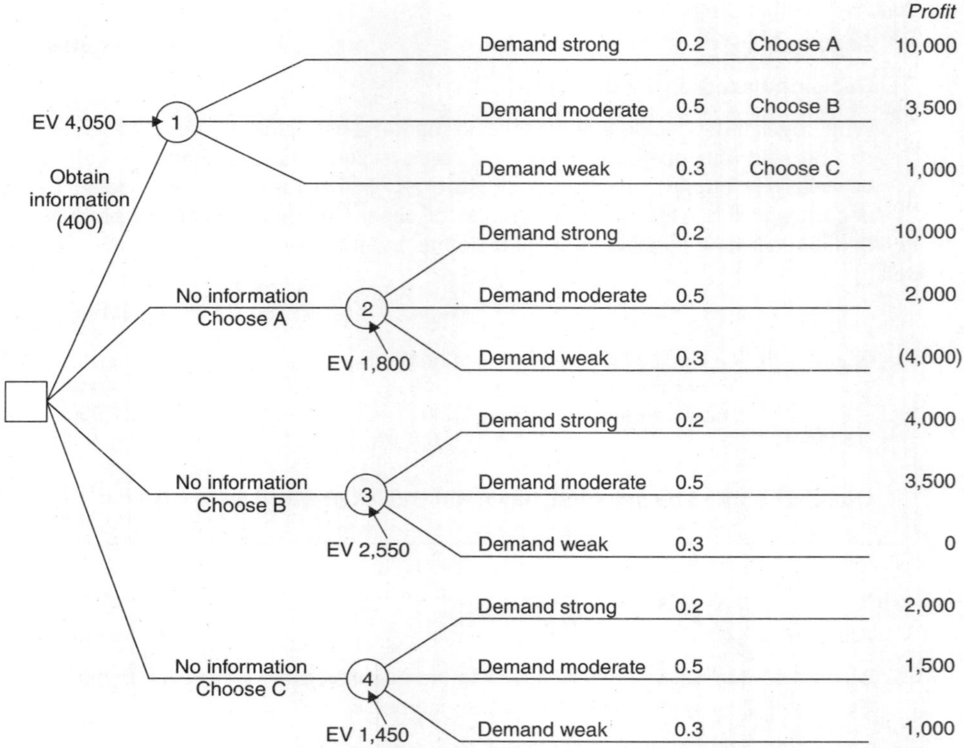

The decision would be to obtain perfect information, since the EV of profit is £4,050 – £400 = £3,650.

Note. You should check carefully that you understand the logic of this decision tree and that you can identify how the EVs at outcome boxes 1, 2, 3 and 4 have been calculated.

2.3 The value of imperfect information

There is one serious drawback to the technique we have just looked at: in practice **useful information is never perfect** unless the person providing it is the sole source of the uncertainty. Market research findings or information from pilot tests and so on are likely to be reasonably accurate, but they can still be wrong: they provide imperfect information. It is possible, however, to arrive at an assessment of **how much it would be worth paying for such imperfect information, given that we have a rough indication of how right or wrong it is likely to be.**

Suppose we are considering the sex and hair colour of people in a given group or population consisting of 70% men and 30% women. We have established the probabilities of hair colourings as follows:

	Men	*Women*
Brown	0.60	0.35
Blonde	0.35	0.55
Red	0.05	0.10

This shows, for example, that 5% of men in such a sample have red hair. These probabilities of sex and hair colouring might be referred to as **prior probabilities.**

Posterior probabilities consider the situation in reverse or retrospect, so that we can ask the question: 'Given that a person taken at random from the population is brown-haired what is the probability that the person is male (or female)?'

The information can be presented in a table. Let's suppose that the population consists of 1,000 people.

	Male	*Female*	*Total*
Brown	420 (W3)	105 (W4)	525 (W5)
Blonde	245	165	410
Red	35	30	65
	700 (W1)	300 (W2)	1,000

Workings

1 1,000 × 70%
2 1,000 – 700
3 700 × 60% (the other two values in the column being calculated in a similar way)
4 300 × 35% (the other two values in the column being calculated in a similar way)
5 420 + 105 (the other two values in the column being calculated in a similar way)

∴ P(Person selected is a male, given that that person is brown-haired) = 420/525 = 0.8

EXAMPLE: THE VALUE OF IMPERFECT INFORMATION

Suppose that the Small Oil Company (SOC) is trying to decide whether or not to drill on a particular site. The chief engineer has assessed the probability that there will be oil, based on past experience, as 20%, and the probability that there won't be oil as 80%.

It is possible for SOC to hire a firm of international consultants to carry out a complete survey of the site. SOC has used the firm many times before and has estimated that if there really is oil, there is a 95% chance that the report will be favourable, but if there is no oil, there is only a 10% chance that the report will indicate that there is oil.

Required

Determine whether drilling should occur.

SOLUTION

Read the information given carefully. We are given *three* sets of probabilities.

(a) The probability that there will be oil (0.2) or there will not be (0.8). These outcomes are mutually exclusive.

(b) The probability that, if there is oil, the report will say there is oil (0.95) or say there is no oil (0.05).

(c) The probability that, if there is no oil, the report will say there is oil (0.1) or say there is no oil (0.9).

Both (b) and (c) describe conditional events, since the existence of oil or otherwise influences the chances of the survey report being correct.

SOC, meanwhile, faces a number of choices which we can show as a decision tree.

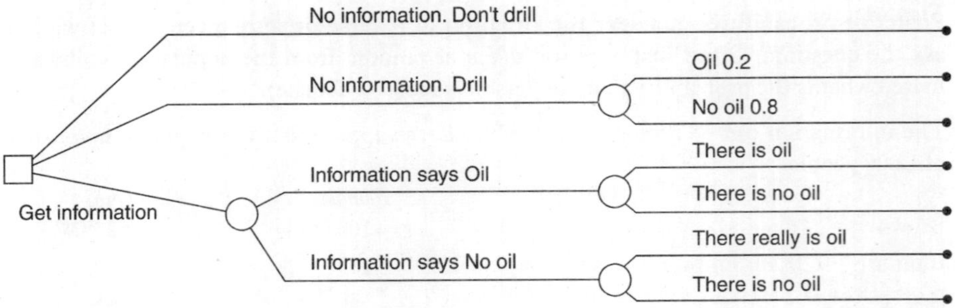

We must now calculate the probabilities of the following outcomes:

- The information will say 'oil' or 'no oil'
- The information will be right or wrong if it says 'oil'
- The information will be right or wrong if it says 'no oil'

If you check the information given in the problem, you will find that these probabilities are not given.

(a) We are told that the engineer has assessed that there is a 20% chance of oil and an 80% chance of no oil (ignoring information entirely). These are the **prior probabilities** of future possible outcomes.

(b) The **probabilities that there will be oil or no oil once the information has been obtained are posterior probabilities.**

Step 1 We can tabulate the various probabilities as percentages.

		Actual outcome					
		Oil		*No oil*		*Total*	
Survey	oil	19	(W2)	8	(W3)	27	(W4)
result:	no oil	1		72		73	
Total		20	(W1)	80		100	

Workings

1. The engineer estimates 20% probability of oil and 80% of no oil.
2. If there is oil, ie in 20 cases out of 100, the survey will say so in 95% of these cases, ie in $20 \times 0.95 = 19$ cases. The 1 below the 19 is obtained by subtraction.
3. In the 80 per 100 cases where there is in fact no oil, the survey will wrongly say that there is oil 10% of the time; ie $80 \times 0.10 = 8$ cases. The 72 below the 8 is obtained by subtraction.
4. The horizontal totals are given by addition.

Step 2 We can now provide all the probabilities needed to complete the tree.

P (survey will say there is oil)		= 27/100	= 0.27
P (survey will say there is no oil)		= 73/100	= 0.73
If survey says oil	P (there is oil)	= 19/27 = 0.704	
	P (there is no oil)	= 8/27 = 0.296 (or 1–0.704)	
If survey says no oil	P (there is oil)	= 1/73 = 0.014	
	P (there is no oil)	= 72/73 = 0.986 (or 1–0.014)	

Step 3 We can now go on to complete the decision tree. Let us make the following assumptions. (In an exam question such information would have been given to you from the start.)

- The cost of drilling is £10m.
- The value of the benefits if oil is found is £70m, giving a net 'profit' of £60m.
- The cost of obtaining information from the consultants would be £3m.

An assumption is made that the decision-maker will take whichever decision the information indicates is the best. If the information says 'oil', the company will drill, and if the information says 'no oil' it will not drill.

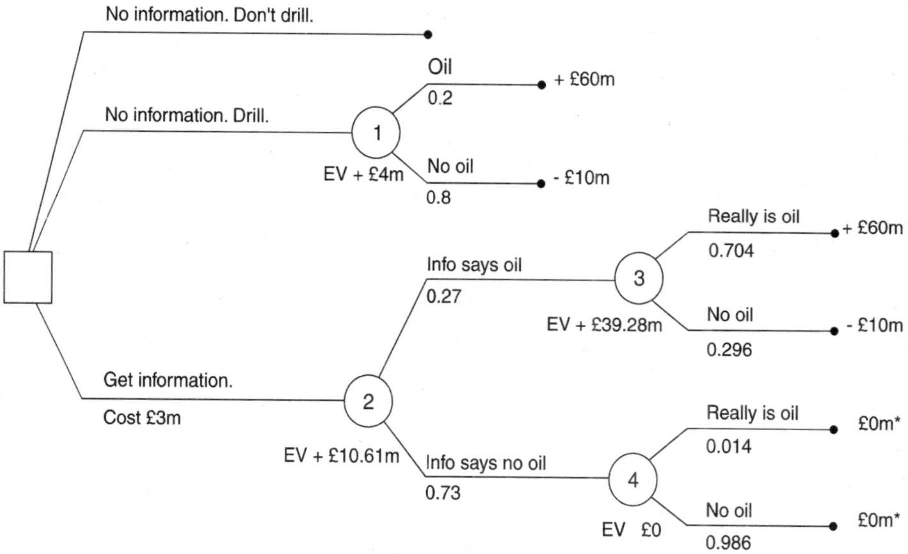

* The information is 'no oil', so the company won't drill, regardless of whether there really is oil or not.

Step 4 We can now perform rollback analysis.

		£m
EV at point 3 =	0.704 × £60m	42.24
	0.296 × (£10m)	(2.96)
		+ 39.28

		£m
EV at point 2 =	0.27 × £39.28m	10.61
	0.73 × £0	0.00
		+ 10.61

Step 5 There are three choices.

		EV
(a)	Do not obtain information and do not drill	£0
(b)	Do not obtain information and drill	+£4 million
(c)	Obtain information first, decide about drilling later (£(10.61m – 3m))	+£7.61 million

The decision should be to obtain the information from a survey first.

Step 6 The value of the imperfect information is the difference between (b) and (c), £3.61 million.

3 SENSITIVITY ANALYSIS

Sensitivity analysis
Sensitivity example
Introduction
'What if' analysis

3.1 Introduction

We will encounter sensitivity analysis in relation to a number of techniques throughout this text. Here we look at it in more general terms.

Definition

Sensitivity analysis is a modelling and risk assessment procedure in which changes are made to significant variables in order to determine the effect of these changes on the planned outcome. Particular attention is thereafter paid to variables identified as being of special significance.

Two useful approaches to sensitivity analysis

(a) Estimate by how much costs and revenues would need to differ from their estimated values before the decision would change.

(b) Estimate whether a decision would change if estimated costs were x% higher than estimated, or estimated revenues y% lower than estimated.

The essence of the approach is therefore to carry out the calculations with one set of values for the variables and then substitute other possible values for the variables to see how this affects the overall outcome.

EXAMPLE: SENSITIVITY ANALYSIS

SS has estimated the following sales and profits for a new product which it may launch on to the market.

		£	£
Sales	(2,000 units)		4,000
Variable costs:	materials	2,000	
	labour	1,000	
			3,000
Contribution			1,000
Less incremental fixed costs			800
Profit			200

Required

Analyse the sensitivity of the project.

SOLUTION

The **margin of safety** = ((budgeted sales – breakeven sales)/budgeted sales) × 100%

The breakeven point = fixed costs/contribution per unit
= £800/(£1,000/2,000 units) = 1,600 units

∴ Margin of safety = ((2,000 – 1,600)/2,000) × 100% = 20%

If any of the **costs increase by more than £200**, the profit will disappear and there will be a **loss.**

Changes in variables which would result in a loss

- More than ((200/800) × 100%) 25% increase in incremental **fixed costs**
- More than ((200/2,000) × 100%) 10% increase in unit cost of **materials**
- More than ((200/1,000) × 100%) 20% increase in **unit labour costs**
- More than ((200/4,000) × 100%) 5% drop in **unit selling price**

Management would now be able to judge more clearly whether the product is likely to be profitable. The **items to which profitability is most sensitive** in this example are the **selling price** (5%) and **material costs** (10%). Sensitivity analysis can help to **concentrate management attention on the most important forecasts.**

'What if' analysis

'What if' analysis looks at the results of varying a model's key variables, parameters or estimates.

Sensitivity analysis is a 'what if' technique that examines how a result will change if the original predicted values are not achieved or if an underlying assumption changes.

In its **simplest form** 'what if' analysis can be carried out using a **hand-held calculator. Spreadsheet packages** can be used for more complex scenarios, with answers to 'what if' questions obtained quickly and simply. **Commercial software packages** are now available for the most complex tasks.

4 SIMULATION MODELS

Simulation models
Introduction
The Monte Carlo method

4.1 Introduction

One of the chief problems encountered in decision-making is the uncertainty of the future. Where only a few factors are involved, probability analysis and expected value calculations can be used to find the most likely outcome of a decision. Often, however, in real life, there are so **many uncertain variables** that this approach does not give a true impression of possible variations in outcome. To get an idea of what will happen in real life one possibility is to use a **simulation model** in which the **values and the variables are selected at random**. Obviously this is a situation **ideally suited to a computer** (large volume of data, random number generation).

4.2 The Monte Carlo method

The **Monte Carlo method of simulation** makes use of random numbers.

The term 'simulation' model is often used more specifically to refer to modelling which **makes use of random numbers.** This is the 'Monte Carlo' method of simulation. In the business environment it can, for example, be used to examine inventory, queuing, scheduling and forecasting problems.

EXAMPLE: INVENTORY SYSTEM

In an inventory system, it may be decided to examine inventory levels at the end of each day or each week.

Suppose that a computer has been programmed to generate the weekly demand for an item of inventory to be, in units, 15, 22, 12, 17, 10, 5, 14, and 20 over a period of eight weeks. If the simulation model also assumes that 50 units of inventory are ordered at the end of any week when the balance of units in inventory falls below 20, and that the delivery takes one week, a simulation model might produce the following report of inventory levels at the end of each week:

Week	*Event*	*End of week inventory level*
0		50
1	Demand 15 units	35
2	Demand 22 units	13
	Order 50 units	
3	Demand 12 units	1
	50 units delivered	51
4	Demand 17 units	34
5	Demand 10 units	24
6	Demand 5 units	19
	Order 50 units	
7	Demand 14 units	5
	50 units delivered	55
8	Demand 20 units	35

The simulation model **shows how inventory levels might vary**, and **what average inventory and inventory costs might be**. It would also be possible to **test whether the reorder level should be altered** to a different amount by changing the parameter that the reorder level should be '20 or less at the end of the week'. A reorder level of, say '15 or less' could be tested, re-running the model over a simulated period of time to determine the balance in inventory or the number of inventory-outs each week, and the expected **cost of inventory holding, re-ordering and inventory-outs could then be estimated.**

Chapter roundup

- **Decision trees** are diagrams which illustrate the choices and possible outcomes of a decision.
- **Rollback analysis** evaluates the EV of each decision option. You have to work from right to left and calculate EVs at each outcome point.
- **Perfect information** is guaranteed to predict the future with 100% accuracy. **Imperfect information** is better than no information at all but could be wrong in its prediction of the future.
- The **value of perfect information** is the difference between the EV of profit with perfect information and the EV of profit without perfect information.
- **Two useful approaches to sensitivity analysis**
  - Estimate by how much costs and revenues would need to differ from their estimated values before the decision would change.
  - Estimate whether a decision would change if estimated costs/ revenues were x%/y% higher/lower than estimated.
- The **Monte Carlo method of simulation** makes use of random numbers.

Quick quiz

1 If the decision-maker is trying to maximise the figure, what figure would the decision-maker choose at point B in the diagram below?

A 40,000
B 11,800
C 13,900
D 22,000

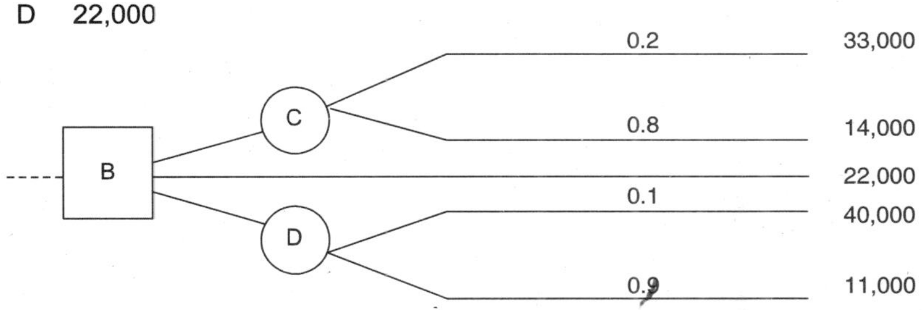

2 Given the probability distribution shown below, what are the ranges of numbers that are needed to reach a value in order to run a simulation model?

Probability	*Numbers assigned*
0.132	....
0.410	....
0.315	....
0.083	....
0.060	....

3 Define a decision tree.

4 Match the symbol with its meaning:

□, ○ ; The decision point, the outcome point.

5 If the win on a lottery card is £25 and the probability of winning is 1 in 50, what is the expected value?

6 What are the limitations of evaluating decisions using decision trees?

7 What is 'what if' analysis?

Answers to quick quiz

1 D Choice between ((0.2 × 33,000) + (0.8 × 14,000)) = 17,800 at C, 22,000, and ((0.1 × 40,000) + (0.9 × 11,000)) = 13,900 at D.

2

Probability	*Numbers assigned*
0.132	000-131
0.410	132-541
0.315	542-856
0.083	857-939
0.060	940-999

3 A decision tree is a pictorial method of showing a sequence of interrelated decisions and their expected outcomes.

4 □ is the decision point

○ is the outcome point

5 1 in 50 = probability of 0,02

Therefore EV = £25 × 0.02 = £0.50

6 Evaluating decisions by using decision trees has a number of limitations:

(a) The time value of money may not be taken into account.

(b) Decision trees are not very suitable for use in complex situations.

(c) The outcome with the highest EV may have the greatest risks attached to it. Managers may be reluctant to take risks which may lead to losses.

(d) The probabilities associated with different branches of the 'tree' are likely to be estimates, and possibly unreliable or inaccurate.

7 'What if' analysis looks at the results of varying a model's key variables, parameters or estimates.

Answers to activities

1 **The correct answer is A.**

The various outcomes must be evaluated using expected values.

EV at point B: (0.75 × 10,000) + (0.25 × 8,000) = 9,500

EV at point D: (0.6 × 20,000) + (0.4 × (4,000)) = 10,400

EV at point C: Choice between 10,400 and 11,000

EV at point A: Choice between B (9,500), C (10,400 or 11,000) and choice 3 (9,000).

If we are trying to maximise the figure, option 2 and then option 7 are chosen to give 11,000.

2 (a) All values in £'000

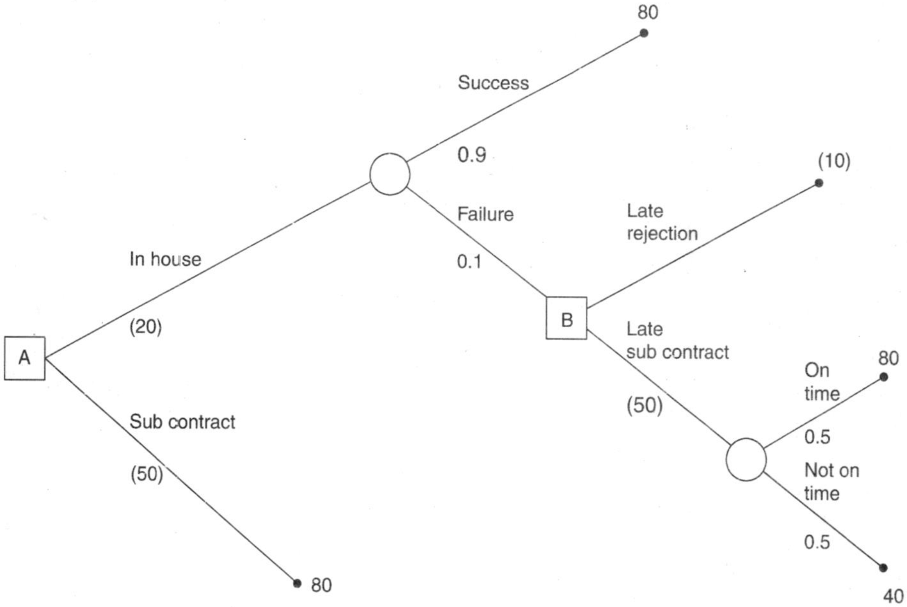

(b) **At decision point B**

EV of late rejection = –10
EV of late sub-contract = (80 × 0.5) + (40 × 0.5) – 50 = 10
The optimum strategy at B is therefore to subcontract with EV = 10.

At decision point A

EV of sub-contract = 80 – 50 = 30
EV of in-house = (80 × 0.9) + (10* × 0.1) – 20 = 53
The optimum strategy at A is therefore to produce in-house with EV = 53.

*This is the optimum EV at decision point B.

Conclusions

The decisions which will maximise expected profits are to attempt initially to produce in-house and if this fails to sub-contract. The expected profit is £53,000.

Assuming that the probabilities have been correctly estimated, the company has a 90% chance of making a profit of £60,000, a 5% chance of making £10,000 and a 5% chance of making a £30,000 loss. If the company is not willing to risk making a loss, the initial option of subcontracting should be taken since this offers a guaranteed profit of £30,000.

3 **The correct answer is option B and so the statement is true.**

Without perfect information, the option with the highest EV of profit will be chosen.

	Option A (National)		*Option B (Regional)*		*Option C (Area)*	
Probability	*Profit*	*EV*	*Profit*	*EV*	*Profit*	*EV*
	£	£	£	£	£	£
0.3	(4,000)	(1,200)	0	0	1,000	300
0.5	2,000	1,000	3,500	1,750	1,500	750
0.2	10,000	2,000	4,000	800	2,000	400
		1,800		2,550		1,450

Marketing regionally (option B) has the highest EV of profit, and would be selected.

4 **The correct answer is £1,500.**

If perfect information about the state of consumer demand were available, option A would be preferred if the forecast demand is strong and option C would be preferred if the forecast demand is weak.

Demand	*Probability*	*Choice*	*Profit*	*EV of profit*
			£	£
Weak	0.3	C	1,000	300
Moderate	0.5	B	3,500	1,750
Strong	0.2	A	10,000	2,000
V of profit with perfect information				4,050
EV of profit, selecting option B				2,550
Value of perfect information				1,500

Chapter 7 :
LINEAR PROGRAMMING

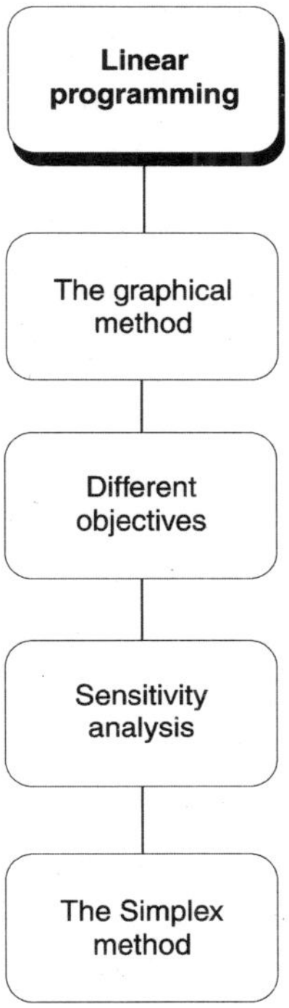

Introduction

In the previous chapter we saw how to determine the profit-maximising allocation of resources when an organisation is faced with just one resource constraint. When there is **more than one resource constraint**, the technique of **linear programming** can be used. This technique can be applied to problems with the following features.

- There is a single objective, which is to maximise or minimise the value of a certain function. The objective in commercial decision making is usually to maximise contribution and thus maximise profit.
- There are several constraints, typically scarce resources, that limit the value of the objective function.

There are two linear programming techniques. The graphical method is used for problems involving two products. The Simplex method is used if the problem involves more than two products.

The first part of the chapter provides a **detailed step-by-step approach** to graphical linear programming. Make sure that you really understand how to carry out each step before you move on to the next.

The graphical method of linear programming can only be used for decision problems with a maximum of two decision variables. For more complex problems the **simplex** method is needed as it can deal with two or more decision variables.

Your objectives

In this chapter you will learn about the following:

- The graphical method of linear programming
- Different objectives than linear programming might solve
- Sensitivity analysis
- The Simplex method

1 GRAPHICAL METHOD

Graphical method
Limiting factors
Formulating the problem
Graphing the problem
Finding the optimum allocation of resources
Using simultaneous equations

1.1 Limiting factors

A **scarce resource** is a resource of which there is a limited supply. Once a scarce resource affects the ability of an organisation to earn profits, a scarce resource becomes known as a **limiting factor**.

Definition

> A **limiting factor** or **key factor** is anything which limits the activity of an entity. An entity seeks to optimise the benefit it obtains from the limiting factor.

Limiting factor analysis

- An organisation might be faced with just one limiting factor (other than maximum sales demand) but there might also be several scarce resources, with two or more of them putting an effective limit on the level of activity that can be achieved.
- Examples of limiting factors such as sales demand and production constraints include
  - Labour. The limit may be either in terms of total quantity or of particular skills.
  - Materials. There may be insufficient available materials to produce enough units to satisfy sales demand.

   - Manufacturing capacity. There may not be sufficient machine capacity for the production required to meet sales demand.

- It is assumed in limiting factor analysis that management would make a product mix decision or service mix decision based on the option that would maximise profit.

If resources are limiting factors, **profit** will be **maximised** by earning the biggest possible profit per unit of limiting factor.

Where there is just one limiting factor, the technique for establishing the product or service mix is to rank the products or services in order of profit per unit of limiting factor.

We have looked at the problem of one limiting factor. We now move on to look at situations where there are more products and more limiting factors.

1.2 Formulating the problem

Let us suppose that WX manufactures two products, A and B. Both products pass through two production departments, mixing and shaping. The organisation's objective is to maximise contribution to fixed costs.

Product A is sold for £1.50 whereas product B is priced at £2.00. There is unlimited demand for product A but demand for B is limited to 13,000 units per annum. The machine hours available in each department are restricted to 2,400 per annum. Other relevant data are as follows:

Machine hours required	*Mixing*	*Shaping*
	Hrs	*Hrs*
Product A	0.06	0.04
Product B	0.08	0.12

Variable cost per unit	£
Product A	1.30
Product B	1.70

Before we work through the steps involved in solving this constraints problem using the graphical approach to linear programming, it is worth reading the definition of linear programming to get a glimpse of what we will be doing.

Definition

> **Linear programming** is 'The use of a series of linear equations to construct a mathematical model. The objective is to obtain an optimal solution to a complex operational problem, which may involve the production of a number of products in an environment in which there are many constraints.'

Activity 1 **(3 minutes)**

Constraints

What are the constraints in the situation facing WX?

(i) Machine hours in each department
(ii) Labour hours in each department
(iii) Sales demand for product B
(iv) Selling price of product A

A (i) and (iii)
B (i) only
C (ii) and (iv)
D (i), (ii) and (iii)

The **steps in the graphical method** are as follows:

- Define variables
- Establish objective function
- Establish constraints
- Draw a graph of the constraints
- Establish the feasible region
- Determine the optimal product mix

Let's start solving WX's problem.

Step 1 **Define variables**

What are the **quantities that WX can vary**? Obviously not the number of machine hours or the demand for product B. The only things which it can vary are the **number of units of each type of product produced.** It is those numbers which the company has to determine in such a way as to obtain the maximum possible profit. Our variables (which are usually products being produced) will therefore be as follows:

Let x = number of units of product A produced.
Let y = number of units of product B produced.

Step 2 **Establish objective function**

The **objective function** is a quantified statement of the aim of a resource allocation decision.

We now need to introduce the question of contribution or profit. We know that the **contribution on each type of product** is as follows:

		£ per unit
Product A	£(1.50 – 1.30) =	0.20
Product B	£(2.00 – 1.70) =	0.30

The **objective of the company is to maximise contribution** and so the **objective function to be maximised** is as follows:

Contribution (C) = 0.2x + 0.3y

Step 3 **Establish constraints**

Definition

A **constraint** is an activity, resource or policy that limits the ability to achieve objectives.

The **value of the objective function** (the maximum contribution achievable from producing products A and B) is **limited by the constraints** facing WX, however. To incorporate this into the problem we need to **translate the constraints into inequalities involving the variables** defined in Step 1. An inequality is an equation taking the form 'greater than or equal to' or 'less than or equal to'.

(a) Consider the **mixing department machine hours** constraint.

(i) **Each unit of product A** requires 0.06 hours of machine time. Producing five units therefore requires 5 × 0.06 hours of machine time and, more generally, **producing x units will require 0.06x hours.**

(ii) Likewise producing **y units of product B will require 0.08y hours.**

(iii) The total machine hours needed in the mixing department to make x units of product A and y units of product B is 0.06x + 0.08y.

(iv) We know that this **cannot be greater than 2,400 hours** and so we arrive at the following inequality.

$\mathbf{0.06x + 0.08y \leq 2{,}400}$

Activity 2 **(5 minutes)**

Inequalities

How can the constraint facing the shaping department be written as an inequality?

A $0.4x + 0.012y \geq 2{,}400$
B $0.04x + 0.12y \leq 2{,}400$
C $0.4x + 0.012y \leq 2{,}400$
D $0.04x + 0.12y \geq 2{,}400$

(b) The final inequality is easier to obtain. The **number of units of product B produced and sold is y** but this has to be **less than or equal to 13,000**. Our inequality is therefore as follows:

$\mathbf{y \leq 13{,}000}$

(c) We also need to add **non-negativity constraints** ($x \geq 0$, $y \geq 0$) since negative numbers of products cannot be produced. (Linear programming is simply a mathematical tool and so there is nothing in this method which guarantees that the answer will 'make sense'. An unprofitable product may produce an answer which is negative. This is mathematically correct but nonsense in operational terms. Always remember to include the non-negativity constraints. The examiner will not appreciate 'impossible' solutions.)

The **problem** has now been **reduced** to the following **four inequalities** and **one equation.**

Maximise contribution (C) = 0.2x + 0.3y, subject to the following constraints:

$$\begin{aligned} 0.06x + 0.08y &\leq 2{,}400 \\ 0.04x + 0.12y &\leq 2{,}400 \\ 0 \leq y &\leq 13{,}000 \\ 0 &\leq x \end{aligned}$$

Activity 3 **(10 minutes)**

Formulation of linear programming model

An organisation makes two products, X and Y. Product X has a contribution of £124 per unit and product Y £80 per unit. Contribution per unit is equal to the selling price per unit less variable cost per unit. Both products pass through two departments for processing and the times in minutes per unit are as follows:

	Product X	*Product Y*
Department 1	150	90
Department 2	100	120

Currently there is a maximum of 225 hours per week available in department 1 and 200 hours in department 2. The organisation can sell all it can produce of X but EU quotas restrict the sale of Y to a maximum of 75 units per week. The organisation, which wishes to maximise contribution, currently makes and sells 30 units of X and 75 units of Y per week.

Required

Assume x and y are the number of units of X and Y produced per week. Formulate a linear programming model of this problem, filling in the blanks in (a) and (b) below.

(a) The objective function is to maximise weekly contribution, given by C = ...

(b) The constraints are:

Department 1 .... EU quota ....

Department 2 .... Non-negativity ....

1.3 Graphing the problem

A **graphical solution** is **only possible** when there are **two variables** in the problem. One variable is represented by the **x axis** of the graph and one by the **y axis**. Since non-negative values are not usually allowed, the graph shows **only zero and positive values of x and y.**

Graphing equations and constraints

A linear equation with one or two variables is shown as a **straight line on a graph.** Thus y = 6 would be shown as follows:

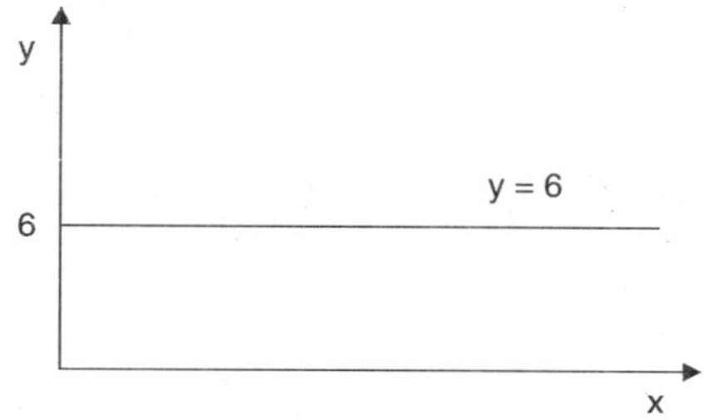

If the problem included a **constraint that y could not exceed 6,** the **inequality y ≤ 6** would be represented by the **shaded area of the graph below:**

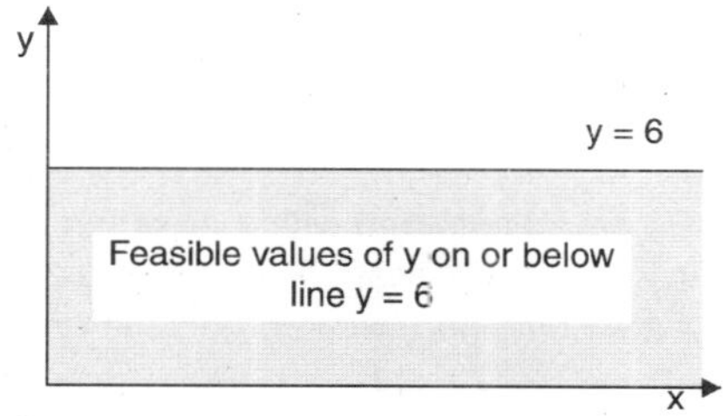

The equation 4x + 3y = 24 is also a straight line on a graph. To **draw any straight line,** we **need only to plot two points and join them up.** The easiest points to plot are the following:

- x = 0 (in this example, if x = 0, 3y = 24, y = 8)
- y = 0 (in this example, if y = 0, 4x = 24, x = 6)

By plotting the points, (0, 8) and (6, 0) on a graph, and joining them up, we have the line for 4x + 3y = 24.

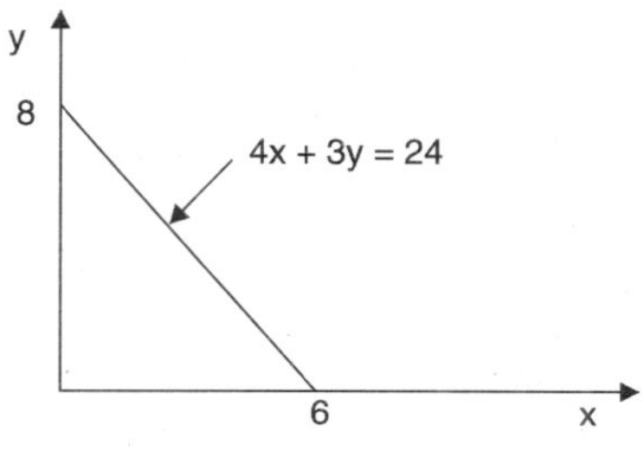

Any combination of values for x and y on the line satisfies the equation. Thus at a point where x = 3 and y = 4, 4x + 3y = 24. Similarly, at a point where x = 4.5 and y = 2, 4x + 3y = 24.

If we had a constraint 4x + 3y ≤ 24, any combined value of x and y within the shaded area below (on or below the line) would satisfy the constraint.

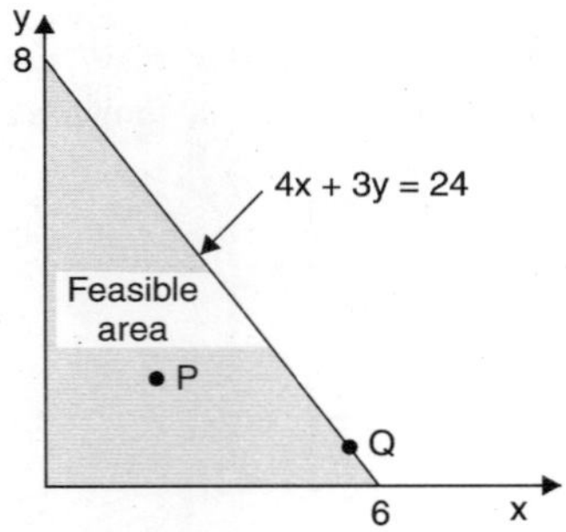

Consider point P which has coordinates of (2, 2). Here, $4x + 3y = 14$, which is less than 24; and at point Q where $x = 5\frac{1}{2}$, $y = 2/3$, $4x + 3y = 24$. **Both P and Q lie within the feasible area or feasible region. A feasible area enclosed on all sides may also be called a feasible polygon.**

Definition

> A **feasible region** is the area contained within all of the constraint lines shown on a graphical depiction of a linear programming problem. All feasible combinations of output are contained within or located on the boundaries of the feasible region.

When there are **several constraints**, the **feasible area** of combinations of values of x and y must be an area **where all the inequalities are satisfied.** Thus, if **$y \leq 6$ and $4x + 3y \leq 24$** the **feasible area** would be the **shaded area** in the following graph:

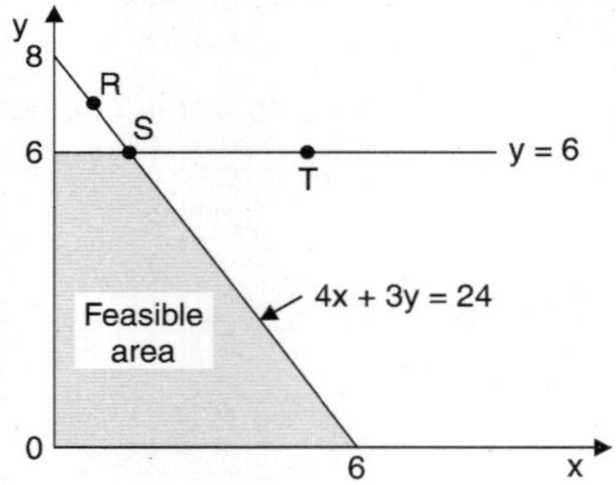

(a) Point R ($x = 0.75$, $y = 7$) is not in the feasible area because, although it satisfies the inequality $4x + 3y \leq 24$, it does not satisfy $y \leq 6$.

(b) Point T ($x = 5$, $y = 6$) is not in the feasible area because, although it satisfies the inequality $y \leq 6$, it does not satisfy $4x + 3y \leq 24$.

(c) Point S ($x = 1.5$, $y = 6$) satisfies both inequalities and lies just on the boundary of the feasible area since $y = 6$ exactly, and $4x + 3y = 24$. Point S is thus at the intersection of the two lines.

Similarly, if y ≥ 6 and 4x + 3y ≥ 24 but x is ≤ 6, the feasible area would be the shaded area in the graph below:

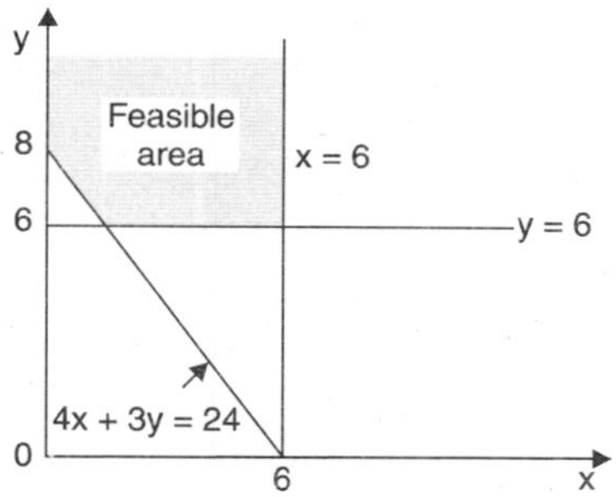

Activity 4 **(15 minutes)**

Feasible region

Draw the feasible region which arises from the constraints facing WX on the graph below:

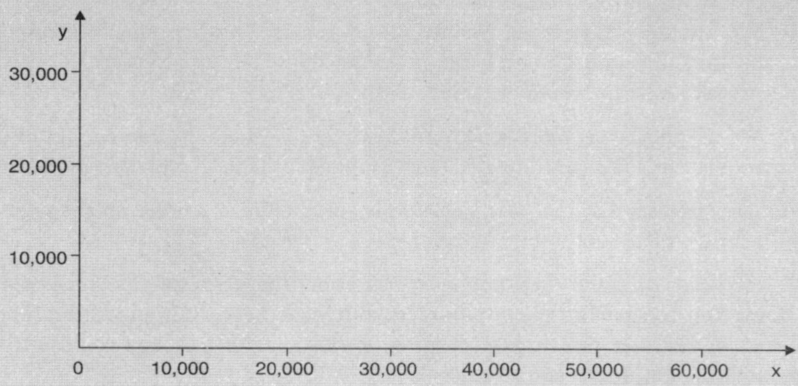

1.4 Finding the optimum allocation of resources

The **optimal solution** can be found by 'sliding the iso-contribution (or profit) line out'.

Having found the feasible region (which includes all the possible solutions to the problem) we need to **find which of these possible solutions is 'best'** or **optimal** in the sense that it yields the maximum possible contribution.

Look at the feasible region of the problem faced by WX (see the solution to the question above). Even in such a simple problem as this, there are a **great many possible solution points within the feasible area**. Even to write them all down would be a time-consuming process and also an unnecessary one, as we shall see.

Here is the graph of WX's problem:

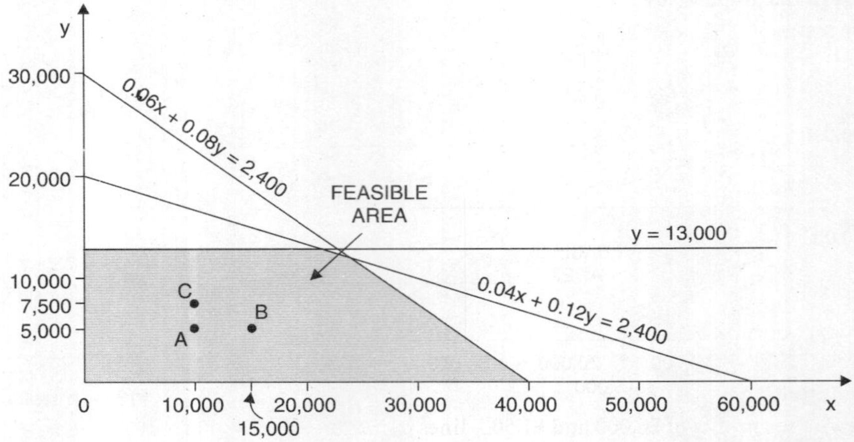

(a) Consider point A at which 10,000 units of product A and 5,000 units of product B are being manufactured. This will yield a contribution of (10,000 × £0.20) + (5,000 × £0.30) = £3,500.

(b) We would clearly get more contribution at point B, where the same number of units of product B are being produced but where the number of units of product A has increased by 5,000.

(c) We would also get more contribution at point C where the number of units of product A is the same but 2,500 more units of product B are being produced.

This argument suggests that the **'best' solution** is going to be at a **point on the edge of the feasible area** rather than in the middle of it.

This still leaves us with quite a few points to look at but there is a way in which we can **narrow down still further the likely points at which the best solution will be found.** Suppose that WX wishes to earn contribution of £3,000. The company could sell the following combinations of the two products:

(a) 15,000 units of A, no B
(b) No A, 10,000 units of B
(c) A suitable mix of the two, such as 7,500 A and 5,000 B

The **possible combinations required to earn contribution of £3,000** could be **shown by the straight line 0.2x + 0.3y = 3,000.**

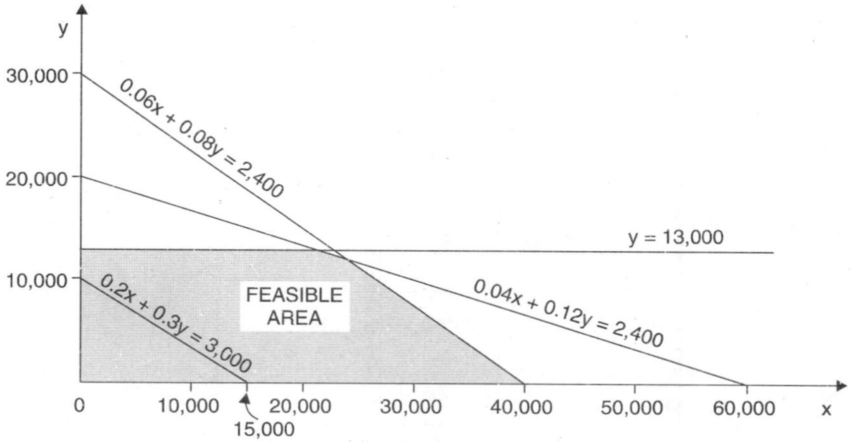

Likewise for profits of £6,000 and £1,500, lines of 0.2x + 0.3y = 6,000 and 0.2x + 0.3y = 1,500 could be drawn **showing the combination of the two products** which would **achieve contribution of £6,000 or £1,500.**

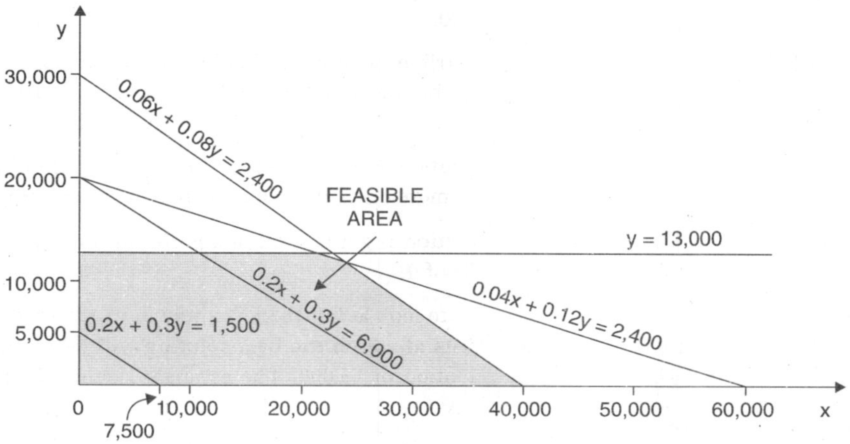

The **contribution lines are all parallel**. (They are called **iso-contribution lines,** 'iso' meaning equal.) A similar line drawn for any other total contribution would also be parallel to the three lines shown here. **Bigger contribution is shown by lines further from the origin** (0.2x + 0.3y = 6,000), and smaller contribution by lines closer to the origin (0.2x + 0.3y = 1,500). As WX tries to increase possible contribution, we need to 'slide' any contribution line outwards from the origin, while always keeping it parallel to the other contribution lines.

As we do this there will come a point at which, if we were to **move the contribution line out any further, it would cease to lie in the feasible region**. Greater contribution could not be achieved, because of the constraints. In our example concerning WX this will happen, as you should test for yourself, where the contribution line just passes through the intersection of 0.06x + 0.08y = 2,400 and 0.04x + 0.12y = 2,400 (at coordinates (24,000, 12,000)). The point (24,000, 12,000) will therefore give us the optimal allocation of resources (to produce 24,000 units of A and 12,000 units of B).

We can usefully summarise the graphical approach to linear programming as follows:

Step 1 Define variables
Step 2 Establish objective function
Step 3 Establish constraints
Step 4 Graph the problem
Step 5 Define feasible area
Step 6 Determine optimal solution

EXAMPLE: THE GRAPHICAL SOLUTION WITH A TWIST

This example shows that it is not always necessarily easy to identify the decision variables in a problem.

DCC operates a small plant for the manufacture of two joint chemical products X and Y. The production of these chemicals requires two raw materials, A and B, which cost £5 and £8 per litre respectively. The maximum available supply per week is 2,700 litres of A and 2,000 litres of B.

The plant can operate using either of two processes, which have differing operating costs and raw materials requirements for the production of X and Y, as follows:

Process	*Raw materials consumed Litres per processing hour*		*Output Litres per hour*		*Cost £ per hour*
	A	*B*	*X*	*Y*	
1	20	10	15	20	500
2	30	20	20	10	230

The plant can run for 120 hours per week in total, but, for safety reasons, process 2 cannot be operated for more than 80 hours per week.

X sells for £18 per litre, Y for £24 per litre.

Required

Formulate a linear programming model, and then solve it, to determine how the plant should be operated each week.

SOLUTION

Step 1 **Define variables**

You might decide that there are two decision variables in the problem, the quantity of X and the quantity of Y to make each week. If so, begin by letting these be x and y respectively.

You might also readily recognise that the aim should be to maximise the total weekly contribution, and so the objective function should be expressed in terms of maximising the total contribution from X and Y.

The contribution per litre from X and Y cannot be calculated because the operating costs are expressed in terms of processing hours.

		Process 1			Process 2	
		£ per hour	£ per hour		£ per hour	£ per hour
Costs:						
Material A			100			150
Material B			80			160
Operating cost			500			230
			680			540
Revenue:						
X	(15 × £18)	270		(20 × £18)	360	
Y	(20 × £24)	480		(10 × £24)	240	
			750			600
Contribution			70			60

The **decision variables** should be **processing hours in each process**, rather than litres of X and Y. If we let the processing hours per week for process 1 be P_1 and the processing hours per week for process 2 be P_2 we can now formulate an objective function, and constraints, as follows:

Step 2 **Establish objective function**

Maximise $70P_1 + 60P_2$(total contribution) subject to the constraints below.

Step 3 **Establish constraints**

$20P_1 + 30P_2$	≤	2,700	(material A supply)
$10P_1 + 20P_2$	≤	2,000	(material B supply)
P_2	≤	80	(maximum time for P_2)
$P_1 + P_2$	≤	120	(total maximum time)
P_1, P_2	≥	0	

Step 4 **Graph the problem**

The graphical solution looks like this:

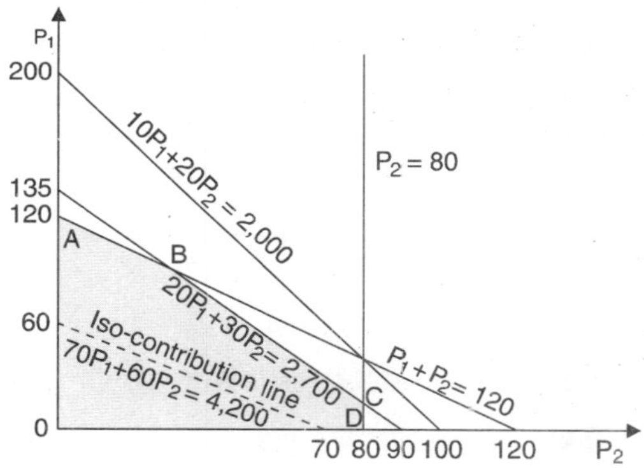

Step 5 **Define feasible area**

The material B constraint is not critical, and the feasible area for a solution is shown as ABCDO on the graph.

Step 6 **Determine optimal solution**

The optimal solution, determined using the iso-contribution line $70P_1 + 60P_2 = 4{,}200$, is at point A, where $P_1 = 120$ and $P_2 = 0$.

Production would be (120 × 15) 1,800 litres of X and (120 × 20) 2,400 litres of Y.

Total contribution would be (120 × £70) = £8,400 per week.

Activity 5 **(30 minutes)**

Determining the optimal solution

On 20 days of every month GS makes two products, the Crete and the Corfu. Production is carried out in three departments – tanning, plunging and watering. Relevant information is as follows:

	Crete	*Corfu*
Contribution per unit	£75	£50
Minutes in tanning department per unit	10	12
Minutes in plunging department per unit	15	10
Minutes in watering department per unit	6	15
Maximum monthly sales (due to government quota restrictions)	3,500	4,000

	Tanning	*Plunging*	*Watering*
Number of employees	7	10	5
Hours at work per day per employee	7	6	10
Number of idle hours per day per employee	0.5	1	0.25

Due to union restrictions, employees cannot be at work for longer than the hours detailed above.

Required

Use the graphical method of linear programming to determine the optimum monthly production of Cretes and Corfus and the monthly contribution if GS's objective is to maximise contribution.

1.5 The graphical method using simultaneous equations

Instead of a 'sliding the contribution line out' approach, **simultaneous equations** can be used to determine the optimal allocation of resources, as shown in the following example.

The optimal solution can also be found using **simultaneous equations**.

EXAMPLE: USING SIMULTANEOUS EQUATIONS

An organisation manufactures plastic-covered steel fencing in two qualities: standard and heavy gauge. Both products pass through the same processes involving steel forming and plastic bonding.

The standard gauge sells at £15 a roll and the heavy gauge at £20 a roll. There is an unlimited market for the standard gauge but outlets for the heavy gauge are limited to 13,000 rolls a year. The factory operations of each process are limited to 2,400 hours a year. Other relevant data is given below:

Variable costs per roll

	Direct material £	Direct wages £	Direct expense £
Standard	5	7	1
Heavy	7	8	2

Processing hours per 100 rolls

	Steel forming Hours	Plastic bonding Hours
Standard	6	4
Heavy	8	12

Required

Calculate the allocation of resources and hence the production mix which will maximise total contribution.

SOLUTION

Step 1 **Define variables**

Let the number of rolls of standard gauge to be produced be x and the number of rolls of heavy gauge be y.

Step 2 **Establish objective function**

Standard gauge produces a contribution of £2 per roll (£15 – £(5 + 7 + 1)) and heavy gauge a contribution of £3 (£20 – £(7 + 8 + 2)).

Therefore the objective is to maximise contribution (C) = 2x + 3y subject to the constraints below.

Step 3 **Establish constraints**

The constraints are as follows:

$0.06x + 0.08y \leq 2{,}400$	(steel forming hours)
$0.04x + 0.12y \leq 2{,}400$	(plastic bonding hours)
$y \leq 13{,}000$	(demand for heavy gauge)
$x, y \geq 0$	(non-negativity)

Step 4 **Graph problem**

The graph of the problem can now be drawn.

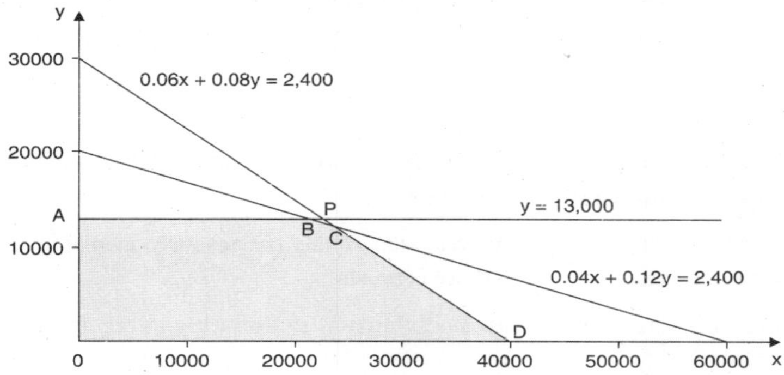

Step 5 **Define feasible area**

The combinations of x and y that satisfy all three constraints are represented by the area OABCD.

Step 6 **Determine optimal solution**

Which combination will maximise contribution? Obviously, the more units of x and y, the bigger the contribution will be, and the optimal solution will be at point B, C or D. It will not be at A, since at A, y = 13,000 and x = 0, whereas at B, y = 13,000 (the same) and x is greater than zero.

Using simultaneous equations to calculate the value of x and y at each of points B, C and D, and then working out total contribution at each point from this, we can establish the contribution-maximising product mix.

Point B

y	=	13,000	(1)
$0.04x + 0.12y$	=	2,400	(2)
$0.12y$	=	1,560	(3) ((1) × 0.12)
$0.04x$	=	840	(4) ((2) – (3))
x	=	21,000	(5)

Total contribution = (21,000 × £2) + (13,000 × £3) = £81,000.

Point C

$0.06x + 0.08y$	=	2,400	(1)
$0.04x + 0.12y$	=	2,400	(2)
$0.12x + 0.16y$	=	4,800	(3) ((1) × 2)
$0.12x + 0.36y$	=	7,200	(4) ((2) × 3)
$0.2y$	=	2,400	(5) ((4) – (3))
y	=	12,000	(6)
$0.06x + 960$	=	2,400	(7) (substitute in (1))
x	=	24,000	(8)

Total contribution = (24,000 × £2) + (12,000 × £3) = £84,000.

Point D

Total contribution = 40,000 × £2 = £80,000.

Comparing B, C and D, we can see that contribution is maximised at C, by making 24,000 rolls of standard gauge and 12,000 rolls of heavy gauge, to earn a contribution of £84,000.

Slack and surplus

Slack occurs when maximum availability of a resource is not used. **Surplus** occurs when more than a minimum requirement is used.

If, at the optimal solution, the resource used equals the resource available there is **no spare capacity** of a resource and so there is **no slack**.

If a resource which has a **maximum availability** is **not binding** at the optimal solution, there will be **slack**.

In the example above, the optimal solution is x = 24,000, y = 12,000.

If we substitute these values into the inequalities representing the constraints, we can determine whether the constraints are binding or whether there is slack.

Steel forming hours: $(0.06 \times 24{,}000) + (0.08 \times 12{,}000) = 2{,}400$ = availability
Constraint is **binding.**

Plastic bonding hours: $(0.04 \times 24{,}000) + (0.12 \times 12{,}000) = 2{,}400$ = availability
Constraint is **binding.**

Demand: Demand of $12{,}000 \leq$ maximum demand of 13,000
There is **slack.**

Note that because we had already determined the optimal solution to be at the intersection of the steel forming hours and plastic bonding hours constraints, we knew that they were binding!

If a minimum quantity of a resource must be used and, at the optimal solution, **more than that quantity is used,** there is a **surplus** on the minimum requirement.

For example, suppose in a particular scenario a minimum of 8,000 grade A labour hours had to be worked in the production of products x and y, such that (say) $3x + 2y \geq 8{,}000$. If 10,000 hours are used to produce the optimal solution, there is a **surplus** of 2,000 hours.

We will be looking at this form of constraint in the next section.

2 DIFFERENT OBJECTIVES

Different objectives
Minimisation problem
Minimising costs

So far the objective in the problems we have been looking at has been to maximise contribution. But linear programming can be used to allocate scarce resources between competing activities, products and so on, in order to **maximise or minimise a range of numerical quantities including contribution.**

For example, problems might include determining the mix of ingredients to minimise costs, the mix of products to maximise revenue or the portfolio of investments to maximise worth. It can also be used for transport routing, production scheduling and personnel resource planning, the objective being to minimise costs.

Whatever the objective, the **optimal solution** is the one that yields the **largest value for the objective in the case of a maximisation problem,** the **smallest value in the case of a minimisation problem.**

In a **minimisation problem** (minimise costs), the optimal solution is the point at which the total cost line touches the feasible polygon at a tangent as close to the origin as possible.

2.1 Minimisation problem

Although decision problems concerned with resource constraints usually involve the maximisation of contribution, there may be a **requirement to minimise costs.** The approach is similar to the one we have been looking at, with the exception that, instead of finding a contribution line touching the feasible polygon at a tangent as far away from the origin as possible, we **look for a total cost line touching the feasible polygon at a tangent as close to the origin as possible.**

EXAMPLE: MINIMISING COSTS

BS has undertaken a contract to supply a customer with at least 260 units in total of two products, X and Y, during the next month. At least 50% of the total output must be units of X. The products are each made by two grades of labour, as follows:

	X	*Y*
	Hrs	*Hrs*
Grade A labour	4	6
Grade B labour	4	2

Although additional labour can be made available at short notice, the company wishes to make use of 1,200 hours of grade A labour and 800 hours of grade B labour which have already been assigned to working on the contract next month. The total variable cost per unit is £120 for X and £100 for Y.

BS wishes to minimise expenditure on the contract next month.

Required

Calculate the number of units of X and Y that should be supplied in order to meet the terms of the contract.

SOLUTION

Step 1 **Define variables**

Let the number of units of X supplied be x, and the number of units of Y supplied be y.

Step 2 **Define objective function**

Minimise 120x + 100y (costs) subject to the constraints below.

Step 3 **Establish constraints**

$x + y \geq 260$		(supply total)
$x \geq 0.5\,(x + y)$		(proportion of x in total)
$4x + 6y \geq 1{,}200$		(grade A labour)
$4x + 2y \geq 800$		(grade B labour)
$x, y \geq 0$		

The constraint $x \geq 0.5\,(x + y)$ needs simplifying further.

If $x \geq 0.5\,(x + y)$

then $2x \geq x + y$

and $x \geq y$

Steps 4 and 5 **Graph the problem and define the feasible area**

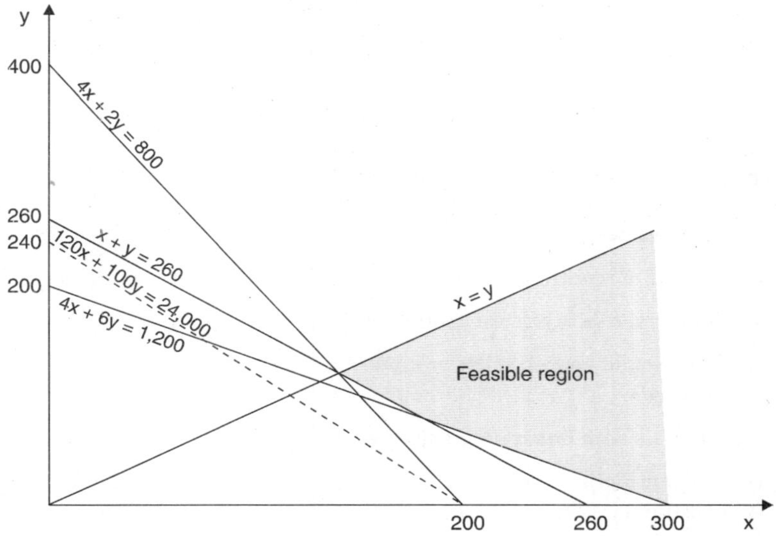

Step 6 **Determine the optimal solution**

The cost line 120x + 100y = 24,000 has been drawn to show the slope of every cost line 120x + 100y. Costs are minimised where a cost line touches the feasible region at a tangent, as close as possible to the origin of the graph. This occurs where the constraints line 4x + 2y = 800 crosses the line x + y = 260. At this point

	$x + y = 260$	.... (1)
	$4x + 2y = 800$	.... (2)
Divide (2) by 2	$2x + y = 400$	.... (3)
Subtract (1) from (3)	$x = 140$	
Substitute in (1)	$y = 120$	

Costs will be minimised by supplying the following output.

	Unit cost	*Total cost*
	£	£
140 units of X	120	16,800
120 units of Y	100	12,000
		28,800

The proportion of units of X in the total would exceed 50%, and demand for grade A labour would exceed the 1,200 hours minimum.

So far we have looked at how to solve linear programming problems. We are now going to examine how the information can be understood and interpreted.

3 SENSITIVITY ANALYSIS

Sensitivity analysis
Limiting factor sensitivity analysis
Sales price sensitivity analysis

Once a graphical linear programming solution has been found, it should be possible to provide further information by interpreting the graph more fully to see what would happen if certain values in the scenario were to change.

(a) What if the contribution from one product was £1 lower than expected?

(b) What if the sales price of another product was raised by £2?

(c) What would happen if less or more of a limiting factor were available, such as material?

Sensitivity analysis with **linear** programming can be carried out in one of two ways:

(a) By considering the value of each limiting factor or binding resource constraint

(b) By considering sale prices (or the contribution per unit)

3.1 Limiting factor sensitivity analysis

We use the shadow price to carry out sensitivity analysis on the availability of a limiting factor.

Shadow prices

The **shadow price** of a resource which is a limiting factor on production is the amount by which total contribution would fall if the organisation were deprived of one unit of the resource. The shadow price also indicates the amount by which total contribution would rise if the organisation were able to obtain one extra unit of the resource, provided that the resource remains an effective constraint on production and provided also that the extra unit of resource can be obtained at its normal variable cost.

Activity 6 **(5 minutes)**

Shadow prices

Choose the correct words from those highlighted.

A shadow price is the **increase/decrease** in **contribution/revenue** created by the availability of an extra unit of a **resource/limiting resource** at **its original cost/a premium price**.

So, in terms of linear programming, the shadow price is the **extra contribution or profit that may be earned by relaxing by one unit a binding resource constraint.**

Suppose the availability of materials is a binding constraint. If one extra kilogram becomes available so that an alternative production mix becomes optimal, with a resulting increase over the original production mix contribution of £2, the shadow price of a kilogram of material is £2.

Note, however, that this increase in contribution of £2 per extra kilogram of material made available is calculated on the **assumption** that the **extra kilogram would cost the normal variable amount.**

Note the following points:

(a) The shadow price therefore represents the maximum **premium** above the basic rate that an organisation should be **willing to pay for one extra unit** of a resource

(b) Since shadow prices indicate the effect of a one unit change in a constraint, they provide a measure of the **sensitivity** of the result

(c) The **shadow price** of a constraint that is **not binding** at the optimal solution is **zero**

(d) Shadow prices are **only valid for a small range** before the constraint becomes non-binding or different resources become critical

Depending on the resource in question, shadow prices enable management to make **better informed decisions** about the payment of overtime premiums, bonuses, premiums on small orders of raw materials and so on.

Calculating shadow prices

In the earlier example of WX, the availability of time in both departments are limiting factors because both are used up fully in the optimal product mix. Let us therefore calculate the effect if **one extra hour of shaping department machine time** was made available so that 2,401 hours were available.

The **new optimal product mix would be at the intersection of the two constraint lines** $0.06x + 0.08y = 2{,}400$ and $0.04x + 0.12y = 2{,}401$.

Solution by simultaneous equations gives $x = 23{,}980$ and $y = 12{,}015$.

(You should solve the problem yourself if you are doubtful about the derivation of the solution.)

Product	*Units*	*Contribution per unit* £	*Total contribution* £
A	23,980	0.20	4,796.0
B	12,015	0.30	3,604.5
			8,400.5
Contribution in original problem ((24,000 × £0.20) + (12,000 × £0.30))			8,400.0
Increase in contribution from one extra hour of shaping time			0.5

The **shadow price of an hour of machining time in the shaping department is therefore £0.50.**

The **shadow price** of a limiting factor also shows by **how much contribution would fall if the availability of a limiting resource fell by one unit.** The **shadow price** (also called **dual price**) of an hour of machine time in the shaping department would again be calculated as £0.50. This is the **opportunity cost** of deciding to put an hour of shaping department time to an alternative use.

We can now make the following points:

(a) The management of WX should be prepared to **pay up to £0.50 extra per hour** (ie £0.50 over and above the normal price) of shaping department machine time to obtain more machine hours.

(b) This **value** of machine time **only applies as long as shaping machine time is a limiting factor**. If more and more machine hours become available, there will eventually be so much machine time that it is no longer a limiting factor.

Activity 7 **(10 minutes)**

Shadow prices

What is the shadow price of one hour of machine time in the mixing department?

A £3
B £7
C £10.50
D £1,193

Ranges for limiting factors

We can calculate **how many hours will be available before machine time in the shaping department ceases to be a limiting factor**.

Look back at the third graph in Section 1.4. As more hours become available the constraint line moves out away from the origin. It ceases to be a limiting factor when it passes through the intersection of the sales constraint and the mixing department machine time constraint which is at the point (22,667, 13,000).

So, if x = 22,667 and y = 13,000, our new constraint would be 0.04x + 0.12y = H (hours) where H = (0.04 × 22,667) + (0.12 × 13,000) = 2,466.68 hours.
The shadow price of shaping department machine time is therefore £0.50 but only up to a maximum supply of 2,466.68 hours (that is 66.68 hours more than the original 2,400 hours). Extra availability of machine time above 2,466.68 hours would not have any use, and the two limiting factors would become sales demand for product B and machine time in the mixing department.

3.2 Sales price sensitivity analysis

Sales price sensitivity analysis is carried out by changing the slope of the 'iso-contribution' line.

The optimal solution in our WX example was to make 24,000 units of product A and 12,000 units of product B. Would this solution change if the **unit sales price of A increased by 10p?**

The **contribution would increase** to 0.3x + 0.3y (in place of 0.2x + 0.3y). The **iso-contribution lines would now have a steeper slope** than previously, parallel (for example) to 0.3x + 0.3y = 3,000.

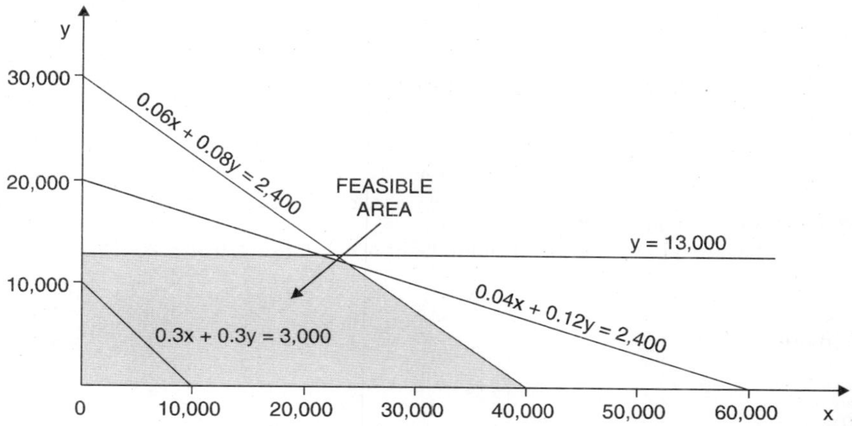

If you were to place a ruler along the iso-contribution line and move it away from the origin as usual, you would find its **last point within the feasible region** was the point (40,000, 0).

Therefore if the sales price of A is raised by 10p, WX's contribution-maximising product mix would be to produce 40,000 units of A and none of B.

EXAMPLE: SENSITIVITY ANALYSIS

SW makes two products, X and Y, which each earn a contribution of £8 per unit. Each unit of X requires four labour hours and three machine hours. Each unit of Y requires three labour hours and five machine hours.

Total weekly capacity is 1,200 labour hours and 1,725 machine hours. There is a standing weekly order for 100 units of X which must be met. In addition, for technical reasons, it is necessary to produce at least twice as many units of Y as units of X.

Required

(a) Determine the contribution-maximising production plan each week.

(b) Calculate the shadow price of the following:

(i) Machine hours
(ii) Labour hours
(iii) The minimum weekly demand for X of 100 units

SOLUTION (a): Production plan

The linear programming problem may be formulated as follows:

Step 1 **Define variables**
Let x = number of units of X produced and y = number of units of Y produced.

Step 2 **Establish objective function**
Maximise contribution (c) = 8x + 8y subject to the constraints below.

Step 3 **Establish constraints**

$4x + 3y \leq 1{,}200$	(labour hours)
$3x + 5y \leq 1{,}725$	(machine hours)
$x \geq 100$	(minimum demand)
$y \geq 2x$	(technical constraint)
$y \geq 0$	(non-negativity)

Step 4 **Graph the problem**

The graph of this problem would be drawn as follows, using $8x + 8y = 2{,}400$ as an iso-contribution line:

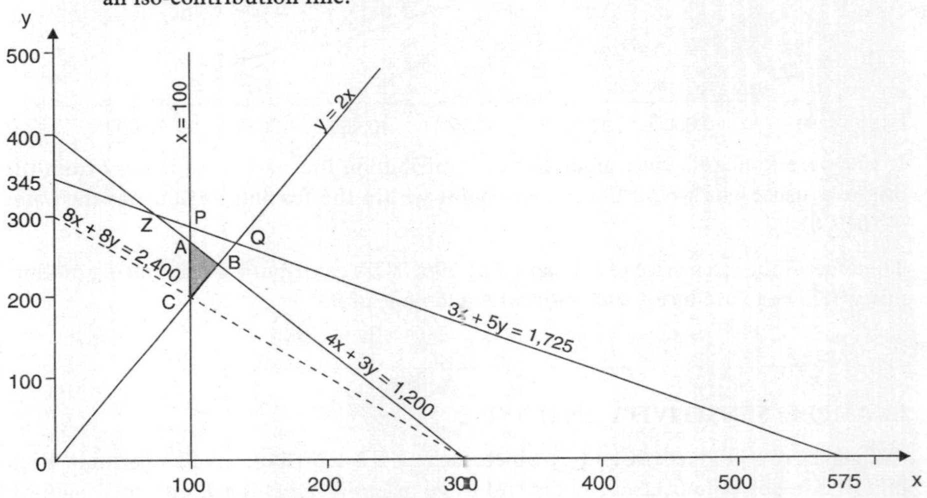

Step 5 **Establish feasible polygon**

The feasible polygon is ABC. Using the slope of the iso-contribution line, we can measure that the contribution-maximising point is point A.

Step 6 **Determine optimal solution**

At point A, the effective constraints are $x = 100$ and $4x + 3y = 1{,}200$.

$\therefore$ If $x = 100$, $(4 \times 100) + 3y = 1{,}200$

$\therefore 3y = 1{,}200 - 400$ and so $y = 266^2/_3$

It is important to be aware that, in linear programming, the optimal solution is likely to give values to the decision variables which are in fractions of a unit. In this example, contribution will be maximised by making $266^2/_3$ units of Y:

	Contribution £
Make 100 units of X	800.00
$266^2/_3$ units of Y	2,133.33
Total weekly contribution	2,933.33

SOLUTION (b): Sensitivity analysis

(i) **Machine hours** are not fully utilised in the optimal solution. 100 units of X and $266^2/_3$ units of Y need $(300 + 1{,}333.33) = 1{,}633.33$ machine hours, leaving 91.67 **machine hours unused**. Machine hours, not being an effective constraint in the optimal solution, have a **shadow price of £0**. Obtaining one extra machine hour would add nothing to the contribution.

(ii) The shadow price of **labour hours** would be obtained by calculating the total weekly contribution if the labour hours constraint were 1,201 hours. It should be possible to see fairly easily that the **new optimal solution** would be where $x = 100$ and $4x + 3y = 1{,}201$. Therefore $x = 100$, $y = 267$ and total weekly contribution would be $(100 + 267) \times £8 = £2{,}936$.

Since contribution with 1,200 labour hours as the constraint was £2,933.33, the shadow price of labour hours is £(2,936 – 2,933.33) = £2.67 per hour. This is the amount by which total contribution would rise if one extra labour hour per week were made available.

Note that there is a limitation to the number of extra labour hours that could be used to earn extra contribution. As more and more labour hours are added, the constraint line will move further and further away from the origin. For example if we added 800 labour hours capacity each week, the constraint $4x + 3y \leq (1{,}200 + 800)$ (ie $4x + 3y \leq 2{,}000$) would be so much further away from the origin that it would no longer be an effective constraint. Machine hours would now help to impose limitations on production, and the profit-maximising output would be at point P on the graph.

Labour hours could only be added to earn more contribution up to point P, after which they would cease to be an effective constraint. At point P, $x = 100$ and $3x + 5y = 1{,}725$. Therefore $y = 285$.

The labour hours required to make 100 units of X and 285 units of Y are $(4 \times 100) + (3 \times 285) = 1{,}255$ hours, which is 55 hours more than the initial constraint limit.

Total contribution at point P = $(100 + 285) \times £8 = £3{,}080$. Since total contribution at point A, where labour hours were limited to 1,200 hours, was £2,933.33, the extra contribution from the 55 extra labour hours would be £(3,080 – 2,933.33)/55 = £2.67 per hour (as calculated previously).

Thus, the shadow price of labour hours is £2.67 per hour, for a maximum of 55 extra hours per week, after which additional labour hours would add nothing to the weekly contribution.

(iii) The shadow price of the **minimum weekly demand for X** may be obtained by calculating the weekly contribution if the minimum demand is reduced by one unit to 99, so that $x \geq 99$, given no change in the other original constraints in the problem.

The new optimal solution would occur where $x = 99$ and $4x + 3y = 1{,}200$. Therefore $y = 268$.

Total contribution per week when $x = 99$ and $y = 268$ is $(99 + 268) \times £8 = £2{,}936$. Since the contribution when $x \geq 100$ was £2,933.33, the **shadow price** of the minimum demand for X is £(2,936 – 2,933.33) = **£2.67 per unit**. In other words, by reducing the minimum demand for X, the weekly contribution can be raised by £2.67 for each unit by which the minimum demand is reduced below 100 per week.

As with the constraint on labour hours, this shadow price is **only applicable up to a certain amount**. If you refer back to the graph of the problem, you should be able to see that if the minimum constraint on X is reduced beyond point Z, it will cease to be an effective constraint in the optimal solution, because at point Z the machine hours limitation will begin to apply.

Activity 8 **(10 minutes)**

Ranges for shadow prices

By how many units per week can the minimum demand be reduced before the shadow price of £2.67 per unit referred to above ceases to apply?

A 300 units
B 100 units
C 75 units
D 25 units

In the final part of this chapter we will look at another method of solving linear programming problems. This is the simplex method.

4 THE PRINCIPLES OF THE SIMPLEX METHOD

The Simplex method
General points
Formulating the problem
The tableau

The **simplex method** is a method of solving linear programming problems with two or more decision variables.

The formulation of the problem using the **simplex method** is similar to that required when the graphical method is used but **slack variables** must be incorporated into the constraints and the objective function.

4.1 General points about the simplex method

A **slack variable** represents the amount of a constraint that is unused.

In any feasible solution, if a problem involves n constraints and m variables (decision plus slack), n variables will have a positive value and (m–n) variables will have a value of zero.

Feasible solutions to a problem are shown in a **tableau**.

Before introducing an example to explain the technique, we will make a few introductory points. Don't worry if you get confused, working through the example will make things clearer.

(a) The simplex method involves **testing one feasible solution after another**, in a **succession of tables or tableaux, until the optimal solution is found**. It can be used for problems with **any number of decision variables, from two upwards.**

(b) In addition to the decision variables, the method introduces additional variables, known as **slack variables** or **surplus variables**. There will be **one slack (or surplus) variable for each constraint in the problem (excluding non-negativity constraints).**

For example, if a linear programming problem has three decision variables and four constraints, there will be four slack variables. With the three decision variables, there will therefore be a total of seven variables and four constraints in the problem.

(c) The technique is a **repetitive, step-by-step process**, with each step having the following **purposes**.

  (i) To **establish a feasible solution** (in other words, a feasible combination of decision variable values and slack variable values) and the **value of the objective function** for that solution.

  (ii) To **establish** whether that particular **solution** is one that **optimises** the value of the objective function.

(d) Each feasible solution is tested by drawing up a **matrix** or **tableau** with the following rows and columns:

  (i) **One row per constraint, plus a solution row**

  (ii) **One column per decision variable and per slack variable, plus a solution column**

(e) **Every variable**, whether a decision variable, slack variable or surplus variable, **must be ≥ 0 in any feasible solution.**

(f) A feature of the simplex method is that if there are **n constraints**, there will be **n variables with a value greater than 0 in any feasible solution.** Thus, if there are seven variables in a problem, and four constraints, there will be four variables with a positive value in the solution, and three variables with a value equal to 0.

Keep these points in mind as we work through an example.

Note that you do not need to be able to test solutions in the exam. You simply need to be able to prepare the appropriate formulae and formulate the appropriate initial tableau, interpret the final (optimal solution) tableau and apply the information contained in that optimal solution. The November 2005 exam included a nine-part question requiring the interpretation of values in a final simplex solution.

4.2 Formulating the problem

EXAMPLE: THE SIMPLEX METHOD

An organisation produces and sells two products, X and Y. Relevant information is as follows:

	Materials units	*Labour hours*	*Machine time hours*	*Contribution per unit* £
X, per unit	5	1	3	20
Y, per unit	2	3	2	16
Total available, each week	3,000	1,750	2,100	

Required

Use the simplex method to determine the profit-maximising product mix.

We have just two decision variables in this problem, but we can still use the simplex method to solve it.

Step 1 **Define variables**

Let x be the number of units of X that should be produced and sold.
Let y be the number of units of Y that should be produced and sold.

Step 2 **Establish objective function**

Maximum contribution (C) = $20x + 16y$ subject to the constraints below.

Step 3 **Establish constraints**

The constraints are as follows:

Materials	$5x + 2y \leq 3,000$	Machine time	$3x + 2y \leq 2,100$
Labour	$x + 3y \leq 1,750$	Non-negativity	$x \geq 0, y \geq 0$

Step 4 **Introduce slack variables**

Begin by turning each constraint (ignoring the non-negativity constraints now) into an equation. This is done by introducing slack variables.

Let a be the quantity of unused materials, b be the number of unused labour hours and c be the number of unused machine hours.

Definition

> **Slack variable** is the amount of each resource which will be unused if a specific linear programming solution is implemented.

Activity 9 **(5 minutes)**

Slack variables

A problem to be solved using linear programming has three decision variables, six constraints (including two non-negativity constraints) and one objective function.

How many slack variables will be required if the simplex method is used?

A 3
B 4
C 5
D 6

We can now express the original constraints as equations.

$$5x + 2y + a = 3{,}000$$
$$x + 3y + b = 1{,}750$$
$$3x + 2y + c = 2{,}100$$

The slack variables a, b and c will be equal to 0 in the final solution only if the combined production of X and Y uses up all the available materials, labour hours and machine hours.

Step 5 **Values of variables – non-negative or zero?**

In this example, there are **five variables** (x, y, a, b and c) and **three equations,** and so in any **feasible solution** that is tested, **three variables** will have a **non-negative value** (since there are three equations) which means that **two variables** will have a value of **zero.**

Activity 10 **(20 minutes)**

Values of variables

A problem to be solved using linear programming has seven variables and four equations based on the original constraints.

How many variables will have a value of zero in any feasible solution determined using the simplex method?

A 7
B 5
C 4
D 3

Step 6 **Express objective function as an equation**

It is usual to express the objective function as an equation with the right-hand side equal to zero. In order to keep the problem consistent, the slack (or surplus) variables are inserted into the objective function equation, but as the quantities they represent should have no effect on the objective function they are given zero coefficients. In our example, the objective function will be expressed as follows:

Maximise contribution (C) given by C – 20x – 16y + 0a + 0b + 0c = 0.

4.3 The tableau

Drawing up the initial tableau and testing the initial feasible solution

We begin by testing a solution that **all the decision variables have a zero value, and all the slack variables have a non-negative value.**

Obviously, this is **not going to be the optimal solution,** but it gives us a starting point from which we can develop other feasible solutions.

Simplex tableaux can be **drawn in several different ways,** and if you are asked to interpret a given tableau in an examination question, you may need to adapt your understanding of the tableau format in this Study Text to the format in the question. The following points apply to all tableaux, however:

(a) There should be a **column for each variable** and also a **solution column**

(b) It helps to add a **further column on the left,** to **indicate the variable which is in the solution to which the corresponding value in the solution column relates**

(c) There is a **row for each equation** in the problem, and a **solution row**

Here is the initial matrix for our problem. Information on how it has been derived is given below:

Variables in solution	*x*	*y*	*a*	*b*	*c*	*Solution*
a	5	2	1	0	0	3,000
b	1	3	0	1	0	1,750
c	3	2	0	0	1	2,100
Solution	–20	–16	0	0	0	0

(a) The **figures in each** row correspond with the **coefficients of the variables in each of the initial constraints.** The bottom row or **solution row** holds the **coefficients of the objective function.** For example the materials constraint 5x + 2y + a = 3,000 gives us the first row, 5 (number of x's), 2 (number of y's), 1 (number of a's), then zeros in the b and c columns (since these do not feature in the constraint equation) and finally 3,000 in the solution column.

(b) The **variables in the solution are a, b and c** (the unused resources).

   (i) The **value of each variable is shown in the solution column.** We are testing a solution that all decision variables have a zero value, so there is no production and hence no resources are used. The total resource available is therefore unused.

   (ii) The **column values** for each variable in the solution are as follows:

   - 1 in the variable's own solution row
   - 0 in every other row, including the solution row

(c) The **contribution per unit obtainable from x and y** is given in the **solution row.** These are the **dual prices** or **shadow prices** of the products X and Y.

The minus signs are of no particular significance, except that in the solution given here they have the following meanings:

(i) A **minus shadow price** indicates that the **value of the objective function can be increased by the amount of the shadow price per unit** of the variable that is introduced into the solution, given no change in the current objective function or existing constraints

(ii) A **positive shadow price** indicates the amount by which the **value of the objective function would be decreased** per unit of the variable introduced into the solution, given no change in the current objective function or the existing constraints

4.4 Interpreting the tableau and testing for improvement

We can see that the **solution is testing a = 3,000, b = 1,750 and c = 2,100, contribution = 0. The co-efficients for the variables not in this solution, x and y, are the dual prices or shadow prices** of these variables, given the solution being tested. A **negative value** to a dual price means that the **objective function can be increased**; therefore the **solution in the tableau is not the optimal solution.**

The **shadow prices** in the initial solution (tableau) **indicate** the following:

(a) The profit would be increased by £20 for every extra unit of x produced (because the shadow price of x is £20 per unit)

(b) Similarly, the profit would be increased by £16 for every extra unit of y produced (because its shadow price is £16 per unit)

Since the **solution is not optimal,** the **contribution may be improved by introducing either x or y into the solution.**

4.5 The next step

The next step is to **test another feasible solution.** We do this by **introducing one variable into the solution, in the place of one variable that is now removed.** In our example, we **introduce x or y in place of a, b or c.**

The simplex technique continues in this way, producing a feasible solution in each successive tableau, until the optimal solution is reached.

4.6 Interpreting the final tableau

If the **shadow prices** on the bottom (solution) row of a tableau are all positive, the tableau shows the optimal solution.

- The solution column shows the optimal production levels and the units of unused resource.
- The figure at the bottom of the solution column/right-hand side of the solution row shows the value of the objective function.
- The figures in the solution row indicate the shadow prices of resources.

After a number of iterations, the following tableau is produced:

Variables in solution	*x*	*y*	*a*	*b*	*c*	*Solution column*
x	1	0	0	–0.2857	0.4286	400
a	0	0	1	0.5714	–1.8571	100
y	0	1	0	0.4286	–0.1429	450
Solution row	0	0	0	1.1428	6.2858	15,200

This can be interpreted as follows:

(a) The solution in this tableau is the **optimal** one, because the **shadow prices on the bottom row are all positive**

(b) The optimal solution is to **make and sell 400 units of X** and **450 units of Y, to earn a contribution of £15,200**

(c) The solution will leave **100 units of material unused** but will use up all available labour and machine time

(d) The **shadow price of labour time (b) is £1.1428 per hour,** which **indicates the amount by which contribution could be increased if more labour time could be made available at its normal variable cost**

(e) The **shadow price of machine time (c) is £6.2858 per hour,** which **indicates the amount by which contribution could be increased if more machine time could be made available, at its normal variable cost**

(f) The **shadow price of materials is nil,** because there are 100 units of **unused** materials in the solution

Activity 11  **(20 minutes)**

Formulation of problem

TDS manufactures two products, X and Y, which earn a contribution of £8 and £14 per unit respectively. At current selling prices, there is no limit to sales demand for Y, but maximum demand for X would be 1,200 units. The company aims to maximise its annual profits, and fixed costs are £15,000 per annum.

In the year to 30 June 20X2, the company expects to have a limited availability of resources and estimates of availability are as follows:

Skilled labour	maximum 9,000 hours
Machine time	maximum 4,000 hours
Material M	maximum 1,000 tonnes

The usage of these resources per unit of product are as follows:

	X	*Y*
Skilled labour time	3 hours	4 hours
Machine time	1 hour	2 hours
Material M	½ tonne	¼ tonne

Required

(a) Formulate the problem using the simplex method of linear programming.

(b) Determine how many variables will have a positive value and how many a value of zero in any feasible solution.

Chapter roundup

- The **graphical method** of linear programming is used for problems involving two products.
- The **steps in the graphical method** are as follows:
  - Define variables
  - Establish objective function
  - Establish constraints
  - Draw a graph of the constraints
  - Establish the feasible region
  - Determine the optimal product mix
- The **optimal solution** can be found by 'sliding the iso-contribution (or profit) line out'.
- The optimal solution can also be found using **simultaneous equations.**
- **Slack** occurs when maximum availability of a resource is not used. **Surplus** occurs when more than a minimum requirement is used.
- In a **minimisation problem** (minimise costs), the optimal solution is the point at which the total cost line touches the feasible polygon at a tangent as close to the origin as possible.
- The **shadow price** of a resource which is a limiting factor on production is the amount by which total contribution would fall if the organisation were deprived of one unit of the resource. The shadow price also indicates the amount by which total contribution would rise if the organisation were able to obtain one extra unit of the resource, provided that the resource remains an effective constraint on production and provided also that the extra unit of resource can be obtained at its normal variable cost.
- **Sales price sensitivity analysis** is carried out by changing the slope of the 'iso-contribution' line.
- The formulation of the problem using the **simplex method** is similar to that required when the graphical method is used but **slack variables** must be incorporated into the constraints and the objective function.
- A **slack variable** represents the amount of a constraint that is unused.
- In any feasible solution, if a problem involves n constraints and m variables (decision plus slack), n variables will have a positive value and (m–n) variables will have a value of zero.
- Feasible solutions to a problem are shown in a **tableau**.

Quick quiz

1 *Fill in the blanks in the statements below with one of the following terms:*

Objective function; decision variable; constraint; inequality; non-negativity constraints.

(a) .... should be included when formulating linear programming solutions to ensure that the answer makes sense in operational terms.

(b) An .... is an equation taking the form 'greater than or equal to' or 'less than or equal to'.

(c) An .... is a quantified statement of the aim of a resource allocation decision.

2 *Choose the correct words from those highlighted.*

A feasible **polygon/area** enclosed on all sides is known as a feasible **polygon/area**.

3 *Put the following steps in the graphical approach to linear programming in the correct order:*

Draw a graph of the constraints
Define variables
Establish the feasible region
Establish constraints
Establish objective function
Determine optimal product mix

4 *Choose the correct words from those highlighted.*

When dealing with a problem in which there is a requirement to minimise costs, we look for a total cost line touching the feasible area at a tangent **as close to/as far from** the origin as possible.

5 The shadow price of a scarce resource is not the same as its dual price. *True* or *false?*

6 In what circumstances does slack arise?

A At the optimal solution, when the resource used equals the resource available

B At the optimal solution, when a minimum quantity of a resource must be used, and more than that quantity is used

C At the optimal solution, when the resource used is less than the resource available

D At the optimal solution, when a minimum quantity of resource is used

7 Draw the feasibility polygon for the following inequalities:

$2x + 3y \leq 12$
$y \geq 2x$
$x \geq 0, y \geq 0$

8 *Choose the correct words from those highlighted.*

If a **maximum/minimum** quantity of a resource must be used and, at the optimal solution, **more than/ less than** that quantity is used, there is a surplus on the **minimum/maximum** requirement.

9 Choose the correct words from those highlighted.

The simplex method can be used for problems with **one / two / three / more than three / any number of** decision variables.

10 Fill in the blanks.

If a linear programming problem has four decision variables and five constraints (excluding non-negativity constraints), there will be .... slack variables and a total of .... variables. Each feasible solution matrix will have .... rows and .... columns. There will be .... variables with a value greater than 0 in any feasible solution.

11 A slack variable represents the amount of constraining resource that is used. *True* or *false?*

Answers to quick quiz

1 (a) Non-negativity constraints
(b) Inequality
(c) Objective function

2 area
polygon

3 Define variables
Establish objective function
Establish constraints
Draw a graph of the constraints
Establish the feasible region
Determine optimal product mix

4 as close to

5 False

6 C. If a resource has a maximum availability and it's not binding at the optimal solution, there will be slack.

7 Start with the inequality $y \geq 2x$. The equation $y = 2x$ is a straight line, and you need to plot two points to draw it, such as (0, 0) and (2, 4).

Since $y \geq 2x$, feasible combinations of x and y lie above this line (for example if $x = 2$, y must be 4 or more).

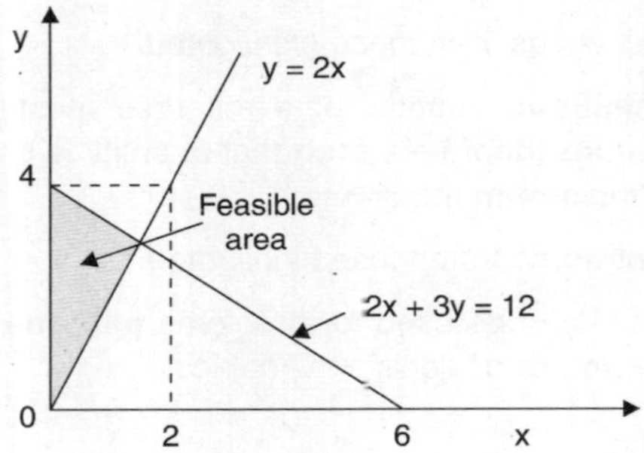

8 minimum
more than
minimum

9 any number of

10 five slack variables
total of nine variables
six rows
ten columns
five variables with a value greater than 0

11 False. It represents the amount unused.

Answers to activities

1 **The correct answer is A.** There is no restriction on the availability of labour hours. Selling price cannot be a constraint.

2 **The correct answer is B.** The constraint has to be a 'less than equal to' inequality, because the amount of resource used (0.04x + 0.12y) has to be 'less than equal to' the amount available of 2,400 hours.

3 (a) The objective function is to maximise weekly contribution, given by C = 124x + 80y.

(b) The constraints are

Department 1	150x + 90y	≤	225 × 60 minutes
Department 2	100x + 120y	≤	200 × 60 minutes
EU quota	y	≤	75
Non-negativity	x, y	≥	0

These constraints can be simplified to

Department 1	15x + 9y	≤	1,350
Department 2	10x + 12y	≤	1,200
EU quota	y	≤	75
Non-negativity	x, y	≥	0

4 If 0.06x + 0.08y = 2,400, then if x = 0, y = 30,000 and if y = 0, x = 40,000.
If 0.04x + 0.12y = 2,400, then if x = 0, y = 20,000 and if y = 0, x = 60,000.

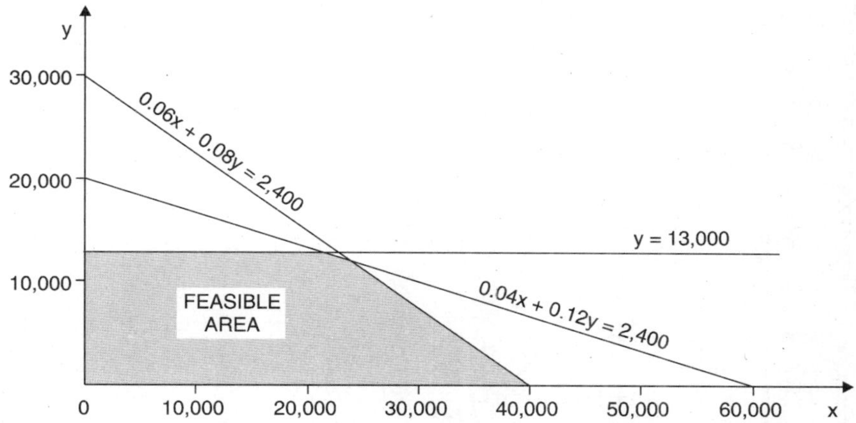

5 **Calculate the number of productive hours worked in each department each month**

Number of employees × number of productive hours worked each day × number of days each month.

Tanning = 7 × (7 – 0.5) × 20 = 910 hours
Plunging = 10 × (6 – 1) × 20 = 1,000 hours
Watering = 5 × (10 – 0.25) × 20 = 975 hours

Step 1 **Define variables**

Let the number of Cretes produced each month = x and the number of Corfus produced each month = y.

Step 2 **Establish objective function**

The contribution is £75 per Crete and £50 per Corfu. The objective function is therefore maximise C = 75x + 50y subject to the constraints below.

Step 3 **Establish constraints**

Tanning	$x/6 + y/5 \leq 910$
Plunging	$x/4 + y/6 \leq 1,000$
Watering	$x/10 + y/4 \leq 975$
Monthly sales units	$x \leq 3,500$, $y \leq 4,000$
Non-negativity	$x \geq 0$, $y \geq 0$

Step 4 **Graph the problem**

The problem can be solved using the following graph which includes a sample contribution line 75x + 50y = 150,000.

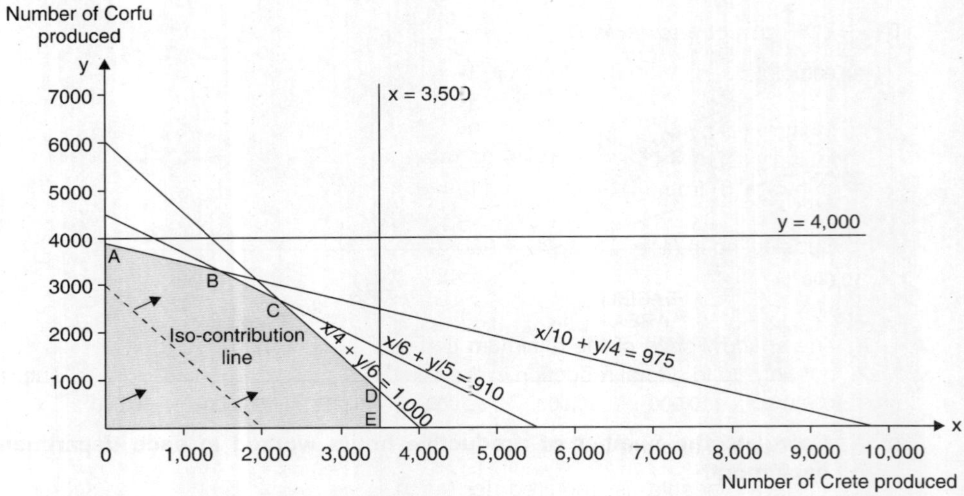

Step 5 **Define the feasible area**

The feasible region for a solution is OABCDE.

Step 6 **Determine the optimal solution**

Moving the sample contribution line across the feasible region it can be seen that the optimum solution is at any point along the line x/4 + y/6 = 1,000 between C and D (as the sample contribution line has the same gradient as the plunging constraint). The coordinates of point C are (2,175, 2,737.5) while those of point D are (3,500, 750).

The contribution from any of these solutions is £((75 × 3,500) + (50 × 750)) = £300,000 (using the coordinates of D).

6 **The correct answer is:** A shadow price is the **increase** in **contribution** created by the availability of an extra unit of a **limiting resource** at its **original cost**.

7 **The correct answer is A.**

If we assume one **less** hour of machine time in the mixing department is available, the new optimal solution is at the intersection of 0.06x + 0.08y = 2,399 and 0.04x + 0.12y = 2,400

Solution by simultaneous equations gives x = 23,970, y = 12,010

Product	Units	*Contribution per unit* £	*Total contribution* £
A	23,970	0.20	4,794
B	12,010	0.30	3,603
			8,397
Contribution in original problem			8,400
Reduction in contribution			3

∴ Shadow price of one hour of machine time in the mixing department is £3.

8 **The correct answer is D.**

At point Z:	$4x + 3y = 1,200$	.... (1)
	$3x + 5y = 1,725$	.... (2)
Multiply (1) by 3	$12x + 9y = 3,600$	.... (3)
Multiply (2) by 4	$12x + 20y = 6,900$	.... (4)
Subtract (3) from (4)	$11y = 3,300$	
	$y = 300$	
Substituting in (1)	$4x + 900 = 1,200$	
	$4x = 300$	
	$x = 75$	

The shadow price of the minimum demand for X is £2.67 per unit demanded, but only up to a total reduction in the minimum demand of (100 – 75) = 25 units per week.

9 **The correct answer is B.**

A slack variable is required for each constraint (ignoring non-negativity constraints). There are 6 – 2 = 4 such constraints.

10 **The correct answer is D.**

Four variables will have a non-negative value (since there are four equations), which means that 7 – 4 = 3 variables will have a value of zero.

11 (a) The linear programming problem would be formulated as follows.

Define variables

Let x and y be the number of units made and sold of product X and product Y respectively.

Establish objective function

Maximise contribution (C) = 8x + 14y subject to the constraints below.

Establish constraints

$3x + 4y$	$\leq$	9,000	(skilled labour)*
$x + 2y$	$\leq$	4,000	(machine time)
$0.5x + 0.25y$	$\leq$	1,000	(material M)
x	$\leq$	1,200	(demand for X)
x, y	$\geq$	0	

* This constraint is that skilled labour hours cannot exceed 9,000 hours, and since a unit of X needs 3 hours and a unit of Y needs four hours, 3x + 4y cannot exceed 9,000. The other constraints are formulated in a similar way.

Introduce slack variables

Introduce a slack variable into each constraint, to turn the inequality into an equation.

Let a	=	the number of unused skilled labour hours
b	=	the number of unused machine hours
c	=	the number of unused tonnes of material M
d	=	the amount by which demand for X falls short of 1,200 units

Then

$$3x + 4y + a = 9{,}000 \text{ (labour hours)}$$
$$x + 2y + b = 4{,}000 \text{ (machine hours)}$$
$$0.5x + 0.25y + c = 1{,}000 \text{ (tonnes of M)}$$
$$x + d = 1{,}200 \text{ (demand for X)}$$

and maximise contribution (C) given by $C - 8x - 14y + 0a + 0b + 0c + 0d = 0$

(b) There are six variables (x, y, a, b, c, d) and four equations. In any feasible solution four variables will have a non-negative value (as there are four equations), while two variables will have a value of zero.

Chapter 8 :

REGRESSION AND TIME SERIES

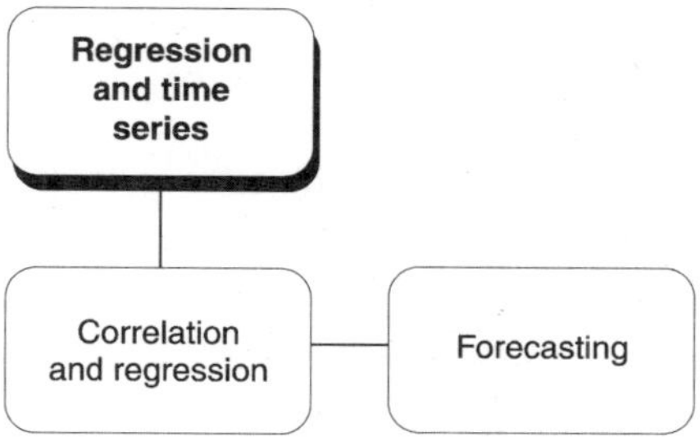

Introduction

We looked at scatter diagrams in Chapter 2. In the first half of this chapter we are going to look at how the inter-relationship shown between variables in a scatter diagram can be described and calculated. The first two sections deal with **correlation,** which is concerned with assessing the strength of the relationship between two variables.

We will then see how, if we assume that there is a **linear relationship** between two variables (such as selling costs and sales volume), we can determine the equation of a straight line to represent the relationship between the variables and use that equation to make **forecasts** or **predictions.**

We conclude the first half of the chapter by looking very briefly at multiple regression.

In some situations, there are no independent variables from which to forecast a dependent variable. In the second half of this chapter we will be looking at a technique called **time series analysis.** With this **forecasting** method we look at **past data** about the variable which we want to forecast (such as sales levels) to see if there are **any patterns.** We then assume that these patterns will continue into the future. We are then able to forecast what we believe will be the value of a variable at some particular point of time in the future.

Your objectives

In this chapter you will learn about the following:

- Correlation
- The correlation coefficient
- Lines of best fit
- Least square regression
- The components of time series
- Finding trends
- Finding seasonal variations
- Forecasting
- The limitations of forecasting models

1 CORRELATION AND REGRESSION

Correlation and regression
- Correlation
- The correlation and coefficient of determination
- Lines of best fit
- Least square regression
- Multiple regression

1.1 Correlation

When the value of one variable is related to the value of another, they are said to be **correlated**.

Two variables are said to be correlated if a change in the value of one variable is accompanied by a change in the value of another variable. This is what is meant by **correlation**.

EXAMPLES OF VARIABLES WHICH MIGHT BE CORRELATED

- A person's height and weight
- The distance of a journey and the time it takes to make it

Scatter diagrams

One way of showing the correlation between two related variables is on a **scatter diagram**, plotting a number of pairs of data on the graph. For example, a scatter diagram showing monthly selling costs against the volume of sales for a 12-month period might be as follows:

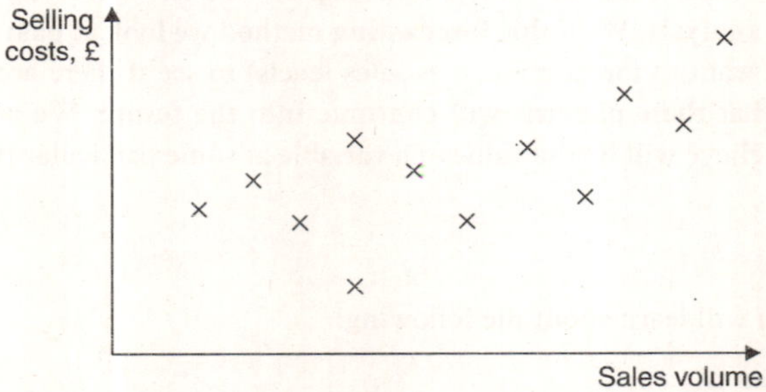

The **independent** variable (the cause) is plotted on the **horizontal** (x) axis and the **dependent** variable (the effect) is plotted on the **vertical** (y) axis.

This scattergraph suggests that there is some correlation between selling costs and sales volume, so that, as sales volume rises, selling costs tend to rise as well.

Degrees of correlation

Two variables might be perfectly correlated, partly correlated or uncorrelated. Correlation can be positive or negative.

These differing degrees of correlation can be illustrated by scatter diagrams.

Perfect correlation

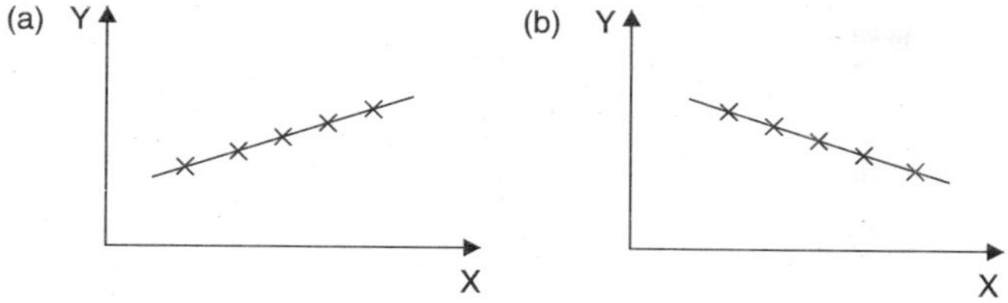

All the pairs of values lie on a straight line. An exact **linear relationship** exists between the two variables.

Partial correlation

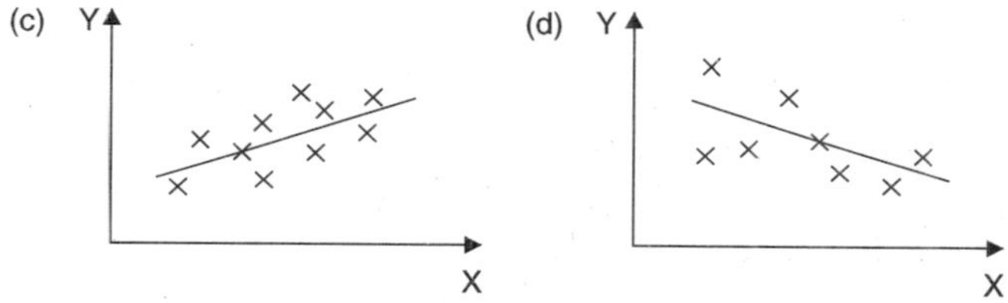

In (c), although there is no exact relationship, low values of X tend to be associated with low values of Y, and high values of X with high values of Y.

In (d) again, there is no exact relationship, but low values of X tend to be associated with high values of Y and vice versa.

No correlation

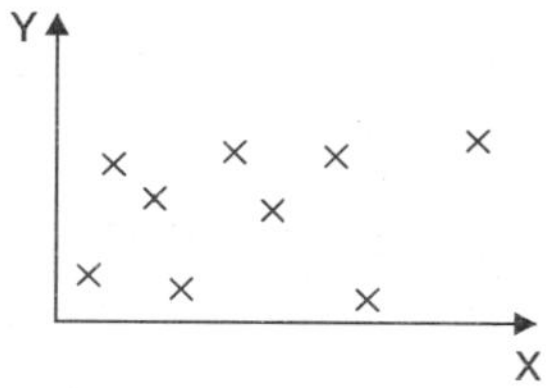

The values of these two variables are not correlated with each other.

Positive and negative correlation

Correlation, whether perfect or partial, can be **positive** or **negative**.

Definitions

- **Positive correlation** means that low values of one variable are associated with low values of the other, and high values of one variable are associated with high values of the other.
- **Negative correlation** means that low values of one variable are associated with high values of the other, and high values of one variable with low values of the other.

1.2 The correlation coefficient and the coefficient of determination

The **degree of correlation** between two variables is measured by **correlation coefficient, r.** This is also called **Pearson's correlation coefficient.** The nearer r is to +1 or –1, the stronger the relationship.

The correlation coefficient

The correlation coefficient, r is used to measure how strong the connection is between two variables, known as the degree of correlation.

It is calculated using a formula which will be given to you in the assessment. It looks complicated but with a systematic approach and plenty of practice, you will be able to answer correlation questions in the assessment.

$$\textbf{Correlation coefficient, r} = \frac{n\Sigma XY - \Sigma X\Sigma Y}{\sqrt{[n\Sigma X^2 - (\Sigma X)^2][n\Sigma Y^2 - (\Sigma Y)^2]}}$$

Where X and Y represent pairs of data for two variables X and Y

n = the number of pairs of data used in the analysis

The correlation coefficient range

The correlation coefficient, r must always fall between –1 and +1. If you get a value outside this range you have made a mistake.

- r = +1 means that the variables are **perfectly positively correlated**
- r = –1 means that the variables are **perfectly negatively correlated**
- r = 0 means that the variables are **uncorrelated**

EXAMPLE: THE CORRELATION COEFFICIENT

The cost of output at a factory is thought to depend on the number of units produced. Data have been collected for the number of units produced each month in the last six months, and the associated costs, as follows:

Month	*Output* *'000s of units* X	*Cost* *£'000* Y
1	2	9
2	3	11
3	1	7
4	4	13
5	3	11
6	5	15

Required

Assess whether there is there any correlation between output and cost.

SOLUTION

$$r = \frac{n\sum XY - \sum X \sum Y}{\sqrt{[n\sum X^2 - (\sum X)^2][n\sum Y^2 - (\sum Y)^2]}}$$

We need to find the values for the following:

(a) $\sum XY$ Multiply each value of X by its corresponding Y value, so that there are six values for XY. Add up the six values to get the total.

(b) $\sum X$ Add up the six values of X to get a total. $(\sum X)^2$ will be the square of this total.

(c) $\sum Y$ Add up the six values of Y to get a total. $(\sum Y)^2$ will be the square of this total.

(d) $\sum X^2$ Find the square of each value of X, so that there are six values for X^2. Add up these values to get a total.

(e) $\sum Y^2$ Find the square of each value of Y, so that there are six values for Y^2. Add up these values to get a total.

Set out your workings in a table.

Workings

X	*Y*	*XY*	*X²*	*Y²*
2	9	18	4	81
3	11	33	9	121
1	7	7	1	49
4	13	52	16	169
3	11	33	9	121
5	15	75	25	225
$\sum X$ = 18	$\sum Y$ = 66	$\sum XY$ = 218	$\sum X^2$ = 64	$\sum Y^2$ = 766

$(\sum X)^2 = 18^2 = 324$
$(\sum Y)^2 = 66^2 = 4,356$

$n = 6$

$$r = \frac{(6 \times 218) - (18 \times 66)}{\sqrt{[(6 \times 64) - 324] \times [(6 \times 766) - 4,356]}}$$

$$= \frac{1,308 - 1,188}{\sqrt{(384 - 324) \times (4,596 - 4,356)}}$$

$$= \frac{120}{\sqrt{60 \times 240}} = \frac{120}{\sqrt{14,400}} = \frac{120}{120} = 1$$

There is **perfect positive correlation** between the volume of output at the factory and costs which means that there is a perfect linear relationship between output and costs.

Activity 1 **(15 minutes)**

Correlation

A company wants to know if the money they spend on advertising is effective in creating sales. The following data have been collected:

Monthly advertising expenditure £'000	*Sales in following month £'000*
1.2	132.5
0.9	98.5
1.6	154.3
2.1	201.4
1.6	161.0

Required

Calculate the correlation' coefficient for the data and explain the result.

The coefficient of determination, r^2

The **coefficient of determination, r^2** measures the proportion of the total variation in the value of one variable that can be explained by variations in the value of the other variable.

Unless the correlation coefficient r is exactly or very nearly +1, –1 or 0, its meaning or significance is a little unclear. For example, if the correlation coefficient for two variables is +0.8, this would tell us that the variables are positively correlated, but the correlation is not perfect. It would not really tell us much else. A more meaningful analysis is available from **the square of the correlation coefficient, r,** which is called the **coefficient of determination, r^2.**

Interpreting r^2

In the question above, r = –0.992, therefore r^2 = 0.984. This means that over 98% of variations in sales can be explained by the passage of time, leaving 0.016 (less than 2%) of variations to be explained by other factors.

Similarly, if the correlation coefficient between a company's output volume and maintenance costs was 0.9, r^2 would be 0.81, meaning that 81% of variations in maintenance costs could be explained by variations in output volume, leaving only 19% of variations to be explained by other factors (such as the age of the equipment).

Note, however, that if r^2 = 0.81, we would say that 81% of **the variations in y can be explained by variations in x.** We do not necessarily conclude that 81% of variations in y are *caused* by the variations in x. We must beware of reading too much significance into our statistical analysis.

Correlation and causation

If two variables are well correlated, either positively or negatively, this may be due to **pure chance** or there may be a **reason** for it. The larger the number of pairs of data collected, the less likely it is that the correlation is due to chance, though that possibility should never be ignored entirely.

If there is a reason, it may not be **causal**. For example, monthly net income is well correlated with monthly credit to a person's bank account, for the logical (rather than causal) reason that for most people the one equals the other.

Even if there is a causal explanation for a correlation, it does not follow that variations in the value of one variable cause variations in the value of the other. For example, sales of ice cream and of sunglasses are well correlated, not because of a direct causal link but because the weather influences both variables.

Having looked at correlation we are now going on to look at lines of best fit.

1.3 Lines of best fit

Strength of a relationship

Correlation enables us to determine the **strength of any relationship between two variables** but it does not offer us any method of **forecasting** values for one variable, Y, given values of another variable, X.

Equation of a straight line

If we assume that there is a **linear relationship** between the two variables and we determine the **equation of a straight line (Y = a + bX)** which is a good fit for the available data plotted on a scattergraph, we can use the equation for forecasting. We do this by substituting values for X into the equation and deriving values for Y.

Estimating the equation

There are a number of techniques for estimating the equation of a line of best fit. We will be looking at the **scattergraph method** and **simple linear regression analysis**. Both provide a technique for estimating values for a and b in the equation, $y = a + bx$.

The scattergraph method

The scattergraph method involves the use of judgement to draw what seems to be a line of best fit through plotted data.

EXAMPLE: THE SCATTERGRAPH METHOD

Suppose we have the following pairs of data about output and costs for a company – Oscar Ltd:

Month	*Output* '*000 units*	*Costs* *£'000*
1	20	82
2	16	70
3	24	90
4	22	85
5	18	73

(a) These pairs of data can be plotted on a **scattergraph** (the **horizontal** axis representing the **independent** variable and the **vertical** axis the **dependent**) and a line of best fit might be judged as the one shown below. It is drawn to pass through the middle of the data points, thereby having as many data points below the line as above it.

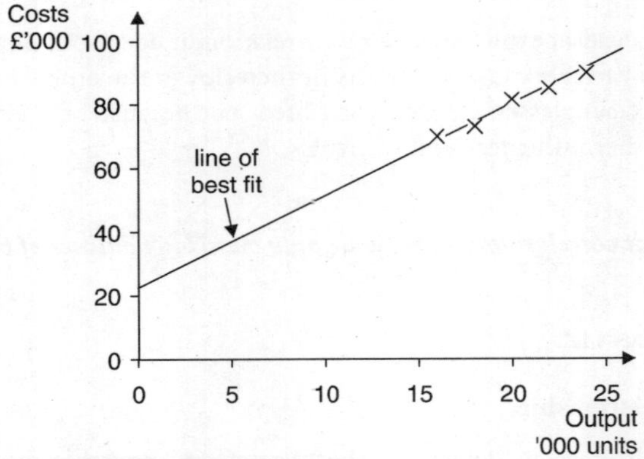

(b) **A formula for the line of best fit** can be found. In our example, suppose that we read the following data from the graph:

(i) When X = 0, Y = 22,000. This must be the value of **a** in the formula Y = a + bX.

(ii) When X = 20,000, Y = 82,000. Since Y = a + bX, and a = 22,000,
82,000 = 22,000 + (b × 20,000)
b × 20,000 = 60,000
b = 3

(c) In this example the estimated equation from the scattergraph is Y = 22,000 + 3X.

Forecasting and scattergraphs

If the company to which the data for Oscar Ltd above relates wanted to predict costs at a certain level of output (say 13,000 units), the value of 13,000 could be substituted into the equation Y = 22,000 + 2.95X and an estimate of costs made.

If X = 13, Y = 22,000 + (3 × 13,000)

∴ Y = £61,000

Predictions can be made directly from the scattergraph, but this will usually be less accurate.

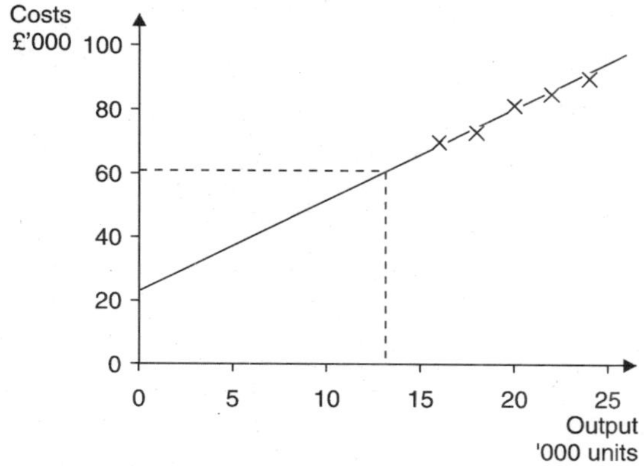

The prediction of the cost of producing 13,000 units from the scattergraph is £61,000.

1.4 Least square regression

Linear regression analysis (the **least squares method**) is one technique for estimating a line of best fit. Once an equation for a line of best fit has been determined, forecasts can be made.

The **least squares method of linear regression analysis** involves using the following formulae for a and b in Y = a + bX:

$$b = \frac{n\Sigma XY - \Sigma X \Sigma Y}{n\Sigma X^2 - (\Sigma X)^2}$$

$$a = \bar{Y} - b\bar{X}$$

Where n is the number of pairs of data

$\bar{X}$ is the mean X value of all the pairs of data

$\bar{Y}$ is the mean Y value of all the pairs of data

Some helpful hints

(a) The value of b must be calculated first as it is needed to calculate a.

(b) $\bar{X}$ is the mean of the X values $= \frac{\Sigma X}{n}$

$\bar{Y}$ is the mean of the Y values $= \frac{\Sigma Y}{n}$

(c) Remember that X is the independent variable and Y is the dependent variable.

(d) Set your workings out in a table to find the figures to put into the formulae.

EXAMPLE: LINEAR REGRESSION ANALYSIS – OSCAR LTD

(a) Given that there is a fairly high degree of correlation between the output and the costs detailed for Oscar Ltd above (so that a linear relationship can be assumed), calculate an equation to determine the expected level of costs, for any given volume of output, using the least squares method.

(b) Prepare a budget for total costs if output is 22,000 units.

(c) Confirm that the degree of correlation between output and costs is high by calculating the correlation coefficient.

SOLUTION

(a) *Workings*

X	Y	XY	X^2	Y^2
20	82	1,640	400	6,724
16	70	1,120	256	4,900
24	90	2,160	576	8,100
22	85	1,870	484	7,225
18	73	1,314	324	5,329
$\Sigma X = 100$	$\Sigma Y = 400$	$\Sigma XY = 8{,}104$	$\Sigma X^2 = 2{,}040$	$\Sigma Y^2 = 32{,}278$

n = 5 (There are five pairs of data for x and y values)

$$b = \frac{n\Sigma XY - \Sigma X \Sigma Y}{n\Sigma X^2 - (\Sigma X)^2} = \frac{(5 \times 8{,}104) - (100 \times 400)}{(5 \times 2{,}040) - 100^2}$$

$$= \frac{40{,}520 - 40{,}000}{10{,}200 - 10{,}000} = \frac{520}{200} = 2.6$$

$$a = \overline{Y} - b\overline{X} = \frac{400}{5} - 2.6 \times \left(\frac{100}{5}\right) = 28$$

$$Y = 28 + 2.6X$$

Where Y = total cost, in thousands of pounds
X = output, in thousands of units

Compare this equation to that determined in the example on page 237.

Note that the fixed costs are £28,000 (when X = 0 costs are £28,000) and the variable cost per unit is £2.60.

(b) If the output is 22,000 units, we would expect costs to be

$28 + (2.6 \times 22) = 85.2 =$ £85,200.

(c)
$$r = \frac{520}{\sqrt{200 \times (5 \times 32{,}278 - 400^2)}} = \frac{520}{\sqrt{200 \times 1{,}390}} = \frac{520}{527.3} = +\,0.986$$

Activity 2 **(10 minutes)**

Linear regression analysis

If $\Sigma x = 79$, $\Sigma y = 1,466$, $\Sigma x^2 = 1,083$, $\Sigma y^2 = 363,076$, $\Sigma xy = 19,736$ and $n = 6$, then the value of b, the gradient, to two decimal places, is

A 10.12
B 111.03
C 13.62
D -8.53

Activity 3 **(5 minutes)**

Forecasting

In a forecasting model based on $y = a + bx$, the intercept is £262. If the value of y is £503 and x is 23, then the value of the gradient, to two decimal places, is

A –20.96
B –10.48
C 10.48
D 20.96

1.5 Multiple regression

So far, all our uses of linear regression have investigated the relationship between two variables only: for example, costs and output or price and sales volume.

However, you will realise that many factors will be influential. For example:

- Sales could depend on price, advertising expenditure and interest rates
- Transportation costs could depend on weight, distance and the time and date of delivery (traffic and weather problems)

Multiple regression recognises that several factors may be at work and attempts to determine their influence on the dependent variable.

As an example, consider a supermarket chain. Investigations have shown that the revenue from a given store depends on

- The population of the catchment area
- The size of the store
- Advertising spend
- Local unemployment rate.

Each of these will provide input which will influence the revenue.

If a linear solution is being sought, the equation will be of the general form:

$$y = a + b_1x_1 + b_2x_2 + b_3x_3 + b_4x_4$$

Total revenue (y) — Constant (a) — Population (b_1x_1) — Floor area (b_2x_2) — Advertising (b_3x_3) — Unemployment (b_4x_4)

The challenge is to find the values of a, b_1, b_2, b_3, b_4, which will make the equation a good predictor of the sales revenue.

To start, data must be collected from each store showing revenue, population, floor area, advertising and local unemployment. That data must the be processed to find the regression equation of best fit.

Although multiple regression analysis can be carried out manually it is much easier to use a computer and many spreadsheet packages come with a multiple regression ability. Of course, before relying on the resulting equation, the correlations should be examined. If low, the multiple regression exercise will have failed to produce a good prediction of revenue.

In the first half of the chapter we looked at correlation and regression. In the second half of the chapter we are going to look at forecasting.

2 FORECASTING

Forecasting
The components of time series
Finding the trend
Finding the seasonal variations
Forecasting
The limitations of forecasting models

2.1 The components of time series

A **time series** is a series of figures or values recorded over time. Any pattern found in the data is then assumed to continue into the future and an **extrapolative forecast** is produced.

Examples of time series

- Output at a factory each day for the last month
- Monthly sales over the last two years
- Total annual costs for the last ten years
- The Retail Prices Index each month for the last ten years
- The number of people employed by a company each year for the last 20 years

There are four components of a time series: trend, seasonal variations, cyclical variations and random variations.

The trend

The **trend** is the underlying long-term movement over time in the values of the data recorded.

EXAMPLE: PREPARING TIME SERIES GRAPHS AND IDENTIFYING TRENDS

	Output per labour hour Units	*Cost per unit* £	*Number of employees*
20X4	30	1.00	100
20X5	24	1.08	103
20X6	26	1.20	96
20X7	22	1.15	102
20X8	21	1.18	103
20X9	17	1.25	98
	(A)	(B)	(C)

(a) In time series (A) there is a **downward trend** in the output per labour hour. Output per labour hour did not fall every year, because it went up between 20X5 and 20X6, but the long-term movement is clearly a downward one.

Graph showing trend of output per labour hour in years 20X4-X9

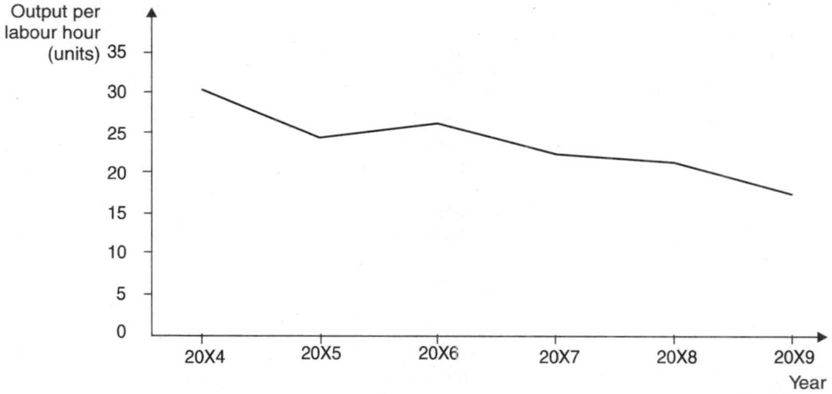

(b) In time series (B) there is an **upward trend** in the cost per unit. Although unit costs went down in 20X7 from a higher level in 20X6, the basic movement over time is one of rising costs.

Graph showing trend of costs per unit in years 20X4-X9

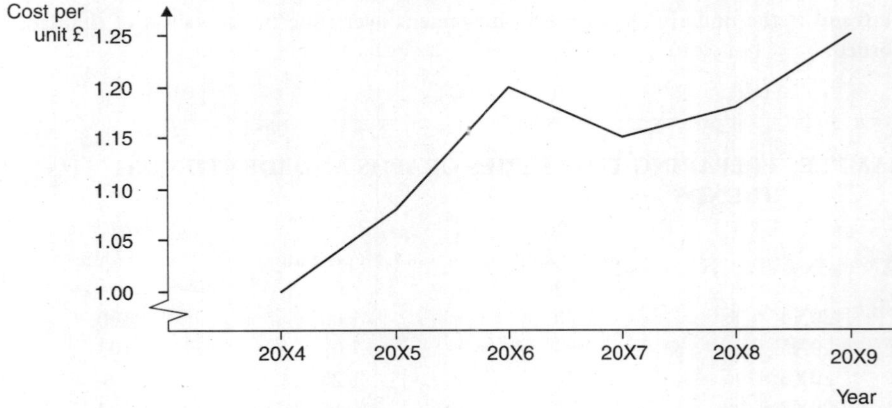

(c) In time series (C) there is no clear movement up or down, and the number of employees remained fairly constant around 100. The trend is therefore a **static,** or **level** one.

Graph showing trend of number of employees in years 20X4-X9

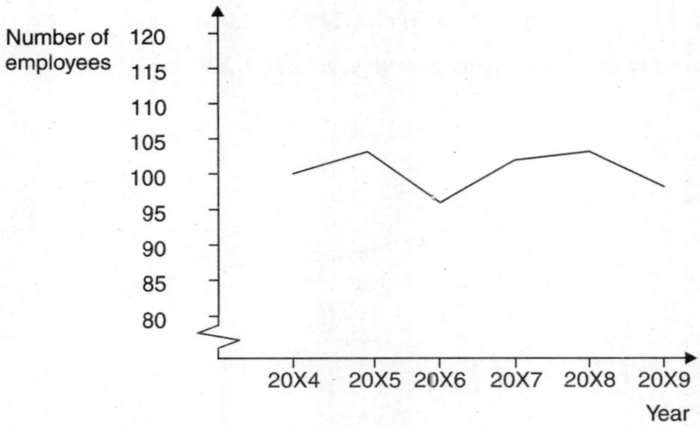

Seasonal variations

Definition 

> **Seasonal variations** are short-term fluctuations in recorded values, due to different circumstances which affect results at different times of the year, on different days of the week or at different times of day and so on.

Examples of seasonal variations

(a) Sales of ice cream will be higher in summer than in winter, and sales of overcoats will be higher in autumn than in spring.

(b) Shops might expect higher sales shortly before Christmas, or in their winter and summer sales.

(c) Sales might be higher on Friday and Saturday than on Monday.

(d) The telephone network may be heavily used at certain times of the day (such as mid-morning and mid-afternoon) and much less used at other times (such as in the middle of the night).

EXAMPLE: THE TREND AND SEASONAL VARIATIONS

The number of customers served by a company of travel agents over the past four years is shown in the following **historigram** (time series graph):

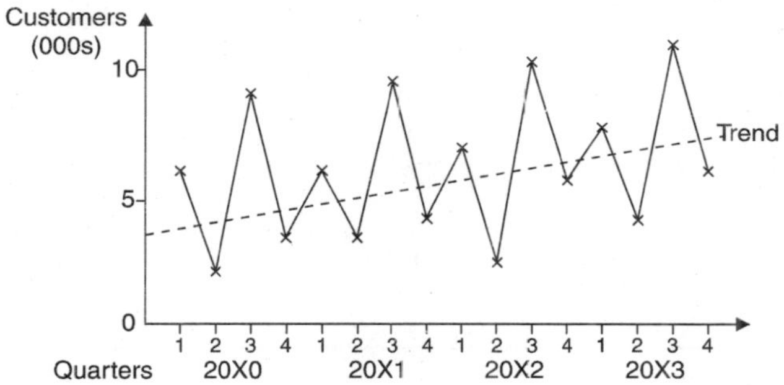

In this example, there would appear to be large **seasonal fluctuations in demand,** but there is also a basic **upward trend.**

Cyclical variations

Cyclical variations are medium-term changes in results caused by circumstances which repeat in cycles.

In business, cyclical variations are commonly associated with **economic cycles,** successive **booms** and **slumps** in the economy. Economic cycles may last a few years. Cyclical variations are **longer** term than seasonal variations.

Though you should be aware of the cyclical component, you will not be expected to carry out any calculation connected with isolating it. The mathematical models which we will use, therefore, exclude any reference to C.

Summarising the components

The components of a time series **combine** to produce a variable in one of two ways:

Additive model: Series = Trend + Seasonal + Random

Y = T + S + R

Multiplicative model: Series = Trend × Seasonal × Random

Y = T × S × R

2.2 Finding the trend

Methods of finding the trend

The main problem we are concerned with in time series analysis is how to **identify the trend** and **seasonal variations.**

Main methods of finding a trend are

(a) A **line of best fit** (the **trend line**) drawn by eye on a graph
(b) **Linear regression analysis**
(c) A technique known as **moving averages**

Finding the trend by moving averages

One method of finding the trend is by the use of **moving averages.**

Definitions

- A **moving average** is an average of the results of a fixed number of periods.
- The **moving averages method** attempts to remove seasonal variations from actual data by a process of averaging.

EXAMPLE: MOVING AVERAGES OF AN ODD NUMBER OF RESULTS

Year	*Sales Units*
20X0	390
20X1	380
20X2	460
20X3	450
20X4	470
20X5	440
20X6	500

Required

Take a moving average of the annual sales over a period of three years.

SOLUTION

(a) Average sales in the three-year period 20X0 – 20X2 were

$$\left(\frac{390+380+460}{3}\right) = \frac{1{,}230}{3} = 410$$

This average relates to the middle year of the period, 20X1.

(b) Similarly, average sales in the three-year period 20X1 – 20X3 were

$$\left(\frac{380+460+450}{3}\right) = \frac{1{,}290}{3} = 430$$

This average relates to the middle year of the period, 20X2.

(c) The average sales can also be found for the periods 20X2–20X4, 20X3–20X5 and 20X4–20X6, to give the following:

Year	*Sales*	*Moving total of 3 years' sales*	*Moving average of 3 years' sales (÷3)*
20X0	390		
20X1	380	1,230	410
20X2	460	1,290	430
20X3	450	1,380	460
20X4	470	1,360	453
20X5	440	1,410	470
20X6	500		

Note the following points:

(i) The moving average series has five figures relating to the years from 20X1 to 20X5. The original series had seven figures for the years from 20X0 to 20X6.

(ii) There is an upward trend in sales, which is more noticeable from the series of moving averages than from the original series of actual sales each year.

Over what period should a moving average be taken?

The above example averaged over a three-year period. Over what period should a moving average be taken? The answer to this question is that **the moving average which is most appropriate will depend on the circumstances and the nature of the time series.** Note the following points:

(a) A moving average which takes an average of the results in many time periods will represent results over a longer-term than a moving average of two or three periods.

(b) On the other hand, with a moving average of results in many time periods, the last figure in the series will be out of date by several periods. In our example, the most recent average related to 20X5. With a moving average of five years' results, the final figure in the series would relate to 20X4.

(c) When there is a known cycle over which seasonal variations occur, such as all the days in the week or all the seasons in the year, the most suitable moving average would be one which covers one full cycle.

Activity 4 **(20 minutes)**

Three-month moving average

Using the following data, complete the following table in order to determine the three-month moving average for the period January-June:

Month	*No of new houses finished*	*Moving total 3 months new houses finished*	*Moving average of 3 months new houses finished*
January	500		
February	450		
March	700		
April	900		
May	1,250		
June	1,000		

Moving averages of an even number of results

When finding the moving average of an **even number of results,** a second moving average has to be calculated so that trend values can relate to specific actual figures.

In the previous example, moving averages were taken of the results in an **odd number of time periods,** and the average then related to the **mid-point of the overall period.** If a moving average were taken of results in an **even number of time periods,** the basic technique would be the same, but **the mid-point of the overall period would not relate to a single period.** For example, suppose an average were taken of the following four results:

Spring	120	
Summer	90	average 115
Autumn	180	
Winter	70	

The average would relate to the mid-point of the period, between summer and autumn. The trend line average figures need to relate to a particular time period; otherwise, seasonal variations cannot be calculated. To overcome this difficulty, we take a **moving average of the moving average.** An example will illustrate this technique.

EXAMPLE: MOVING AVERAGES OVER AN EVEN NUMBER OF PERIODS

Calculate a moving average trend line of the following results:

Year	*Quarter*	*Volume of sales* '000 units
20X5	1	600
	2	840
	3	420
	4	720
20X6	1	640
	2	860
	3	420
	4	740
20X7	1	670
	2	900
	3	430
	4	760

SOLUTION

A moving average of **four** will be used, since the volume of sales would appear to depend on the season of the year, and each year has four **quarterly** results.

The moving average of four does not relate to any specific period of time; therefore a second moving average of two will be calculated on the first moving average trend line.

Year	*Quarter*	*Actual volume of sales* *'000 units* (A)	*Moving total of 4 quarters' sales* *'000 units* (B)	*Moving average of 4 quarters' sales* *'000 units* (B ÷ 4)	*Mid-point of 2 moving averages Trend line* *'000 units* (C)
20X5	1	600			
	2	840			
			2,580	645.0	
	3	420			650.00
			2,620	655.0	
	4	720			657.50
			2,640	660.0	
20X6	1	640			660.00
			2,640	660.0	
	2	860			662.50
			2,660	665.0	
	3	420			668.75
			2,690	672.5	
	4	740			677.50
			2,730	682.5	
20X7	1	670			683.75
			2,740	685.0	
	2	900			687.50
			2,760	690.0	
	3	430			
	4	760			

By taking **a mid point** (a moving average of two) of the original moving averages, we can relate the results **to specific quarters** (from the third quarter of 20X5 to the second quarter of 20X7).

The time series information and moving average trend can be shown on a graph.

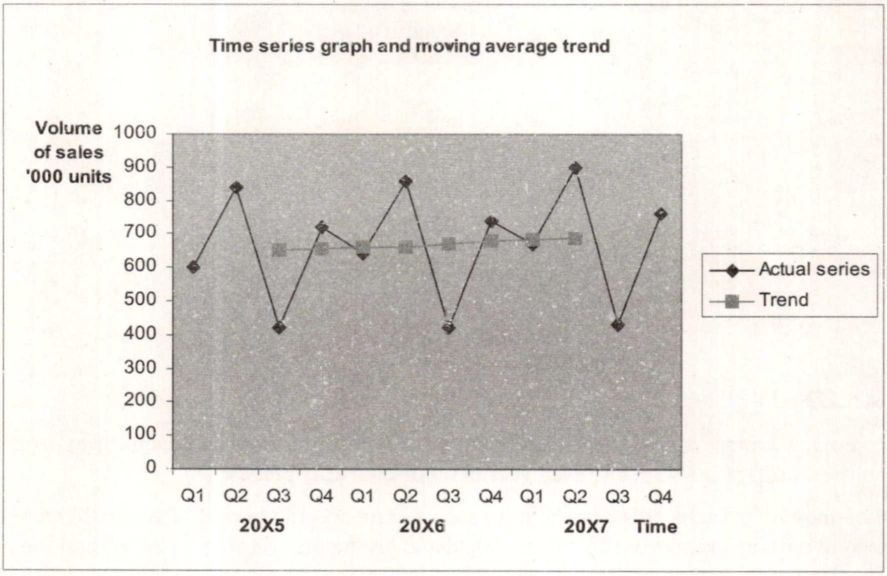

2.3 Finding the seasonal variations

Seasonal variations are the difference between actual and trend figures. An average of the seasonal variations for each time period within the cycle must be determined and then adjusted so that the total of the seasonal variations sums to zero. Seasonal variations can be estimated using the **additive model.**

(Y = T + S + R, with seasonal variations = Y – T) or the **multiplicative model (Y = T × S × R, with seasonal variations = Y ÷ T).**

Finding the seasonal component using the additive model

Once a trend has been established, by whatever method, we can find the **seasonal variations.**

Step 1 The additive model for time series analysis is Y = T + S + R.

Step 2 If we deduct the trend from the additive model, we get Y – T = S + R.

Step 3 If we assume that R, the random, component of the time series is relatively small and therefore negligible, then S = Y – T.

Therefore, the seasonal component, S = Y – T (the de-trended series).

EXAMPLE: THE TREND AND SEASONAL VARIATIONS – KATY LTD

Output at a factory appears to vary with the day of the week. Output over the last three weeks has been as follows:

	Week 1 '000 units	*Week 2* '000 units	*Week 3* '000 units
Monday	80	82	84
Tuesday	104	110	116
Wednesday	94	97	100
Thursday	120	125	130
Friday	62	64	66

Required

Find the seasonal variation for each of the 15 days, and the average seasonal variation for each day of the week using the moving averages method.

SOLUTION

Actual results fluctuate up and down according to the day of the week and so a **moving average of five** will be used. The **difference** between the actual result on any one day (Y) and the trend figure for that day (T) will be the **seasonal variation (S)** for the day. The seasonal variations for the 15 days are as follows:

		Actual (Y)	*Moving total of five days' output*	*Trend (T)*	*Seasonal variation (Y–T)*
Week 1	Monday	80			
	Tuesday	104			
	Wednesday	94	460	92.0	+2.0
	Thursday	120	462	92.4	+27.6
	Friday	62	468	93.6	–31.6
Week 2	Monday	82	471	94.2	–12.2
	Tuesday	110	476	95.2	+14.8
	Wednesday	97	478	95.6	+1.4
	Thursday	125	480	96.0	+29.0
	Friday	64	486	97.2	–33.2
Week 3	Monday	84	489	97.8	–13.8
	Tuesday	116	494	98.8	+17.2
	Wednesday	100	496	99.2	+0.8
	Thursday	130			
	Friday	66			

You will notice that the variation between the actual results on any one particular day and the trend line average is not the same from week to week. This is because Y – T contains not only seasonal variations but **random** variations, and an **average** of these variations can be taken.

	Monday	*Tuesday*	*Wednesday*	*Thursday*	*Friday*
Week 1			+2.0	+27.6	–31.6
Week 2	–12.2	+14.8	+1.4	+29.0	–33.2
Week 3	–13.8	+17.2	+0.8		
Average	–13.0	+16.0	+1.4	+28.3	–32.4

Variations around the basic trend line should cancel each other out, and **add up to 0**. At the moment they do not. **The average seasonal estimates must therefore be corrected so that they add up to zero** and so we spread the total of the daily variations (0.30) across the five days (0.3 ÷ 5) so that the final total of the daily variations goes to zero.

	Monday	*Tuesday*	*Wednesday*	*Thursday*	*Friday*	*Total*
Estimated average daily variation	–13.00	+16.00	+1.40	+28.30	–32.40	0.30
Adjustment to reduce total variation to 0	–0.06	–0.06	–0.06	–0.06	–0.06	–0.30
Final estimate of average daily variation	–13.06	+15.94	+1.34	+28.24	–32.46	0.00

These might be rounded up or down as follows:

Monday –13; Tuesday +16; Wednesday +1; Thursday +28; Friday –32; Total 0.

Activity 5 **(30 minutes)**

Four-quarter moving average trend

Calculate a four-quarter moving average trend centred on actual quarters and then find seasonal variations from the following:

Sales in £'000

	Spring	*Summer*	*Autumn*	*Winter*
20X7	200	120	160	280
20X8	220	140	140	300
20X9	200	120	180	320

Finding the seasonal component using the multiplicative model

The method of estimating the seasonal variations in the additive model is to use the differences between the trend and actual data. **The additive model assumes that the components of the series are independent of each other,** an increasing trend not affecting the seasonal variations for example.

The alternative is to use the **multiplicative model** whereby **each actual figure is expressed as a proportion of the trend.** Sometimes this method is called the **proportional model.**

EXAMPLE: MULTIPLICATIVE MODEL

The additive model example above can be reworked on this alternative basis. The trend is calculated in exactly the same way as before but we need a different approach for the seasonal variations.

The multiplicative model is Y = T × S × R and, just as we calculated S = Y – T for the additive model we can calculate **S = Y/T** for the multiplicative model.

		Actual *(Y)*	*Trend* *(T)*	*Seasonal variation* *(Y/T)*
Week 1	Monday	80		
	Tuesday	104		
	Wednesday	94	92.0	1.022
	Thursday	120	92.4	1.299
	Friday	62	93.6	0.662
Week 2	Monday	82	94.2	0.870
	Tuesday	110	95.2	1.155
	Wednesday	97	95.6	1.015
	Thursday	125	96.0	1.302
	Friday	64	97.2	0.658
Week 3	Monday	84	97.8	0.859
	Tuesday	116	98.8	1.174
	Wednesday	100	99.2	1.008
	Thursday	130		
	Friday	66		

The summary of the seasonal variations expressed in **proportional terms** is as follows:

	Monday	*Tuesday*	*Wednesday*	*Thursday*	*Friday*
Week 1			1.022	1.299	0.662
Week 2	0.870	1.155	1.015	1.302	0.658
Week 3	0.859	1.174	1.008		
Total	1.729	2.329	3.045	2.601	1.320
Average	0.8645	1.1645	1.0150	1.3005	0.6600

Instead of summing to zero, as with the absolute approach, these should **sum** (in this case) **to 5 (an average of 1)**.

They actually sum to 5.0045 so 0.0009 has to be deducted from each one. This is too small to make a difference to the figures above, so we should deduct 0.002 and 0.0025 to each of two seasonal variations. We could arbitrarily decrease Monday's variation to 0.8625 and Tuesday's to 1.162.

When to use the multiplicative model

The multiplicative model is better than the additive model for forecasting when the trend is increasing or decreasing over time. In such circumstances, seasonal variations are likely to be increasing or decreasing too. The additive model simply adds absolute and unchanging seasonal variations to the trend figures whereas the multiplicative model, by multiplying increasing or decreasing trend values by a constant seasonal variation factor, takes account of changing seasonal variations.

Summary

We can summarise the steps to be carried out when calculating the seasonal variation as follows:

Step 1 Calculate the moving total for an appropriate period.

Step 2 Calculate the moving average (the trend) for the period. (Calculate the mid-point of two moving averages if there are an even number of periods.)

Step 3 Calculate the seasonal variation. For an additive model, this is Y – T. For a multiplicative model, this is Y/T.

Step 4 Calculate an average of the seasonal variations.

Step 5 Adjust the average seasonal variations so that they add up to **zero** for an **additive model**. When using the **multiplicative model,** the average seasonal variations should add up to an **average of 1**.

Activity 6 **(15 minutes)**

Average seasonal variations

Find the average seasonal variations for the sales data in the previous question (entitled: Four-quarter moving average trend) using the **multiplicative** model.

Activity 7 **(15 minutes)**

Multiplicative model

In a time series analysis, the multiplicative model is used to forecast sales and the following seasonal variations apply

Quarter	*1*	*2*	*3*	*4*
Seasonal variation	0.8	1.9	0.75	?

The actual sales value for the last two quarters of 20X1 were

Quarter 3: £250,000
Quarter 4: £260,000

(a) The seasonal variation for the fourth quarter is

A 0.55
B –3.45
C 1.00
D 1.45

(b) The trend line for sales:

A remained constant between quarter 3 and quarter 4
B increased between quarter 3 and quarter 4
C decreased between quarter 3 and quarter 4
D cannot be determined from the information given

Seasonally-adjusted data

Definition

Seasonally-adjusted data (deseasonalised) are data which have had any seasonal variations taken out, so leaving a figure which might indicate the trend. Seasonally-adjusted data should indicate whether the overall trend is rising, falling or stationary.

EXAMPLE: SEASONALLY-ADJUSTED DATA

Actual sales figures for four quarters, together with appropriate seasonal adjustment factors derived from previous data, are as follows:

		Seasonal adjustments	
Quarter	*Actual sales*	*Additive model*	*Multiplicative model*
	£'000	*£'000*	
1	150	+3	1.02
2	160	+4	1.05
3	164	–2	0.98
4	170	–5	0.95

Required

Deseasonalise these data.

SOLUTION

We are reversing the normal process of applying seasonal variations to trend figures.

The rules for deseasonalising data are as follows:

- **Additive model** – subtract positive seasonal variations from and add negative seasonal variations to actual results.
- **Multiplicative model** – divide the actual results by the seasonal variation factors.

		Deseasonalised sales	
Quarter	*Actual sales*	*Additive model*	*Multiplicative model*
	£'000	*£'000*	*£'000*
1	150	147	147
2	160	156	152
3	164	166	167
4	170	175	179

Activity 8 **(5 minutes)**

Seasonally adjusted figures

Unemployment numbers actually recorded in a town for the first quarter of 20X9 were 4,700. The underlying trend at this point was 4,400 people and the seasonal factor is 0.85. Using the multiplicative model for seasonal adjustment, the seasonally-adjusted figure (in whole numbers) for the quarter is

A 5,529
B 5,176
C 3,995
D 3,740

2.4 Forecasting

Forecasts can be made by **extrapolating the trend** and **adjusting for seasonal variations.** Remember, however, that all forecasts are subject to error.

Making a forecast

Step 1 **Plot a trend line**: use the line of best fit method, linear regression analysis or the moving averages method.

Step 2 **Extrapolate the trend line.** This means extending the trend line outside the range of known data and forecasting future results from historical data.

Step 3 **Adjust forecast trends** by the applicable average seasonal variation to obtain the actual forecast.

(a) **Additive model** – add positive variations to and subtract negative variations from the forecast trends.

(b) **Multiplicative model** – multiply the forecast trends by the seasonal variation.

EXAMPLE: FORECASTING

Use the trend values and the estimates of seasonal variations calculated for Katy Ltd above to forecast sales in week 4.

SOLUTION

We begin by plotting the trend values on a graph and extrapolating the trend line.

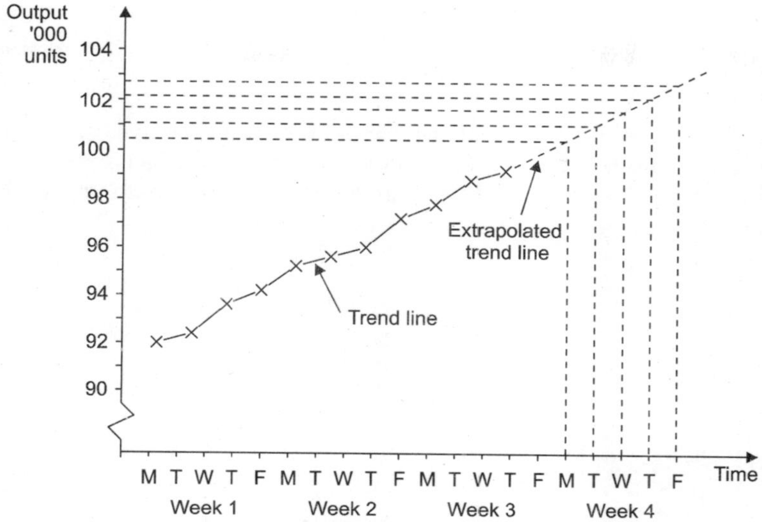

From the extrapolated trend line we can take the following readings and adjust them by the seasonal variations:

Week 4	*Trend line readings*	*Seasonal variations*	*Forecast*
Monday	100.5	–13	87.5
Tuesday	101.5	+16	117.1
Wednesday	101.7	+1	102.7
Thursday	102.2	+28	130.2
Friday	102.8	–32	70.8

If we had been using the multiplicative model the forecast for Tuesday, for example, would be 101.1 × 1.1645 = 117.7.

Forecasting using linear regression analysis

Correlation exists in a time series if there is a relationship between the period of time and the recorded value for that period of time. Time is the X variable and **simplified values for X are used** instead of year numbers.

For example, instead of having a series of years 20X1 to 20X5, we could have values for X from 0 (20X1) to 4 (20X5).

Using linear regression analysis, a trend line is found to be y = 20 – 2.2X where X = 0 in 20X1 and Y = sales level in thousands of units. Using the trend line, predicted sales in 20X6 (X = 5) would be

20 – (2.2 × 5) = 9 ie 9,000 units

Predicted sales in 20X7 (year 6) would be

20 – (2.2 × 6) = 6.8 ie 6,800 units

Activity 9 **(5 minutes)**

Forecast sales

Suppose that a trend line, found using linear regression analysis, is Y = 300 – 4.7X where X is time (in quarters) and Y = sales level in thousands of units. Given that X = 0 represents 20X0 quarter 1 and that the seasonal variations are as set out below:

	Q_1	Q_2	Q_3	Q_4
Seasonal variations ('000 units)	–20	–8	+4	+15

The forecast sales level for 20X5 quarter 4 is [ ] units

Activity 10 **(5 minutes)**

Forecasting

Over a 36-month period, sales have been found to have an underlying linear trend of Y = 14.224 + 7.898X, where Y is the number of items sold and X represents the month. Monthly deviations from trend have been calculated and month 37 is expected to be 1.28 times the trend value.

The forecast number of items to be sold in month 37 is approximately

A 389
B 390
C 391
D 392

2.5 The limitations of forecasting models

Remember that all forecasts are subject to error. There are a number of factors which will affect the reliability of forecasts.

The reliability of time series analysis forecasts

All forecasts are subject to error, but the likely errors vary from case to case.

(a) The further into the future the forecast is for, the more unreliable it is likely to be.

(b) The less data available on which to base the forecast, the less reliable the forecast.

(c) The pattern of trend and seasonal variations cannot be guaranteed to continue in the future.

(d) There is always the danger of random variations upsetting the pattern of trend and seasonal variation.

(e) The extrapolation of the trend line is done by judgement and can introduce error.

The reliability of regression analysis forecasts

There are a number of factors which affect the reliability of forecasts made using regression analysis.

(a) **It assumes a linear relationship exists between the two variables** (since linear regression analysis produces an equation in the linear format) whereas a non-linear relationship might exist.

(b) **It assumes that the value of one variable, Y, can be predicted or estimated from the value of one other variable, X.** In reality the value of Y might depend on several other variables, not just X.

(c) When it is used for forecasting, **it assumes that what has happened in the past will provide a reliable guide to the future.**

(d) When calculating a line of best fit, there will be a range of values for X. In the example in section 1.4, Oscar Ltd, the line $Y = 28 + 2.6X$ was predicted from data with output values ranging from $X = 16$ to $X = 24$. Depending on the degree of correlation between X and Y, we might safely use the estimated line of best fit to predict values for Y in the future, provided that the value of X remains within the range 16 to 24. We would be on less safe ground if we used the formula to predict a value for Y when $X = 10$, or 30, or any other value outside the range 16 to 24, because we would have to **assume that the trend line applies outside the range of X values used to establish the line in the first place.**

(e) As with any forecasting process, **the amount of data available is very important.** Even if correlation is high, if we have fewer than about ten pairs of values, we must regard any forecast as being somewhat unreliable. (It is likely to provide more reliable forecasts than the scattergraph method, however, since it uses all of the available data.)

(f) **The reliability of a forecast will depend on the reliability of the data collected to determine the regression analysis equation.** If the data is not collected accurately or if data used is false, forecasts are unlikely to be acceptable.

Chapter roundup

- When the value of one variable is related to the value of another, they are said to be **correlated**.
- Two variables might be **perfectly correlated**, **partly correlated** or **uncorrelated**. Correlation can be **positive** or **negative**.
- The **degree of correlation** between two variables is measured by the **correlation coefficient, r**. The nearer r is to +1 or –1, the stronger the relationship.
- The **coefficient of determination, r^2**, measures the proportion of the total variation in the value of one variable that can be explained by variations in the value of the other variable.
- The **scattergraph method** involves the use of judgement to draw what seems to be a line of best fit through plotted data.
- **Linear regression analysis** (the **least squares method**) is one technique for estimating a line of best fit. Once an equation for a line of best fit has been determined, forecasts can be made.
- Multiple regression recognises that several factors influence the dependant variable.
- A **time series** is a series of figures or values recorded over time. Any pattern found in the data is then assumed to continue into the future and an **extrapolative forecast** is produced.
- There are four components of a time series: **trend**, **seasonal variations**, **cyclical variations** and **random variations**.
- The **trend** is the underlying long-term movement over time in the values of the data recorded.
- **Seasonal variations** are short-term fluctuations in recorded values, due to different circumstances which affect results at different times of the year, on different days of the week or at different times of the day and so on.
- **Cyclical variations** are medium-term changes in results caused by circumstances which repeat in cycles.
- One method of finding the trend is by the use of **moving averages**.
- When finding the moving average of an **even number of results**, a second moving average has to be calculated so that trend values can relate to specific actual figures.
- **Seasonal variations are the difference between actual and trend figures**. An average of the seasonal variations for each time period within the cycle must be determined and then adjusted so that the total of the seasonal variations sums to zero. Seasonal variations can be estimated using the **additive model (Y = T + S + R, with seasonal variations = Y – T)** or the **multiplicative model (Y = T × S × R, with seasonal variations = Y/T)**.

- **Forecasts** can be made by **extrapolating the trend** and **adjusting for seasonal variations.**
- There are a number of factors which will affect the reliability of forecasts. Remember that all forecasts are subject to error.

Quick quiz

1 .... means that low values of one variable are associated with low values of the other, and high values of one variable are associated with high values of the other.

2 .... means that low values of one variable are associated with high values of the other, and high values of one variable with low values of the other.

3
- Perfect positive correlation, r = ...
- Perfect negative correlation, r = ...
- No correlation, r = ...

The correlation coefficient, r, must always fall within the range .... to ....

4 If the correlation coefficient of a set of data is 0.95, what is the coefficient of determination and how is it interpreted?

5 Complete the following formula:

Coefficient of rank correlation, $R = 1 - \left[\frac{6\Sigma\quad}{n(\qquad)}\right]$

Where n = ...

d = ...

6 (a) The equation of a straight line is given as Y = a + bX. Give two methods used for estimating the above equation.

(b) If Y = a + bX, it is best to use the regression of Y upon X where X is the dependent variable and Y is the independent variable.

True ☐

False ☐

7 What are the four main components of a time series?

8 **Additive model**

Y = T + S + R

Where Y=

T=

S=

R=

9 What is the formula for the multiplicative model?

10 If the trend is increasing or decreasing over time, it is better to use the additive model for forecasting.

True ☐

False ☐

11 List three methods for finding trend lines.

12 **Results** **Method**

Results		Method
Odd number of time periods	?	Calculate 1 moving average
Even number of time periods		Calculate 2 moving averages

13 A = Y – T

B = Y/T

Seasonal variation:

Multiplicative model =

Additive model =

14 When calculating seasonal variations, adjust the average seasonal variations so that they add up to zero for a(n) additive/multiplicative model. When using the additive/multiplicative model, the average seasonal variations should add up to an average of 1.

15 When deseasonalising data, the following rules apply to the additive model:

I Add positive seasonal variations
II Subtract positive seasonal variations
III Add negative seasonal variations
IV Subtract negative seasonal variations

A I and II
B II and III
C II and IV
D I only

16 Time series analysis data can be used to make forecasts by **extrapolating** the trend line. What does extrapolation mean?

17 Cyclical variation is the term used for the difference which is not explained by the trend line and the average seasonal variation.

True ☐

False ☐

18 List the factors that might explain why time series analysis forecasts may not be 100% reliable.

Answers to quick quiz

1 Positive correlation

2 Negative correlation

3
- $r = +1$
- $r = -1$
- $r = 0$

The correlation coefficient, r, must always fall within the range –1 to +1.

4 Correlation coefficient = r = 0.95

Coefficient of determination = $r^2 = 0.95^2 = 0.9025$ or 90.25%

This tells us that over 90% of the variations in the dependent variable (Y) can be explained by variations in the independent variable, X.

5 $$R = 1 - \left[\frac{6\sum d^2}{n(n^2-1)}\right]$$

where n = number of pairs of data
d = difference between the rankings in each set of data

6 (a)
- Scattergraph method (line of best fit)
- Simple linear regression analysis

(b) False. When using the regression of Y upon X, X is the independent variable and Y is the dependent variable (the value of Y will depend upon the value of X).

7
- Trend
- Seasonal variation (fluctuation)
- Cyclical variations
- Random variations

8 Y = the actual time series
T = the trend series
S = the seasonal component
R = the random/irregular component

9 $Y = T \times S \times R$

10 False

11
- Line of best fit
- Linear regression
- Moving averages

12 Odd number of time periods = calculate 1 moving average

Even number of time periods = calculate 2 moving averages

13 Multiplicative model = B = Y/T

Additive model = A = Y – T

14 When calculating seasonal variations, adjust the average seasonal variations so that they add up to **zero** for an **additive model**. When using the **multiplicative model**, the average seasonal variations should add up to an average of **1**.

15 B

16 Extending the trend line outside the range of known data and forecasting future results from historical data.

17 False. The residual is the term used to explain the difference which is not explained by the trend line and the average seasonal variation.

18 (a) The further into the future a forecast is made, the more unreliable it is likely to be.

(b) The less data available for forecasting, the less reliable the forecast.

(c) The trend and seasonal variation patterns identified may not continue in the future.

(d) Random variations may upset the pattern of trend and seasonal variation.

(e) The extrapolation of the trend line is done by judgement and may not be accurate.

Answers to activities

1

Monthly advertising Expenditure	*Sales*			
X	Y	X^2	Y^2	XY
1.2	132.5	1.44	17,556.25	159.00
0.9	98.5	0.81	9,702.25	88.65
1.6	154.3	2.56	23,808.49	246.88
2.1	201.4	4.41	40,561.96	422.94
1.6	161.0	2.56	25,921.00	257.60
7.4	747.7	11.78	117,549.95	1175.07

$(\Sigma X)^2 = 7.4^2 = 54.76$
$(\Sigma Y)^2 = 747.7^2 = 559{,}055.29$

$$r = \frac{(5\times1{,}175.07)-(7.4\times747.7)}{\sqrt{[(5\times11.78)-54.76]\times[5\times117{,}549.95)-559{,}055.29]}}$$

$$= \frac{5{,}875.35-5{,}532.98}{\sqrt{4.14\times28{,}694.46}}$$

$$= \frac{342.37}{\sqrt{118{,}795.06}}$$

$$= \frac{342.37}{344.67} = 0.993$$

0.993 is very close to 1, therefore there is a strong positive correlation and sales are dependent on advertising expenditure.

2 A

$$r = \frac{(6\times19{,}736)-(79\times1{,}466)}{(6\times1{,}083)-79^2}$$

$$= \frac{118{,}416-115{,}814}{6{,}498-6{,}241} = \frac{2{,}602}{257} = 10.12$$

3 C y = a + bx

503 = 262 + (b × 23)

241 = b × 23

b = 10.48

4

Month	*No of new houses finished*	*Moving total 3 months new houses finished*	*Moving average of 3 months new houses finished*
January	500		
February	450	1,650	550
March	700	2,050	683
April	900	2,850	950
May	1,250	3,150	1,050
June	1,000		

5

		Sales (Y)	*4-quarter total*	*8-quarter total*	*Moving average (T)*	*Seasonal variation (Y–T)*
20X7	Spring	200				
	Summer	120				
			760			
	Autumn	160		1,540	192.5	–32.5
			780			
	Winter	280		1,580	197.5	+82.5
			800			
20X8	Spring	220		1,580	197.5	+22.5
			780			
	Summer	140		1,580	197.5	–57.5
			800			
	Autumn	140		1,580	197.5	–57.5
			780			
	Winter	300		1,540	192.5	+107.5
			760			
20X9	Spring	200		1,560	195.0	+5.0
			800			
	Summer	120		1,620	202.5	–82.5
			820			
	Autumn	180				
	Winter	320				

We can now average the seasonal variations.

	Spring	*Summer*	*Autumn*	*Winter*	*Total*
20X7			–32.5	+82.5	
20X8	+22.5	–57.5	–57.5	+107.5	
20X9	+5.0	–82.5			
	+27.5	–140.0	–90.0	+190.0	
Average variations (in £'000)	+13.75	–70.00	–45.00	+95.00	–6.25
Adjustment so sum is zero	+1.5625	+1.5625	+1.5625	+1.5625	+6.25
Adjusted average variations	+15.3125	–68.4375	–43.4375	+96.5625	0

These might be rounded up or down to

spring £15,000, summer –£68,000, autumn –£43,000, winter £97,000

6

	Spring	*Summer*	*Autumn*	*Winter*	*Total*
20X7			*0.83	1.42	
20X8	1.11	0.71	0.71	1.56	
20X9	1.03	0.59			
	2.14	1.30	1.54	2.98	

	Spring	*Summer*	*Autumn*	*Winter*	*Total*
Average variations	1.070	0.650	0.770	1.490	3.980
Adjustment to sum to 4	+ 0.005	+ 0.005	+ 0.005	+ 0.005	0.020
Adjusted average variations	1.075	0.655	0.775	1.495	4.000

* Seasonal variation Y/T = $\frac{160}{192.5}$ = 0.83

7 (a) **The correct answer is A.**

As this is a multiplicative model, the seasonal variations should sum (in this case) to 4 (an average of 1) as there are four quarters.

Let x = seasonal variation in quarter 4.

0.8 + 1.9 + 0.75 + x = 4

$\therefore$ 3.45 + x = 4

x = 4 – 3.45

x = 0.55

(b) **The correct answer is B.**

For a multiplicative model, the seasonal component is as follows:

S = Y/T

$\therefore$ T = Y/S

	Quarter	
	3	*4*
Seasonal component (S)	0.75	0.55
Actual sales (Y)	£250,000	£260,000
Trend (T) (= Y/S)	£333,333	£472,727

The trend line for sales has therefore increased between quarter 3 and quarter 4.

8 **The correct answer is A.**

If you remembered the ruling that you need to **divide** by the seasonal variation factor to obtain seasonally-adjusted figures (using the multiplicative model), then you should have been able to eliminate options C and D. This might have been what you did if you weren't sure whether you divided the **actual results** or the **trend** by the seasonal variation factor.

$$\text{Seasonally adjusted data} = \frac{\text{Actual results}}{\text{Seasonal factor}} = \frac{4{,}700}{0.85} = 5{,}529$$

9 | 206,900 | units

Working

X = 0 corresponds to 20X0 quarter 1

$\therefore$ X = 23 corresponds to 20X5 quarter 4

Trend sales level = 300 – (4.7 × 23) = 191.9 ie 191,900 units

Seasonally-adjusted sales level = 191.9 + 15 = 206.9 ie 206,900 units

10 This is typical of multiple choice questions that you must work through fully if you are to get the right answer.

Y = 14.224 + 7.898X

If X = 37, trend in sales for month 37 = 14.224 + (7.898 × 37)
= 306.45

$\therefore$ Seasonally-adjusted trend value = 306.45 × 1.28
= 392.256

$\therefore$ The correct answer is 392, option D.

Chapter 9 :

PROJECT MANAGEMENT AND NETWORK ANALYSIS

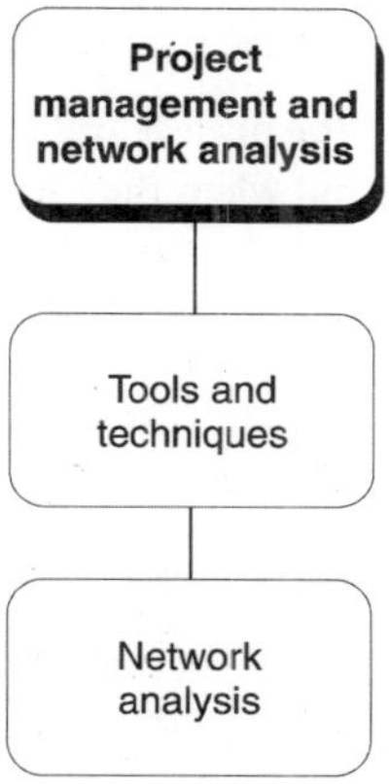

Introduction

Our study of business mathematics concludes by looking at two areas where mathematical skills are especially needed.

In this chapter we look at project management and network analysis.

Managing a project can be very demanding. Effective project management requires thorough planning, monitoring and control.

We start this chapter by studying some of the **management tools and techniques** available to help the project management process.

We then look at network analysis.

Your objectives

In this chapter you will learn about the following:

- Tools and techniques
- Network analysis

1 TOOLS AND TECHNIQUES

Tools and techniques
Work breakdown structure
The project budget
Gantt charts

The techniques we discuss in this section are concerned with the fundamentals of planning projects and controlling their progress. As with most activities, it is difficult to separate the process of planning a project from that of controlling it: planning is likely to continue throughout the life of the project. A **baseline plan** will show the following:

- Start and end dates for the project and its major phases or activities
- The resources needed and when they are required
- Estimates of cost for the project and the major phases or activities

1.1 Work breakdown structure

Definition

> **Work breakdown structure** is an analysis of the work involved in a project into a structure of phases, activities and tasks.

Dependencies determine the order in which tasks must be carried out, while interactions between tasks affect them without imposing order. Work breakdown structure (WBS) is fundamental to project planning and control. Its essence is the **analysis** of the work required to complete the project into **manageable components**.

A good way to approach WBS is to consider the **outputs** (or '**deliverables**') the project is required to produce. This can then be analysed into physical and intangible components, which can in turn be further analysed down to whatever level of simplicity is required. Working backwards in this way helps to **avoid preconceived ideas** of the work the project will involve and the processes that must be undertaken.

For example, a simple domestic project might be to create a vegetable plot in a garden. The output would be a plot of cultivated, well-drained soil that was free of weeds, of a suitable level of fertility and with suitable exposure to sun and rain, together with protection from strong winds. This has obvious implications for what must be done. A plot must be selected; existing vegetation must be cleared; weeds must be dug out; the soil must be improved if necessary, by liming and composting; and a physical boundary or kerb must be provided to prevent invasion by creeping weeds such as grass.

The WBS can allow for several levels of analysis, starting with major project phases and gradually breaking them down into major activities, more detailed sub-activities and individual tasks that will last only a very short time. There is no standardised terminology for the various levels of disaggregation, though an **activity** is sometimes regarded as being composed of **tasks**.

The delivery phase of many projects will break down into significant stages or sub-phases. These are very useful for control purposes, as the completion of each stage is an obvious point for reviewing the whole plan before starting the next one.

Dependencies and interactions

A very important aspect of project planning is the determination of **dependencies** and **interactions.** At any level of WBS analysis, some tasks will be dependent on others; that is to say, **a dependent task cannot commence** until the task upon which it depends is completed. In our vegetable plot example, it is quite obvious that thought must be given to selecting the site of the plot in order to achieve the necessary sun, rain and shelter *before* seizing a spade and starting to dig. Similarly, it would be physically impossible to apply fertiliser if it had not already been positioned at the site. Careful analysis of dependencies is a major step towards a workable project plan, since it provides an **order in which things must be tackled**. Sometimes, of course, the dependencies are limited and it is possible to proceed with tasks in almost any order, but this is unusual. The more complex a project, the greater the need for analysis of dependencies.

Interactions are slightly different; they occur when tasks are linked but not dependent. This can arise for a variety of reasons: a good example is a requirement to share the use of a scarce resource. If we only possessed one spade to prepare our vegetable plot, we could not use it simultaneously both to cultivate the plot itself and to dig the trench in which we wish to place the kerbstones. We could choose to do either of these activities first, but we could not do them both at the same time.

The output from the WBS process is a list of tasks, probably arranged hierarchically to reflect the disaggregation of activities. This then becomes the input into the planning and control processes described in the rest of this section.

1.2 The project budget

The **project budget** plans the allocation of resources to the project and forms a basis for their control. Budgeting may be top-down or bottom-up.

Definition

> **Project budget** is the amount and distribution of resources allocated to a project.

Building a project budget should be an orderly process that attempts to establish a realistic estimate of the cost of the project. There are two main methods for establishing the project budget; **top-down** and **bottom-up**.

Top-down budgeting describes the situation where the budget is imposed 'from above'. Project managers are allocated a budget for the project based on an estimate made by senior management. The figure may prove realistic, especially if similar projects have been undertaken recently. However the technique is often used simply because it is quick, or because only a certain level of funding is available.

In **bottom-up budgeting** the project manager consults the project team, and others, to calculate a budget based on the tasks that make up the project. WBS is a useful tool in this process.

It is useful to collate this information on a **Budgeting Worksheet**.

Budgeting Worksheet				
Project Name: .... **Date worksheet completed:** .... **Project Manager:**				
Task (code)	Responsible staff member or external supplier	Estimated material costs	Estimated labour costs	Total cost of task

Estimates (and therefore budgets) cannot be expected to be 100% accurate. Business **conditions may change,** the project plan may be amended or estimates may simply prove to be incorrect.

Any **estimate** must be accompanied by some **indication of expected accuracy.** Estimates can be **improved** by:

- **Learning** from past mistakes
- Ensuring sufficient design **information**
- Ensuring as **detailed a specification as possible** from the customer
- Properly **analysing the job** into its constituent units.

The overall level of cost estimates will be influenced by

(a) **Project goals**. If a high level of quality is expected costs will be higher.

(b) **External vendors.** Some costs may need to be estimated by outside vendors. To be realistic, these people must understand exactly what would be expected of them.

(c) **Staff availability**. If staff are unavailable, potentially expensive contractors may be required.

(d) **Time schedules**. The quicker a task is required to be done the higher the cost is likely to be – particularly with external suppliers.

The budget may express all resources in monetary amounts, or may show money and other resources – such as staff hours. A monetary budget is often used to establish the current cost variance of the project. To establish this we need

(a) **The Actual Cost of Work Performed (ACWP)**. This is the amount spent to date on the project.

(b) **The Budgeted Cost of Work Scheduled (BCWS)**. The amount that was budgeted to be spent to this point on scheduled activities.

(c) **The Budgeted Cost of Work Performed (BCWP)**. This figure is calculated by pricing the work that has actually been done – using the same basis as the scheduled work.

BCWP – ACWP = The **cost variance** for the project.
BCWP – BCWS = The **schedule variance** for the project.

During the project, actual expenditure is tracked against budget on either a separate **Budget Report**, or as part of a regular **Progress Report**. We will be looking at project documentation and reports later in this chapter.

Budgets should be presented for approval and **sign-off** to the stakeholder who has responsibility for the funds being used.

Before presenting a budget for approval it may have to be revised a number of times. The 'first draft' may be overly reliant on rough estimates, as insufficient time was available to obtain more accurate figures.

On presentation, the project manager may be asked to find ways to cut the budget. If he or she agrees that cuts can be made, the consequences of the cuts should be pointed out – for example, a reduction in quality.

It may be decided that a project costs more than it is worth. If so, scrapping the project is a perfectly valid option. In such cases the budgeting process has highlighted the situation before too much time and effort has been spent on an unprofitable venture.

1.3 Gantt charts

A **Gantt chart** shows the deployment of resources over time.

A **Gantt chart**, named after the engineer *Henry Gantt* who pioneered the procedure in the early 1900s, is a horizontal bar chart used to plan the **time scale** for a project and to estimate the **resources** required.

The Gantt chart displays the time relationships between tasks in a project. Two lines are usually used to show the time allocated for each task, and the actual time taken.

EXAMPLE

A simple Gantt chart, illustrating some of the activities involved in a network server installation project, follows:

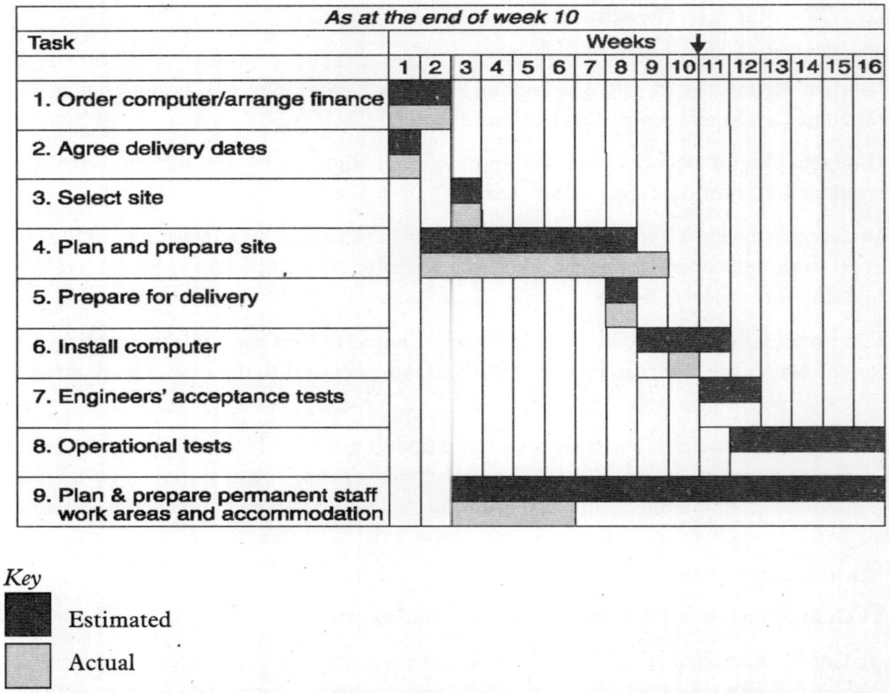

The chart shows that at the end of the tenth week Activity 9 is running behind schedule. More resources may have to be allocated to this activity if the staff accommodation is to be ready in time for the changeover to the new system.

Activity 4 had not been completed on time, and this has resulted in some disruption to the computer installation (Activity 6), which may mean further delays in the commencement of Activities 7 and 8.

A Gantt chart does not show the interrelationship between the various activities in the project as clearly as a **network diagram** (covered later in this chapter). A combination of Gantt charts and network analysis will often be used for project planning and resource allocation.

Activity 1 **(1 minute)**

Terminology

What is the surname of the man who invented the resource planning chart a century ago?

A Gannt
B Gantt
C Ganntt
D Gant

So far we have looked at some of the basic techniques and ideas used in project management. We are now going to look at a very widely used and powerful technique – network analysis.

2 NETWORK ANALYSIS

Network analysis
Introduction
Activity on arrow presentation
Activity-on-node presentation
Finding the critical path
Float ties
Criticisms of critical path/ network analysis
Example
PERT

2.1 Introduction

Network analysis illustrates interactions and dependencies. It is used to plan the sequence of tasks making up project scope and to determine the critical path. PERT uses probabilities to make estimates of likely completion and milestone dates.

Network analysis, also known as **Critical Path Analysis** (CPA), is a useful technique to help with planning and controlling large projects, such as construction projects, research and development projects and the computerisation of systems.

Definition

> **Network analysis** requires breaking down the project into tasks, arranging them into a logical sequence and estimating the duration of each.
>
> This enables the series of tasks that determines the minimum possible duration of the project to be found. These are the **critical activities**.

CPA aims to ensure the progress of a project, so the project is completed in the **minimum amount of time**. It pinpoints the tasks which are **on the critical path,** ie those parts which, if delayed beyond the allotted time, would **delay the completion** of the project as a whole. The technique can also be used to assist in **allocating resources** such as labour and equipment.

Critical path analysis is quite a simple technique. The events and activities making up the whole project are represented in the form of a **diagram**. Drawing the diagram or chart involves the following steps:

Step 1 Estimating the time needed to complete each individual activity or task that makes up a part of the project.

Step 2 Sorting out what activities must be done one after another, and which can be done at the same time, if required.

Step 3 Representing these in a network diagram.

Step 4 Estimating the critical path, which is the longest sequence of consecutive activities through the network.

The duration of the whole project will be fixed by the time taken to complete the longest path through the network. This path is called the **critical path** and activities on it are known as **critical activities**. Activities on the critical path **must be started and completed on time,** otherwise the total project time will be extended. The method of finding the critical path is illustrated in the example below.

Network analysis shows the **sequence** of tasks and how long they are going to take. The diagrams are drawn from left to right. To construct a network diagram you need to know the activities involved in a project, the expected duration of each and the order (or precedences, or dependencies) of the activities.

For example:

Activity	*Expected duration (days)*	*Preceding activity*
A	3	–
B	5	–
C	2	B
D	1	A
E	6	A
F	3	D
G	3	C, E

2.2 Activity on arrow presentation – Katy Ltd

Here is a network diagram showing our example in the form known as **activity on arrow.**

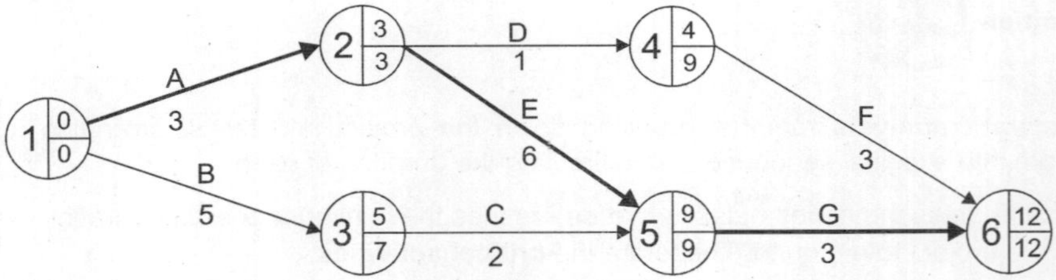

(a) The network is made up of events and activities, represented by circles and arrows respectively. The diagram is laid out to show the dependencies that exist between the activities, working from left to right. The first event is the start of the overall sequence of activities (or the project). Each subsequent event marks the beginning of at least one activity and, therefore, the end of any activities upon which it is dependent. In the network diagram above, for example, event 5 marks the completion of activities E and C and the start of activity G.

(b) Events are numbered, working from left to right and the numbers are entered in the left hand halves of the event circles. Also by convention, the events are numbered so that the event at the end of any activity has a higher number than the one at its start.

(c) Activities are lettered, again working from left to right. The duration of each activity is shown by a number entered against its identifying letter.

(d) When the basic information has been entered on to the network, it becomes possible to determine the **critical path** through it: this is the sequence of activities that takes the longest time and which therefore determines the overall expected duration of the project.

(e) A **forward pass** is made through the network and the **earliest event time** (EET) is entered in the upper right quadrant of each event circle. This time depends on the duration of any sequence of activities leading to the event in question and therefore reflects the dependencies involved. In the diagram, event 5, for example, cannot occur (and activity G therefore cannot begin) until the sequences A–E and B–C are both complete. B–C takes (5 + 2) days, while A–E takes (3 + 6) days. The *earliest* event time for event 5 is therefore 9 days. This is a general rule: the EET for any event shows the **longest duration sequence of activities leading to it**.

(f) When the forward pass is complete, a **rearward pass** is made, starting at the final event and working back to establish the **latest event time** (LET) for each event. The LET for an event is entered in the lower right quadrant of its symbol. Like the EET, the LET depends on the longest sequence of activities involved, but this time it is the sequences of events that follow the event in question that are relevant rather than the ones that precede it. In the example network diagram, event 2 is followed by sequences D–F and E–G with durations (1 + 3) days and (6 + 3) days respectively. If there is to be time to complete the longer sequence E–G, the LET for event 2 must be 3 days.

(g) When both forward and rearward passes are complete, the **critical path** is identifiable as the route through the network that links all the events that have LET equal to EET: there is no **float** on this path. We discuss float times later in this section. The critical path activities are highlighted on the diagram in some way, such as by using double lines or hash marks.

The **critical path** in the diagram above is AEG. Note the **float time** of five days for Activity F. Activity F can begin any time between days 4 and 9, thus giving the project manager a degree of flexibility.

(h) Sometimes it is necessary to use a **dummy activity** in a network diagram. Dummies indicate dependency, but they take no time. The need for them arises from the convention that activity arrows are always straight. Thus, if an activity, C, depends on both activity A and activity B, the presentation below is not used:

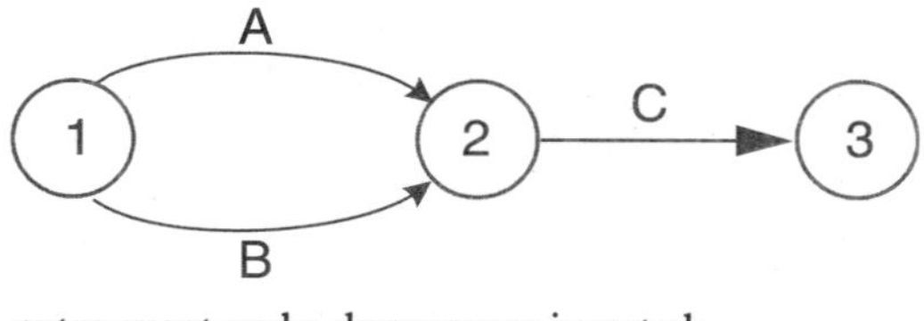

Instead, an extra event and a dummy are inserted:

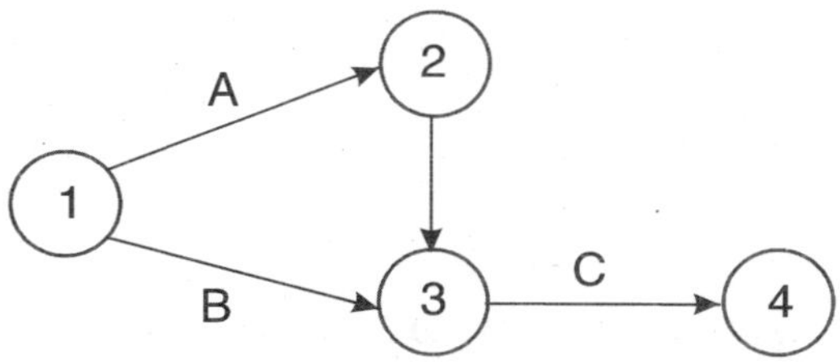

The dummy activity is shown as a broken line. Note also how the dummy starts at an event with a lower number than the one it ends at. Sometimes it is necessary to use a dummy activity not just to comply with the convention, but to **preserve the basic logic** of the network.

Activity 2 **(10 minutes)**

Consider the following example of a project to install a new office telephone system.

Activity	*Preceding Activity*
A: buy equipment	–
B: allocate extension numbers	–
C: install switchboard	A
D: install wiring	B, C
E: print office directory	B

The project is finished when both D and E are complete.

Identify why there may be a need for a dummy activity, and draw the basic network showing it.

Dummy activities are not required when the **activity on node** technique (discussed below) is used for drawing the network.

In our earlier example (Katy Ltd), if activity G had depended on activity D as well as on activities C and E, this would have been shown as a dummy running from event 4 to event 5.

Network diagrams may also be drawn using **activity-on-node** presentation which is similar in style to that used by the **Microsoft Project** software package.

EXAMPLE: ACTIVITY-ON-NODE

Suppose that a project includes three activities, C, D and E. Neither activity D nor E can start until activity C is completed, but D and E could be done simultaneously if required.

This would be represented as follows:

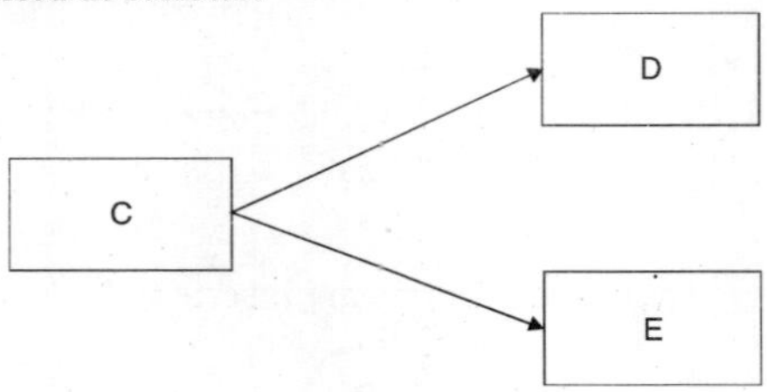

Note the following:

(a) An **activity** within a network is represented by a rectangular box. (Each box is a **node**.)

(b) The **flow** of activities in the diagram should be from **left to right**.

(c) The diagram clearly shows that **D and E must follow C**.

A second possibility is that an activity cannot start until two or more activities have been completed. If activity H cannot start until activities G and F are both complete, then we would represent the situation like this:

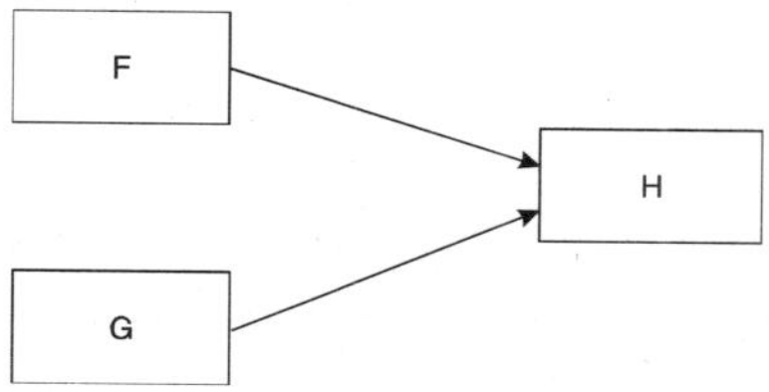

In some conventions an extra node is introduced at the start and end of a network. This serves absolutely no purpose (other than to ensure that all the nodes are joined up), so we recommend that you do not do it. Just in case you ever see a network presented in this way, both styles are shown in the next example.

EXAMPLE: STARTS AND ENDS

Draw a diagram for the following project. The project is finished when both D and E are complete.

Activity	*Preceding activity*
A	–
B	–
C	A
D	B & C
E	B

SOLUTION

Microsoft Project style

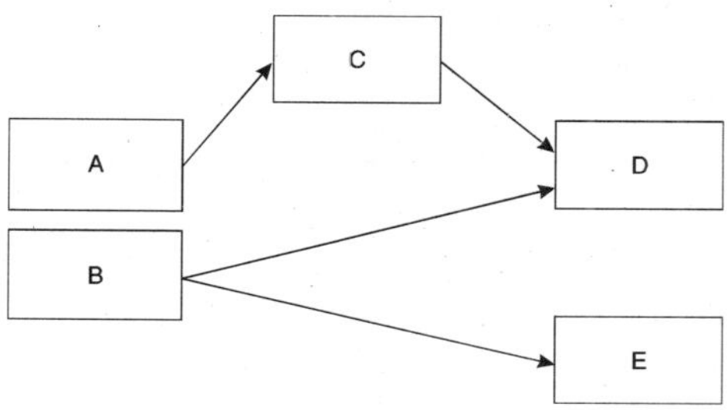

With start and end nodes

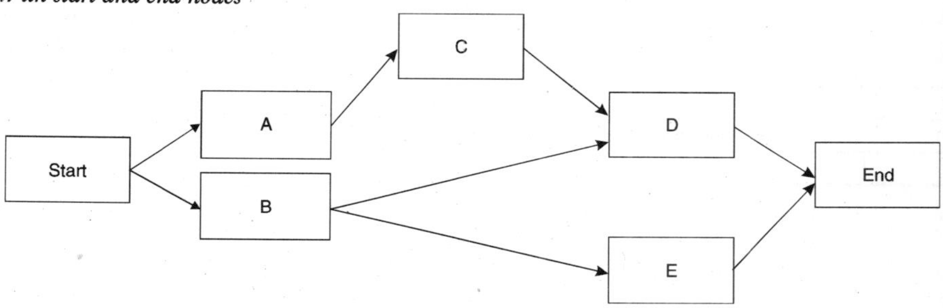

Any network can be analysed into a number of different paths or routes. A path is simply a sequence of activities which can take you from the start to the end of the network. In the example above, there are just three routes or paths.

(a) A C D.
(b) B D.
(c) B E.

The time needed to complete each individual activity in a project must be estimated. This duration is shown within the node as follows. The reason for and meaning of the other boxes will be explained in a moment.

Task A	
	6 days

EXAMPLE: THE CRITICAL PATH

Activity	*Immediately preceding activity*	*Duration (weeks)*
A	–	5
B	–	4
C	A	2
D	B	1
E	B	5
F	B	5
G	C, D	4
H	F	3
I	F	2

(a) What are the paths through the network?
(b) What is the critical path and its duration?

SOLUTION

The first step in the solution is to draw the network diagram, with the time for each activity shown:

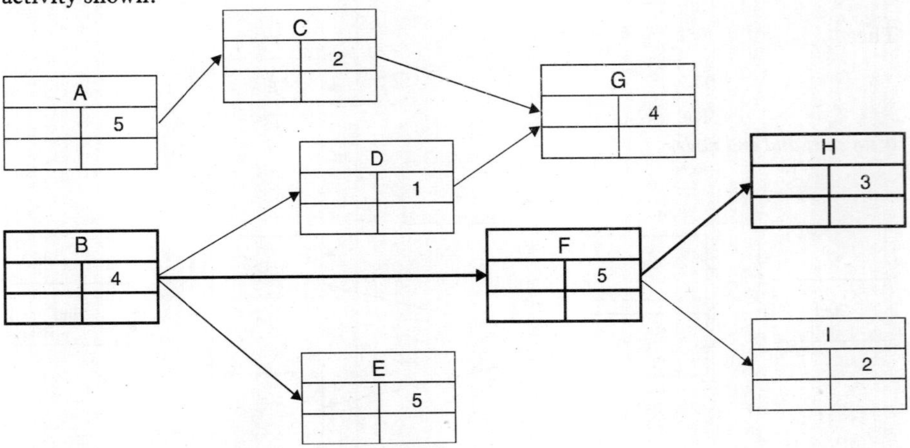

We could list the paths through the network and their overall completion times as follows:

Path	*Duration (weeks)*	
A C G	(5 + 2 + 4)	11
B D G	(4 + 1 + 4)	9
B E	(4 + 5)	9
B F H	(4 + 5 + 3)	12
B F I	(4 + 5 + 2)	11

The critical path is the longest, BFH, with a duration of 12 weeks. This is the minimum time needed to complete the project.

The critical path is indicated on the diagram by drawing thick (or double-line) arrows, as shown above. In Microsoft Project the arrows and the nodes are highlighted in red.

Listing paths through the network in this way should be easy enough for small networks, but it becomes a long and tedious task for bigger and more complex networks. This is why software packages are used in real life.

Project management software packages offer a much larger variety of techniques than can easily be done by hand. Microsoft Project allows each activity to be assigned to any one of a variety of types: 'start as late as possible', 'start as soon as possible', 'finish no earlier than a particular date', 'finish no later than a particular date', and so on.

In real life, too, activity times can be shortened by working weekends and overtime, or they may be constrained by non-availability of essential personnel. In other words, with any more than a few activities, the possibilities are mind-boggling, which is why software is used. Nevertheless, a simple technique is illustrated in the following example.

2.3 Finding the critical path

The procedure for finding the critical path is essentially the same as we used with the activity on arrow example earlier.

One way of showing earliest and latest **start** times for activities is to divide each event node into sections. This is similar to the style used in Microsoft Project except that Project uses real dates, which is far more useful, and the bottom two sections can mean a variety of things, depending what constraints have been set.

These sections record the following things:

(a) The **name** of the activity, for example Task A. This helps humans to understand the diagram.

(b) An **ID number** which is unique to that activity. This helps computer packages to understand the diagram, because it is possible that two or more activities could have the same name. For instance two bits of research done at different project stages might both be called 'Research'.

(c) The **duration** of the activity.

(d) The **earliest start time.** Conventionally for the first node in the network, this is time 0.

(e) The **latest start time.**

(*Note*. Don't confuse start times with the '**event**' times that are calculated when using the **activity-on-arrow** method, even though the approach is the same.)

Task D	
ID number: 4	Duration: 6 days
Earliest start: Day 4	Latest start: Day 11

Earliest start times

To find the earliest start times, always start with activities that have no predecessors and give them an earliest starting time of 0. In the example we have been looking at, this is week 0.

Then work along each path from **left to right** through the diagram calculating the earliest time that the next activity can start, just as with activity on arrow.

For example, the earliest time for activity C is week 0 + 5 = 5. The earliest time activities D, E and F can start is week 0 + 4 = 4.

To calculate an activity's earliest time, simply look at the box for the *preceding* activity and add the bottom left figure to the top right figure.

If *two or more* activities precede an activity take the *highest* figure as the later activity's earliest start time: it cannot start before all the others are finished!

Latest start times

The latest start times are the latest times at which each activity can start **if the project as a whole is to be completed in the earliest possible time,** in other words in 12 weeks in our example.

Work backwards from **right to left** through the diagram calculating the latest time at which the activity can start, if it is to be completed at the latest finishing time. For example the latest start time for activity H is 12 – 3 = week 9 and for activity E is 12 – 5 = week 7.

Activity F might cause difficulties as two activities, H and I, lead back to it.

(a) Activity H must be completed by week 12, and so must start at week 9.
(b) Activity I must also be completed by week 12, and so must start at week 10.

Activity F takes 5 weeks so its latest start time is either 9 – 5 = week 4 or 10 – 5 = week 5. However, if it starts in week 5 it will not be possible to start activity H on time and the whole project will be delayed. We therefore take the *lower* figure.

The final diagram is now as follows:

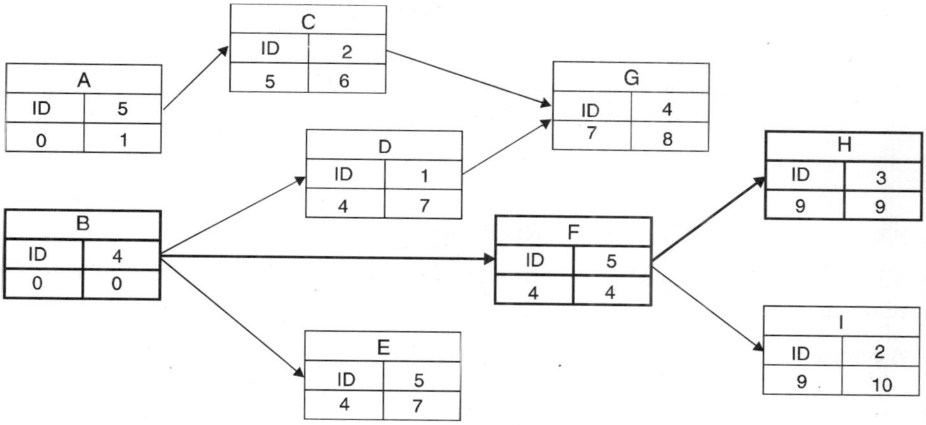

Critical activities are those activities which must be started on time, otherwise the total project time will be increased. It follows that each event on the critical path must have the same earliest and latest start times. The critical path for the above network is therefore B F H.

2.4 Float times

Float time is the time available for unforeseen circumstances.

(a) **Total float** on an activity is the time available (earliest start date to latest finish date) *less* time needed for the job. If, for example, job A's earliest start time was day 7 and its latest end time was day 17, and the job needed four days, total float would be:

$(17 - 7) - 4 = 6$ days

(b) **Free float** is the delay possible in an activity on the assumption that all preceding activities start as early as possible and all subsequent activities also start at the earliest time.

(c) **Independent float** is the delay possible if all preceding jobs have finished as late as possible, and all succeeding jobs are to start as early as possible.

By definition there is no float time on the critical path.

2.5 Criticisms of critical path/network analysis

(a) It is not always possible to devise an effective WBS for a project.

(b) **It assumes a sequential relationship** between activities. It assumes that Activity B starts after Activity A has finished. It is not very good at coping with the possibility that an activity 'later' in the sequence may be relevant to an earlier activity.

(c) There are **problems in estimation**. Where the project is completely new, the planning process may be conducted in conditions of relative ignorance.

(d) Although network analysis plans the use of resources of labour and finance, it does not appear to develop plans for contingencies, other than crashing time.

(e) CPA **assumes a trade-off between time and cost**. This may not be the case where a substantial portion of the cost is **indirect overheads** or where the direct labour proportion of the total cost is limited.

EXAMPLE: GANTT CHARTS AND RESOURCES

This example is provided as an illustration of the use of Gantt charts to manage resources efficiently.

A company is about to undertake a project about which the following data is available:

Activity	*Preceded by activity*	*Duration* Days	*Workers required*
A	–	3	6
B	–	5	3
C	B	2	4
D	A	1	4
E	A	6	5
F	D	3	6
G	C, E	3	3

There is a multi-skilled workforce of nine workers available, each capable of working on any of the activities.

Draw the network to establish the duration of the project and the critical path. Then draw a Gantt chart, using the critical path as a basis, assuming that jobs start at the earliest possible time.

SOLUTION

Here are the diagrams:

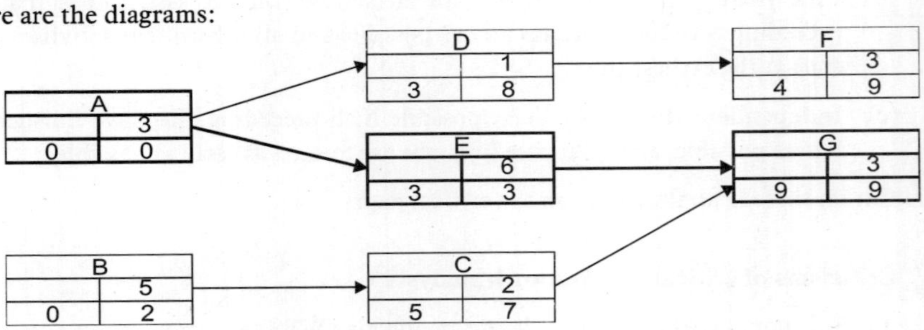

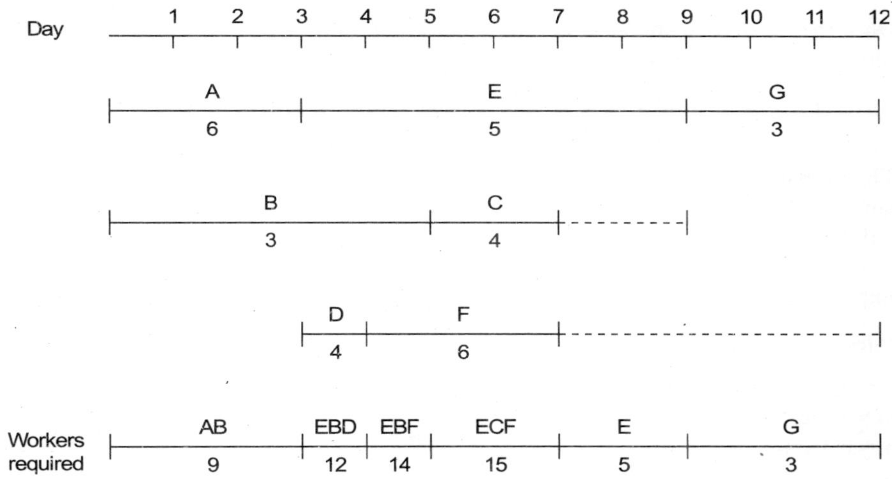

It can be seen that if all activities start at their earliest times, as many as 15 workers will be required on any one day (days 6–7), whereas on other days there would be idle capacity (days 8–12).

The problem can be reduced, or removed, by using up spare time on non-critical activities. Suppose we **deferred the start** of activities D and F until the latest possible days. These would be days 8 and 9, leaving four days to complete the activities by the end of day 12.

The Gantt chart would be redrawn as follows:

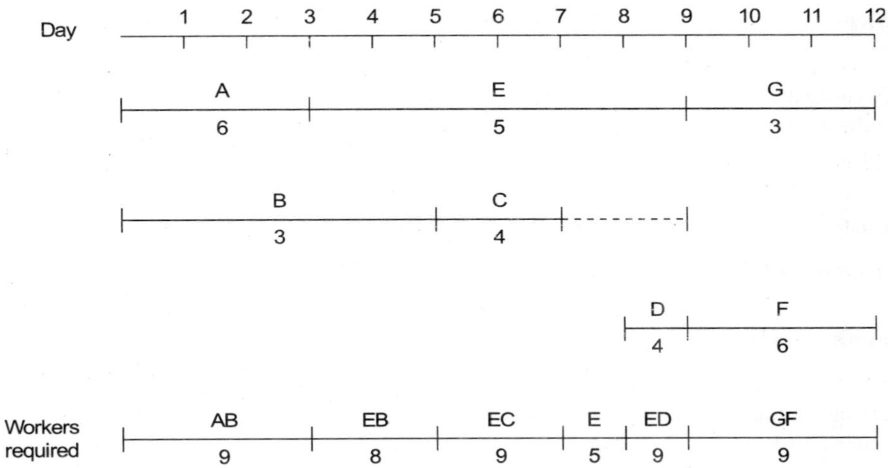

2.6 Project evaluation and review technique (PERT)

Project evaluation and review technique (PERT) is a modified form of network analysis designed to account for **uncertainty**. For each activity in the project, **optimistic, most likely** and **pessimistic** estimates of times are made, on the basis of past experience, or even guess-work. These estimates are converted into a mean time and also a standard deviation.

Once the mean time and standard deviation of the time have been calculated for each activity, it should be possible to do the following:

(a) Establish the duration of the critical path using **expected times**
(b) Calculate a **contingency time allowance**

The **probable** time estimate is based on the assumption that all relevant conditions are normal. The **expected** time is a different concept: like an **expected value** it is an estimate based on the use of probability.

$$\text{Expected time} = \frac{o + 4m + p}{6}$$

where:

o = optimistic estimate
m = probable estimate
p = pessimistic estimate

Contingency time allowances

The standard deviation of the time required for the critical path activities is calculated.

Step 1 Calculate the standard deviation for each critical activity time using the formula $\frac{p - o}{6}$

Step 2 Square the standard deviations to obtain the **variances.**

Step 3 Sum the variances to give the total variance for the critical path.

Step 4 Find the square root of the total variance to give the standard deviation of the duration of the critical path.

A contingency time allowance stated in terms of a number of standard deviations will indicate the probability of completion within the total time allowed, including contingency.

Costs

A similar approach may be employed to deal with uncertainty over costs.

Further analysis

Similar, slightly more complex statistical processes may be used to establish the probability that any given activity or sequence of activities will be completed by a given time. This is useful when staged payments or time penalties are involved.

Chapter roundup

- **Work breakdown structure** is an analysis of the work involved in a project into a structure of phases, activities and tasks. Dependencies determine the order in which tasks must be carried out, while interactions between tasks affect them without imposing order.
- The **project budget** plans the allocation of resources to the project and forms a basis for their control. Budgeting may be top-down or bottom-up.
- A **Gantt chart** shows the deployment of resources over time.
- **Network analysis** illustrates interactions and dependencies. It is used to plan the sequence of tasks making up project scope and to determine the **critical path**. PERT uses probabilities to make estimates of likely completion and milestone dates.

Quick quiz

1 What would you expect a Project Initiation Document to contain?

2 What is Work Breakdown Structure?

3 What is the purpose of a Gantt chart?

4 An approach to project management which uses buffers to flexibly respond to the uncertainties of time estimating is

A Critical Path Analysis
B Project Management Maturity
C Critical Chain Project Management
D PERT

Answers to quick quiz

1 Contents could include: project objectives, the scope of the project, overall budget, final deadlines, the ultimate customer, resources, risks inherent in the project, a preliminary project plan (targets, activities and so on) and details of how the project is to be organised and managed.

2 Work Breakdown Structure (WBS) is the process of breaking-down the project into manageable tasks.

3 A Gantt chart displays the time relationships between tasks in a project. It is a horizontal bar chart used to estimate the amount and timing of resources required.

4 C. (PERT has a similar orientation, in accounting for uncertainty, but is a very different approach.)

Answers to activities

1 The answer is B: Gantt. Some people find this extremely difficult to get right.

2 The problem arises because D can only start when both B and C have been finished, whereas E is only required to follow B. The only way to draw the network is to use a dummy activity:

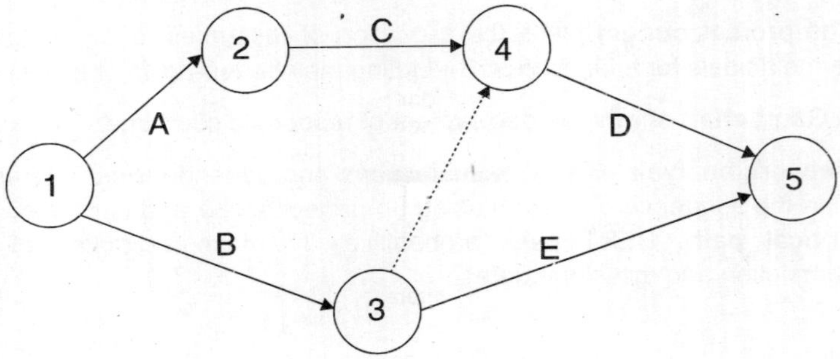

Chapter 10 :
FINANCIAL MATHEMATICS

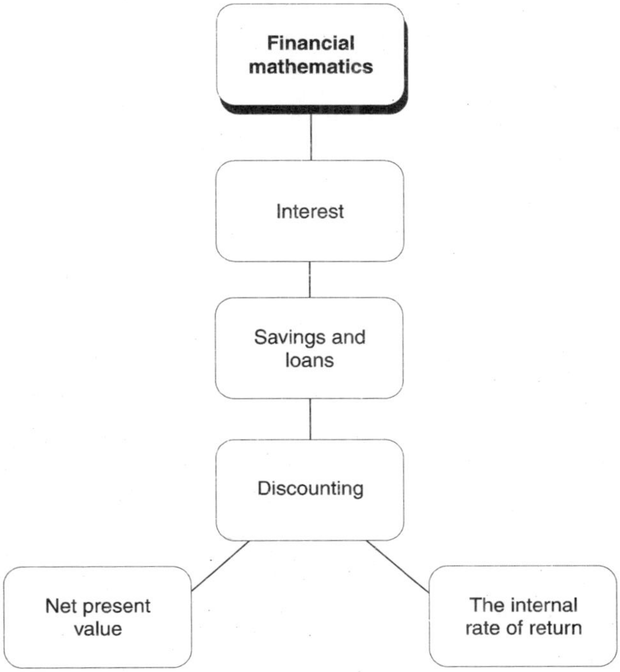

Introduction

This chapter extends the use of mathematics and look at aspects of financial analysis typically undertaken in a business organisation.

In general, financial mathematics deals with problems of **investing money**, or **capital**. If a company (or an individual investor) puts some capital into an investment, a financial return will be expected.

The two major techniques of financial mathematics are **compounding** and **discounting**.

Compounding means that as interest is earned it is added to the original investment and starts to earn interest itself.

Discounting is the reverse of compounding. Its major application in business is in the **evaluation of investments,** to decide whether they offer a satisfactory return to the investor. We will be looking at two methods of using discounting to appraise investments, the **net present value (NPV) method** and the **internal rate of return (IRR) method.**

Your objectives

In this chapter you will learn about the following:

- Simple interest
- Compound interest
- Regular savings and sinking funds
- Loans and mortgages
- The concept of discounting
- The Net Present value (NPV) method
- the Internal Rate of Return (IRR) method

1 INTEREST

Interest
Simple interest
Compound interest
Inflation
Changes in the rate of inflation

1.1 Simple interest

Interest

Interest is the amount of money which an investment earns over time.

Simple interest is interest which is earned in equal amounts every year (or month) and which is a given proportion of the original investment (the principal). The simple interest formula is **S = X + nrX.**

If a sum of money is invested for a period of time, then the amount of simple interest which accrues is equal to the number of periods × the interest rate × the amount invested. We can write this as a formula.

The formula for **simple interest** is as follows:

$S = X + nrX$

Where X = the original sum invested
r = the interest rate (expressed as a proportion, so 10% = 0.1)
n = the number of periods (normally years)
S = the sum invested after n periods, consisting of the original capital (X) plus interest earned.

EXAMPLE: SIMPLE INTEREST

How much will an investor have after five years if he invests £1,000 at 10% simple interest per annum?

SOLUTION

Using the formula $S = X + nrX$

where $X = £1,000$
$r = 10\%$
$n = 5$

$\therefore S = £1,000 + (5 \times 0.1 \times £1,000) = £1,500$

Investment periods

If, for example, the sum of money is invested for three months and the interest rate is a rate per annum, then n =3/12 = 1/4. If the investment period is 197 days and the rate is an annual rate, then n = 197/365.

Simple interest is rarely paid. If you invest money this year you will receive interest. If that interest is then invested it too will give interest. Interest on interest is given the name compound interest.

1.2 Compound interest

Compounding

Interest is normally calculated by means of **compounding**.

Compounding means that, as interest is earned, it is added to the original investment and starts to earn interest itself. The basic formula for compound interest is $\mathbf{S = X(1 + r)^n}$.

If a sum of money, the principal, is invested at a fixed rate of interest such that the interest is added to the principal and no withdrawals are made, then the amount invested will grow by an increasing number of pounds in each successive time period, because **interest earned in earlier periods will itself earn interest in later periods**.

EXAMPLE: COMPOUND INTEREST

Suppose that £2,000 is invested at 10% interest. After one year, the original principal plus interest will amount to £2,200.

	£
Original investment	2,000
Interest in the first year (10%)	200
Total investment at the end of one year	2,200

(a) After two years the total investment will be £2,420.

	£
Investment at end of one year	2,200
Interest in the second year (10%)	220
Total investment at the end of two years	2,420

The second year interest of £220 represents 10% of the original investment, and 10% of the interest earned in the first year.

(b) Similarly, after three years, the total investment will be £2,662.

	£
Investment at the end of two years	2,420
Interest in the third year (10%)	242
Total investment at the end of three years	2,662

Instead of performing the calculations shown above, we could have used the following formula.

The basic formula for **compound interest** is $S = X(1 + r)^n$

Where X = the original sum invested
r = the interest rate, expressed as a proportion (so 5% = 0.05)
n = the number of periods
S = the sum invested after n periods

Using the formula for compound interest, $S = X(1 + r)^n$

where X = £2,000
r = 10% = 0.1
n = 3
S = £2,000 × 1.10^3
= £2,000 × 1.331
= £2,662.

The interest earned over three years is £662, which is the same answer that was calculated above.

Activity 1 **(10 minutes)**

Simon invests £5,000 now. To what value would this sum have grown after the following periods using the given interest rates? State your answer to two decimal places.

Value now	*Investment period*	*Interest rate*	*Final value*
£	Years	%	£
5,000	3	20	
5,000	4	15	
5,000	3	6	

Activity 2 **(10 minutes)**

At what annual rate of compound interest will £2,000 grow to £2,721 after four years?

A 7%
B 8%
C 9%
D 10%

1.3 Inflation

The same compounding formula can be used to **predict future prices** after allowing for **inflation.** For example, if we wish to predict the salary of an employee in five years' time, given that he earns £8,000 now and wage inflation is expected to be 10% per annum, the compound interest formula would be applied as follows:

$$\begin{aligned} S &= X(1 + r)^n \\ &= £8{,}000 \times 1.10^5 \\ &= £12{,}884.08 \end{aligned}$$

say, £12,900.

1.4 Changes in the rate of interest

If the **rate of interest changes during the period** of an investment, the compounding formula must be amended slightly to $S = X(1 + r_1)^y (1 + r_2)^{n-y}$.

The formula for **compound interest** when there are changes in the rate of interest is as follows:

$$S = X(1 + r_1)^y (1 + r_2)^{n-y}$$

Where r_1 = the initial rate of interest

y = the number of years in which the interest rate r_1 applies

r_2 = the next rate of interest

$n - y$ = the (balancing) number of years in which the interest rate r_2 applies.

Activity 3 **(10 minutes)**

(a) If £8,000 is invested now, to earn 10% interest for three years and 8% thereafter, what would be the size of the total investment at the end of five years?

(b) An investor puts £10,000 into an investment for ten years. The annual rate of interest earned is 15% for the first four years, 12% for the next four years and 9% for the final two years. How much will the investment be worth at the end of ten years?

(c) An item of equipment costs £6,000 now. The annual rates of inflation over the next four years are expected to be 16%, 20%, 15% and 10%. How much would the equipment cost after four years?

2 SAVINGS AND LOANS

Saving and loans
Regular savings
Sinking funds
Loans
Mortgages

2.1 Regular savings

Final value or terminal value

An investor may decide to add to his investment from time to time, and you may be asked to calculate the **final value** (or **terminal value**) of an investment to which equal annual amounts will be added. An example might be an individual or a company making annual payments into a pension fund: we may wish to know the value of the fund after n years.

EXAMPLE: REGULAR SAVINGS

A person invests £400 now, and a further £400 each year for three more years. How much would the total investment be worth after four years, if interest is earned at the rate of 10% per annum?

SOLUTION

In problems such as this, we call **now 'Year 0'**, the time **one year from now 'Year 1'** and so on. It is also a good idea to draw a time line in order to establish exactly when payments are made.

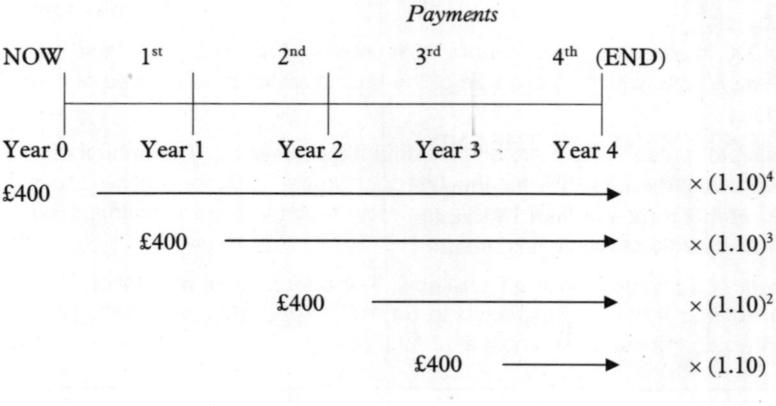

		£
(Year 0)	The first year's investment will grow to £400 $(1.10)^4$	585.64
(Year 1)	The second year's investment will grow to £400 $(1.10)^3$	532.40
(Year 2)	The third year's investment will grow to £400 $(1.10)^2$	484.00
(Year 3)	The fourth year's investment will grow to £400 (1.10)	440.00
		2,042.04

Terminal value calculations

The **final value** (or **terminal value**), S, of an investment to which equal annual amounts will be added is found using the following formula:

$S = \dfrac{(R^n - 1)}{(R - 1)}$ (the formula for a geometric progression).

The solution to the example above can be written as

$(400 \times 1.1) + (400 \times 1.1^2) + (400 \times 1.1^3) + (400 \times 1.1^4)$

with the values placed in reverse order for convenience. This is a **geometric progression** with A (the first term) = (400×1.1), R = 1.1 and n = 4.

The sum of a **geometric progression**, $S = \dfrac{A(R^n - 1)}{R - 1}$

Where A = the first term
R = the common ratio
n = the number of terms

In the example above

A = 400×1.1
R = 1.1
n = 4

If $S = \dfrac{A(R^n - 1)}{R - 1}$

$$S = \frac{400 \times 1.1\,(1.1^4 - 1)}{1.1 - 1}$$

$= £2,042.04$

EXAMPLE: INVESTMENTS AT THE ENDS OF YEARS

(a) If, in the previous example, the investments had been made at the end of each of the first, second, third and fourth years, so that the last £400 invested had no time to earn interest. We can show this situation on the following time line.

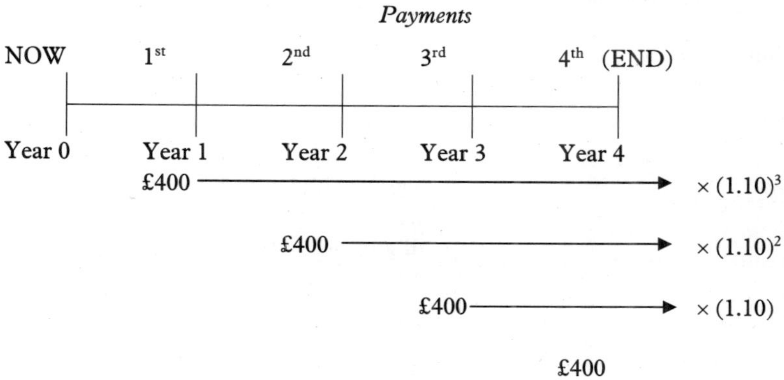

(Year 0) No payment
(Year 1) The first year's investment will grow to £400 × $(1.10)^3$
(Year 2) The second year's investment will grow to £400 × $(1.10)^2$
(Year 3) The third year's investment will grow to £400 × (1.10)
(Year 4) The fourth year's investment remains at £400

The value of the fund at the end of the four years is as follows.

$400 + (400 \times 1.1) + (400 \times 1.1^2) + (400 \times 1.1^3)$

This is a **geometric progression** with

A = £400
R = 1.1
n = 4

$$\text{If} \quad S = \frac{A(R^n - 1)}{R - 1}$$

$$S = \frac{400\,(1.1^4 - 1)}{1.1 - 1}$$

$$= £1,856.40$$

(b) If our investor made investments as in (a) above, but also put in a £2,500 lump sum one year from now, the value of the fund after four years would be

$£1,856.40 + £2,500 \times 1.1^3$

$= £1,856.40 + £3,327.50 = £5,183.90$

That is, we **can compound parts of investments separately, and add up the results.**

Activity 4 **(10 minutes)**

A man invests £1,000 now, and a further £1,000 each year for five more years. How much would the total investment be worth after six years, if interest is earned at the rate of 8% per annum?

2.2 Sinking funds

Definition

A **sinking fund** is an investment into which equal annual instalments are paid in order to earn interest, so that by the end of a given number of years, the investment is large enough to pay off a known commitment at that time. Commitments include the replacement of an asset and the repayment of a mortgage.

With mortgages, the total of the constant annual payments (which are usually paid in equal monthly instalments) plus the interest they earn over the term of the mortgage must be sufficient to pay off the initial loan plus accrued interest. We shall be looking at mortgages later on in this chapter.

When replacing an asset at the end of its life, a company might decide to invest cash in a sinking fund during the course of the life of the existing asset to ensure that the money is available to buy a replacement.

EXAMPLE: SINKING FUNDS

A company has just bought an asset with a life of four years. At the end of four years, a replacement asset will cost £12,000, and the company has decided to provide for this future commitment by setting up a sinking fund into which equal annual investments will be made, starting at year 1 (one year from now). The fund will earn interest at 12%.

Required

Calculate the annual investment.

SOLUTION

Let us start by drawing a time line where £A = equal annual investments:

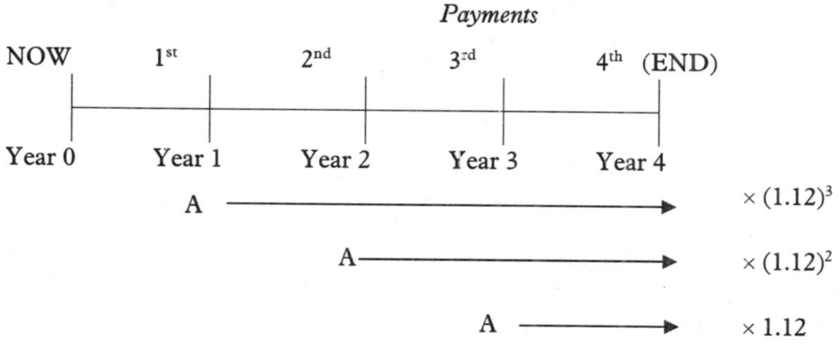

(Year 0)	No payment
(Year 1)	The first year's investment will grow to £A × $(1.12)^3$
(Year 2)	The second year's investment will grow to £A × $(1.12)^2$
(Year 3)	The third year's investment will grow to £A × (1.12)
(Year 4)	The fourth year's investment will remain at £A.

The value of the fund at the end of four years is as follows:

$$A + A(1.12) + A(1.12^2) + A(1.12^3)$$

This is a geometric progression with

A = A
R = 1.12
n = 4

The value of the sinking fund at the end of year 4 is £12,000 (given in the question) therefore

$$£12,000 = \frac{A(1.12^4 - 1)}{1.12 - 1}$$

$$£12,000 = 4.779328A$$

$$\therefore A = \frac{£12,000}{4.779328}$$

$$= £2,510.81$$

Therefore, four investments, each of £2,510.81 should be enough to allow the company to replace the asset.

Activity 5 **(20 minutes)**

Sinking funds

A farmer has just bought a combine harvester which has a life of ten years. At the end of ten years a replacement combine harvester will cost £100,000 and the farmer would like to provide for this future commitment by setting up a sinking fund into which equal annual investments will be made, starting *now*. The fund will earn interest at 10% per annum.

2.3 Loans

Most people will be familiar with the repayment of loans. The repayment of loans is best illustrated by means of an example.

EXAMPLE: LOANS

Timothy Lakeside borrows £50,000 now at an interest rate of 8 percent per annum. The loan has to be repaid through five equal instalments *after* each of the next five years. What is the annual repayment?

SOLUTION

Let us start by calculating the final value of the loan (at the end of year 5).

Using the formula $S = X(1 + r)^n$

Where X = £50,000
r = 8% = 0.08
n = 5
S = the sum invested after 5 years

$\therefore$ S = £50,000 $(1 + 0.08)^5$
= £73,466.40

The value of the initial loan after 5 years (£73,466.40) must equal the sum of the repayments.

A time line will clarify when each of the repayments are made. Let £A = the annual repayments which start a year from now, ie at year 1.

Repayments

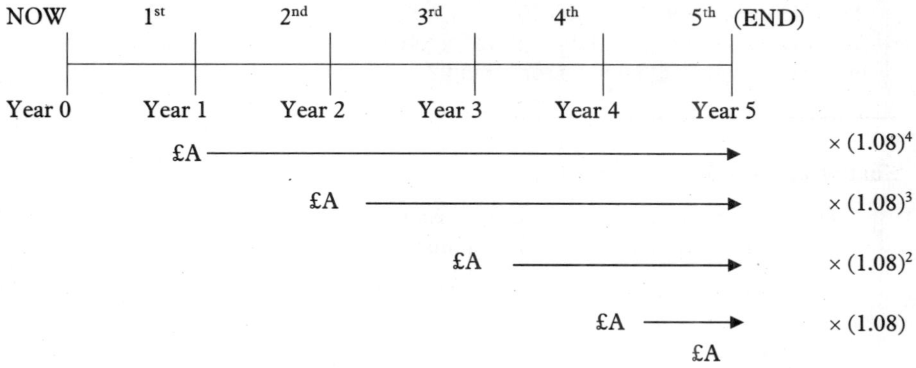

(Year 0)	No payment
(Year 1)	The first year's investment will grow to £A × $(1.08)^4$
(Year 2)	The second year's investment will grow to £A × $(1.08)^3$
(Year 3)	The third year's investment will grow to £A × $(1.08)^2$
(Year 4)	The fourth year's investment will grow to £A × (1.08)
(Year 5)	The fourth year's investment remains at £A.

The value of the repayments at the end of five years is as follows:

$A + (A \times 1.08) + (A \times 1.08^2) + (A \times 1.08^3) + (A \times 1.08^4)$

This is a geometric progression with

A = A
R = 1.08
n = 5

The sum of this geometric progression, $S = \frac{A(R^n - 1)}{R - 1}$ = £73,466.40 since the sum of repayments must **equal** the final value of the loan (ie £73,466.40).

$$S = £73{,}466.40 = \frac{A(1.08^5 - 1)}{1.08 - 1}$$

£73,466.40 = A × 5.86660096

$$A = \frac{£73{,}466.40}{5.86660096}$$

$$= £12{,}522.82$$

The annual repayments are therefore £12,522.82.

Activity 6 **(10 minutes)**

Annual repayments

John Johnstone borrows £50,000 now at an interest rate of 7% per annum. The loan has to be repaid through ten equal instalments after each of the next ten years. What is the annual repayment?

Sinking funds and loans compared

(a) **Sinking funds**. The sum of the **regular savings**, £A per period at r% over n periods *must* equal the sinking fund required at the end of n periods.

(b) **Loan repayments**. The sum of the **regular repayments** of £A per period at r% over n periods *must* equal the final value of the loan at the end of n periods.

The final value of a loan can therefore be seen to be equivalent to a sinking fund.

2.4 Mortgages

As you are probably aware, when a mortgage is taken out on a property over a number of years, there are several ways in which the loan can be repaid. One such way is the **repayment mortgage** which has the following features:

- A certain amount, S, is borrowed to be paid back over n years
- Interest, at a rate r, is added to the loan retrospectively at the end of each year
- A constant amount A is paid back each year

Income tax relief affects repayments but, for simplicity, we will ignore it here.

Mortgage repayments

Consider the repayments on a mortgage as follows:

(a) At the end of one year A has been repaid.

(b) At the end of two years the initial repayment of A has earned interest and so has a value of $A(1 + r)$ and another A has been repaid. The value of the amount repaid is therefore $A(1 + r) + A$.

(c) At the end of three years, the initial repayment will have a value of $A(1 + r)^2$, the second repayment a value of $A(1 + r)$ and a third repayment of A will have been made. The value of the amount repaid is therefore

$A(1 + r)^2 + (1 + r) + A$.

(d) At the end of n years the value of the repayments is therefore

$A(1 + r)^{n-1} + A(1 + r)^{n-2} + ... + A(1 + r)^2 + A(1 + r) + A$.

This is a **geometric progression** with 'A' = A, 'R' = (1 + r) and 'n' = n and hence the **sum of the repayments** $= \frac{A[(1+r)^n - 1]}{r} = \frac{A(R^n - 1)}{R - 1}$

Sum of repayments = final value of mortgage

During the time the repayments have been made, the initial loan has accrued interest.

The repayments must, at the end of n years, repay the initial loan plus the accrued interest.

Therefore the sum of the repayments must equal the final value of the mortgage.

Sum of repayments = final value of mortgage

$$\frac{A(R^n - 1)}{R - 1} = SR^n$$

$$\therefore A = \frac{SR^n \times (R - 1)}{(R^n - 1)}$$

EXAMPLE: MORTGAGES

(a) Sam has taken out a £30,000 mortgage over 25 years. Interest is to be charged at 12%. Calculate the monthly repayment.

(b) After nine years, the interest rate changes to 10%. What is the new monthly repayment?

SOLUTION

(a) **Final value of mortgage** $= £30{,}000 \times (1.12)^{25}$
$= £510{,}002$

Sum of repayments, S

Where A = annual repayment
R = 1.12
n = 25

$$\therefore S = \frac{A(1.12^{25} - 1)}{1.12 - 1}$$

$$= 133.334A$$

Sum of repayments = final value of mortgage

$133.334A = £510{,}002$

$$A = \frac{£510{,}002}{133.334}$$

$A = £3{,}825$

If annual repayment = £3,825

$$\text{Monthly repayment} = \frac{£3{,}825}{12} = £318.75$$

(b) After nine years, the **value of the loan** $= £30{,}000 \times (1.12)^9$
$= £83{,}192$

After nine years, the **sum of the repayments** $= \dfrac{A(R^n - 1)}{R - 1}$

Where A = £3,825
R = 1.12
n = 9

$\therefore$ Sum of repayments $= \dfrac{£3{,}825(1.12^9 - 1)}{1.12 - 1}$

$= £56{,}517$

	£
Value of loan at year 9	83,192
Sum of repayments at year 9	56,517
Loan outstanding at year 9	26,675

A new interest rate of 10% is to be charged on the outstanding loan of £26,675 for 16 years (25 – 9).

Final value of loan $= £26{,}675 \times (1.1)^{16}$
$= £122{,}571$

Sum of repayments $= \dfrac{A(R^n - 1)}{R - 1}$

Where R = 1.1
n = 16
A = annual repayment

$\therefore$ Sum of repayments $= \dfrac{A(1.1^{16} - 1)}{1.1 - 1}$

$= 35.94973A$

Final value of loan = sum of repayments

£122,571 = 35.94973A

$\therefore A = \dfrac{£122{,}571}{35.94973}$

A = £3,410

$\therefore$ monthly repayment $= \dfrac{£3{,}410}{12}$

$= £284$

Note. The final value of a loan/mortgage can be likened to a sinking fund also, since the final value must equate to the sum of the periodic repayments (compare this with a sinking fund where the sum of the regular savings must equal the fund required at some point in the future).

Activity 7 **(10 minutes)**

Monthly repayment

Nicky Eastlacker has taken out a £200,000 mortgage over 25 years. Interest is to be charged at 9%. Calculate the monthly repayment.

The first part of this chapter has examined interest. The second part of the chapter looks at the concept of discounting and two related techniques, net present value and the internal rate of return. These rely on the central idea that money has a time value.

3 DISCOUNTING

3.1 The basic principles of discounting

Discounting is the reverse of compounding. The discounting formula is $X = S \times \frac{1}{(1+r)^n}$

The **basic principle of compounding** is that if we invest £X now for n years at r% interest per annum, we should obtain £X $(1 + r)^n$ in n years' time.

Thus if we invest £10,000 now for four years at 10% interest per annum, we will have a total investment worth £10,000 × 1.10^4 = £14,641 at the end of four years (that is, at year 4 if it is now year 0).

The basic principle of **discounting** is that if we wish to have £S in n years' time, we need to invest a certain sum *now* (year 0) at an interest rate of r% in order to obtain the required sum of money in the future.

EXAMPLE: DISCOUNTING FORMULA

For example, if we wish to have £14,641 in four years' time, how much money would we need to invest now at 10% interest per annum? This is the reverse of the situation described in Paragraph 3.1.

Using our corresponding formula, $S = X(1 + r)^n$

Where X = the original sum invested
r = 10%
n = 4
S = £14,641

$£14{,}641 = X(1 + 0.1)^4$

$£14{,}641 = X \times 1.4641$

$$\therefore X = \frac{£14{,}641}{1.4641} = £10{,}000$$

£10,000 now, with the capacity to earn a return of 10% per annum, is the equivalent in value of £14,641 after four years. We can therefore say that **£10,000 is the present value of £14,641 at year 4, at an interest rate of 10%.**

3.2 Present value

The concept of **present value** can be thought of in two ways.

- It is the value today of an amount to be received some time in the future.
- It is the amount which would be invested today to produce a given amount at some future date.

Definition

The term **'present value'** simply means the amount of money which must be invested now for n years at an interest rate of r%, to earn a given future sum of money at the time it will be due.

The formula for discounting

The **discounting formula** is

$$X = S \times \frac{1}{(1+r)^n}$$

Where S is the sum to be received after n time periods
X is the present value (PV) of that sum
r is the rate of return, expressed as a proportion
n is the number of time periods (usually years)

The rate r is sometimes called a cost of capital.

Note that this equation is just a rearrangement of the compounding formula.

EXAMPLE: DISCOUNTING

(a) Calculate the present value of £60,000 at year 6, if a return of 15% per annum is obtainable.

(b) Calculate the present value of £100,000 at year 5, if a return of 6% per annum is obtainable.

(c) How much would a person need to invest now at 12% to earn £4,000 at year 2 and £4,000 at year 3?

SOLUTION

The discounting formula, $X = S \times \frac{1}{(1+r)^n}$ is required.

(a) S = £60,000
n = 6
r = 0.15

$$PV = 60{,}000 \times \frac{1}{1.15^6}$$
$$= 60{,}000 \times 0.432$$
$$= £25{,}920$$

(b) S = £100,000
n = 5
r = 0.06

$$PV = 100{,}000 \times \frac{1}{1.06^5}$$
$$= 100{,}000 \times 0.747$$
$$= £74{,}700$$

(c) S = £4,000
n = 2 or 3
r = 0.12

$$PV = \left(4{,}000 \times \frac{1}{1.12^2}\right) + \left(4{,}000 \times \frac{1}{1.12^3}\right)$$

$$= 4{,}000 \times (0.797 + 0.712)$$

$$= £6{,}036$$

This calculation can be checked as follows:

	£
Year 0	6,036.00
Interest for the first year (12%)	724.32
	6,760.32
Interest for the second year (12%)	811.24
	7,571.56
Less: withdrawal	(4,000.00)
	3,571.56
Interest for the third year (12%)	428.59
	4,000.15
Less: withdrawal	(4,000.00)
Rounding error	0.15

Activity 8 **(20 minutes)**

Present value

The present value at 7% interest of £16,000 at year 12 is £ ______

Capital expenditure appraisal

Discounted cash-flow techniques can be used to evaluate capital expenditure projects. There are two methods: the **NPV method** and the **IRR method**.

Definition

Discounted cash-flow (DCF) involves the application of discounting arithmetic to the estimated future cash flows (receipts and expenditures) from a project in order to decide whether the project is expected to earn a satisfactory rate of return.

4 THE NET PRESENT VALUE (NPV) METHOD

Net present value
Example
Discount tables
Project comparison
Expected values
Limitations

The **Net Present Value (NPV) method** works out the present values of all items of income and expenditure related to an investment at a given rate of return, and then works out a net total. If it is **positive,** the investment is considered to be **acceptable**. If it is **negative,** the investment is considered to be **unacceptable.**

EXAMPLE: THE NET PRESENT VALUE OF A PROJECT

Dog Ltd is considering whether to spend £5,000 on an item of equipment. The 'cash profits', the excess of income over cash expenditure, from the project would be £3,000 in the first year and £4,000 in the second year.

The company will not invest in any project unless it offers a return in excess of 15% per annum.

Required

Assess whether the investment is worthwhile, or 'viable'.

SOLUTION

(a) In this example, an outlay of £5,000 now promises a return of £3,000 **during** the first year and £4,000 **during** the second year. It is a convention in DCF, however, that cash-flows spread over a year are assumed to occur **at the end of the year,** so that the cash-flows of the project are as follows:

	£
Year 0 (now)	(5,000)
Year 1 (at the end of the year)	3,000
Year 2 (at the end of the year)	4,000

The NPV method takes the following approach:

(i) The project offers £3,000 at year 1 and £4,000 at year 2, for an outlay of £5,000 now.

(ii) The company might invest elsewhere to earn a return of 15% per annum.

(iii) If the company did invest at exactly 15% per annum, how much would it need to invest now, at 15%, to earn £3,000 at the end of year 1 plus £4,000 at the end of year 2?

(iv) Is it cheaper to invest £5,000 in the project, or to invest elsewhere at 15%, in order to obtain these future cash-flows?

(b) If the company did invest elsewhere at 15% per annum, the amount required to earn £3,000 in year 1 and £4,000 in year 2 would be as follows:

Year	*Cash-flow* £	*Discount factor* 15%	*Present value* £
1	3,000	$\frac{1}{1.15} = 0.870$	2,610
2	4,000	$\frac{1}{(1.15)^2} = 0.756$	3,024
			5,634

(c) The choice is to invest £5,000 in the project, or £5,634 elsewhere at 15%, in order to obtain these future cash flows. We can therefore reach the following conclusion:

- It is cheaper to invest in the project, by £634
- The project offers a return of over 15% per annum

(d) The net present value is the difference between the present value of cash inflows from the project (£5,634) and the present value of future cash outflows (in this example, £5,000 × $1/1.15^0$ = £5,000).

(e) An NPV statement could be drawn up as follows:

Year	*Cash-flow* £	*Discount factor* 15%	*Present value* £
0	(5,000)	1.0(	(5,000)
1	3,000	$\frac{1}{1.15} = 0.870$	2,610
2	4,000	$\frac{1}{(1.15)^2} = 0.756$	3,024
		Net present value	+634

The project has a positive net present value, so it is acceptable.

Activity 9 **(15 minutes)**

A company is wondering whether to spend £18,000 on an item of equipment, in order to obtain cash profits as follows:

Year	£
1	6,000
2	8,000
3	5,000
4	1,000

Required

Use the NPV method to assess whether the project is viable.

4.1 Discount tables

Assuming that money earns, say, 10% per annum

(a) The PV (present value) of £1 at year 1 is £1 × $\frac{1}{1.10}$ = £1 × 0.909

(b) Similarly, the PV of £1 at year 2 is £1 × $\frac{1}{(1.10)^2}$ = £1 × 0.826

(c) The PV of £1 at year 3 is £1 × $\frac{1}{(1.10)^3}$ = £1 × 0.751

Discount tables show the value of $1/(1 + r)^n$ for different values of r and n. The 10% discount factors of 0.909, 0.826 and 0.751 are shown in the discount tables at the end of this Study Text in the column for 10%. (You will be given discount tables in your assessment.)

4.2 Project comparison

The NPV method can also be used to compare two or more investment options. For example, suppose that Daisy Ltd can choose between the investment outlined in the previous question above *or* a second investment, which costs £28,000 but which would earn £6,500 in the first year, £7,500 in the second, £8,500 in the third, £9,500 in the fourth and £10,500 in the fifth. Which one should Daisy Ltd choose?

The decision rule is to choose the option with the highest NPV. We therefore need to calculate the NPV of the second option.

Year	*Cash flow*	*Discount factor*	*Present value*
	£	*11%*	£
0	(28,000)	1.000	(28,000)
1	6,500	0.901	5,857
2	7,500	0.812	6,090
3	8,500	0.731	6,214
4	9,500	0.659	6,261
5	10,500	0.593	6,227
			NPV = 2,649

Daisy Ltd should therefore invest in the second option since it has the higher NPV.

4.3 Expected values and discounting

Future cash-flows cannot be predicted with complete accuracy. To take account of this uncertainty an **expected net present value** can be calculated which is a **weighted average net present value based on the probabilities of different sets of circumstances occurring**. Let us have a look at an example.

EXAMPLE: EXPECTED NET PRESENT VALUE

An organisation with a cost of capital of 5% is contemplating investing £340,000 in a project which has a 25% chance of being a big success and producing cash inflows of £210,000 after one and two years. There is, however, a 75% chance of the project not being quite so successful, in which case the cash inflows will be £162,000 after one year and £174,000 after two years.

Required

Calculate an NPV and hence advise the organisation.

SOLUTION

	Discount	*Success*		*Failure*	
Year	*factor*	*Cash-flow*	*PV*	*Cash-flow*	*PV*
	5%	*£'000*	*£'000*	*£'000*	*£'000*
0	1.000	(340)	(340.00)	(340)	(340.000)
1	0.952	210	199.92	162	154.224
2	0.907	210	190.47	174	157.818
			50.39		(27.958)

NPV = (25% × 50.39) + (75% × –27.958) = –8.371

The NPV is –£8,371 and hence the organisation should not invest in the project.

4.4 Limitations of using the NPV method

There are a number of problems associated with using the NPV method in practice.

(a) **The future discount factors** (or interest rates) which are used in calculating NPVs can only be **estimated** and are not known with certainty. Discount rates that are estimated for time periods far into the future are therefore less likely to be accurate, thereby leading to less accurate NPV values.

(b) Similarly, NPV calculations make use of estimated **future cash-flows**. As with future discount factors, cash-flows which are estimated for cash-flows several years into the future cannot really be predicted with any real certainty.

(c) When using the NPV method it is common to assume that all cash-flows occur **at the end of the year**. However, this assumption is also likely to give rise to less accurate NPV values.

There are a number of computer programs available these days which enable a range of NPVs to be calculated for a number of different circumstances (best-case and worst-case situations and so on). Such programs allow some of the limitations mentioned above to be alleviated.

5 THE INTERNAL RATE OF RETURN (IRR) METHOD

Internal rate of return
The IRR method
The Interpolation method

5.1 IRR method

The **IRR method** determines the rate of interest (the IRR) at which the NPV is 0. Interpolation, using the following formula, is often necessary. **The project is viable if the IRR exceeds the minimum acceptable return.**

$$IRR = a\% + \left[\frac{A}{A-B} \times (b-a)\right]\%$$

The **internal rate of return (IRR) method** of evaluating investments is an alternative to the NPV method. The NPV method of discounted cash-flow determines whether an investment earns a **positive or a negative NPV when discounted at a given rate of interest**. If the NPV is zero (that is, the present values of costs and benefits are equal) the return from the project would be exactly the rate used for discounting.

The IRR method will indicate that a project is viable **if the IRR exceeds the minimum acceptable rate of return**. Thus if the company expects a minimum return of, say, 15%, a project would be viable if its IRR is more than 15%.

EXAMPLE: THE IRR METHOD OVER ONE YEAR

If £500 is invested today and generates £600 in one year's time, the internal rate of return (r) can be calculated as follows:

PV of cost = PV of benefits

$$500 = \frac{600}{(1+r)}$$

$$500\,(1 + r) = 600$$

$$1 + r = \frac{600}{500} = 1.2$$

$$r = 0.2 = 20\%$$

5.2 Interpolation method

The arithmetic for calculating the IRR is more complicated for investments and cash-flows extending over a period of time longer than one year. A technique known as the **interpolation method** can be used to calculate an approximate IRR.

EXAMPLE: INTERPOLATION

A project costing £800 in year 0 is expected to earn £400 in year 1, £300 in year 2 and £200 in year 3.

Required

Calculate the internal rate of return.

SOLUTION

The IRR is calculated by first of all finding the NPV at each of two interest rates. Ideally, one interest rate should give a small positive NPV and the other a small negative NPV. The IRR would then be somewhere between these two interest rates: above the rate where the NPV is positive, but below the rate where the NPV is negative.

A very rough guideline for estimating at what interest rate the NPV might be close to zero, is to take

$$\frac{2}{3} \times \left(\frac{\text{profit}}{\text{cost of the project}} \right)$$

In our example, the total profit over three years is £(400 + 300 + 200 – 800) = £100. An approximate IRR is therefore calculated as

$$\frac{2}{3} \times \frac{100}{800} = 0.08 \text{ approx.}$$

A starting point is to try 8%.

(a) Try 8%

Year	*Cash-flow* £	*Discount factor* 8%	*Present value* £
0	(800)	1.000	(800.0)
1	400	0.926	370.4
2	300	0.857	257.1
3	200	0.794	158.8
		NPV	(13.7)

The NPV is negative, therefore the project fails to earn 8% and the IRR must be less than 8%.

(b) Try 6%

Year	*Cash-flow* £	*Discount factor* 6%	*Present value* £
0	(800)	1.000	(800.0)
1	400	0.943	377.2
2	300	0.890	267.0
3	200	0.840	168.0
		NPV	12.2

The NPV is positive, therefore the project earns more than 6% and less than 8%.

The **IRR is now calculated by interpolation**. The result will not be exact, but it will be a close approximation. Interpolation assumes that the NPV falls in a straight line from +12.2 at 6% to –13.7 at 8%.

Graph to show IRR calculation by interpolation

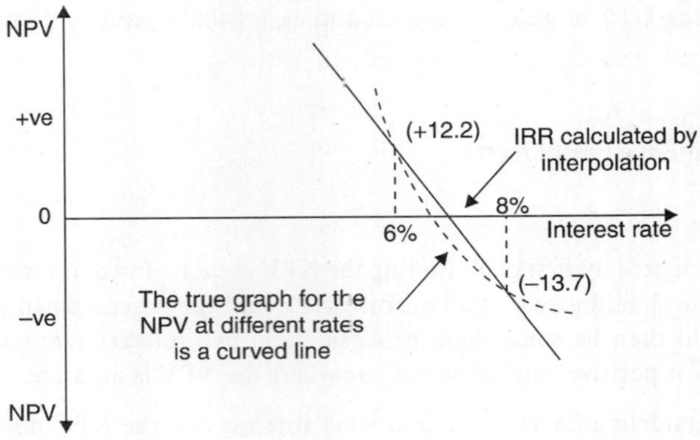

The IRR, where the NPV is zero, can be calculated as follows:

$$\textbf{IRR} = a\% + \left[\frac{A}{A-B} \times (b-a)\right]\%$$

Where a is one interest rate
b is the other interest rate
A is the NPV at rate a
B is the NPV at rate b

(c) Thus, in our example, IRR $= 6\% + \left[\frac{12.2}{(12.2+13.7)} \times (8-6)\right]\%$

$= 6\% + 0.942\%$

$= 6.942\%$ approx

(d) The answer is only an **approximation** because the NPV falls in a slightly curved line and not a straight line between +12.2 and –13.7. Provided that NPVs close to zero are used, the linear assumption used in the interpolation method is nevertheless fairly accurate.

(e) Note that the formula will still work if A and B are both positive, or both negative, and even if a and b are a long way from the true IRR, but the results will be less accurate.

Activity 10 **(10 minutes)**

The net present value of an investment at 15% is £50,000 and at 20% is –£10,000. The internal rate of return of this investment (to the nearest whole number) is

A 16%
B 17%
C 18%
D 19%

Chapter roundup

- **Simple interest** is interest which is earned in equal amounts every year (or month) and which is a given proportion of the original investment (the principal). The simple interest formula is **S = X + nrX**.
- **Compounding** means that, as interest is earned, it is added to the original investment and starts to earn interest itself. The basic formula for compound interest is $\mathbf{S = X(1 + r)^n}$.
- If the **rate of interest changes during the period** of an investment, the compounding formula must be amended slightly to $\mathbf{S = X(1+r_1)^y(1 + r_2)^{n-y}}$.
- A **sinking fund** is an investment into which equal annual instalments are paid in order to earn interest, so that by the end of a given number of years, the investment is large enough to pay off a known commitment at that time. Commitments include the replacement of an asset and the repayment of a mortgage.
- **Discounting** is the reverse of compounding. The discounting formula is $\mathbf{X = S \times 1/(1+r)^n}$.
- The concept of **present value** can be thought of in two ways.
  - It is the value today of an amount to be received some time in the future.
  - It is the amount which would have to be invested today to produce a given amount at some future date.
- The **discounting formula** is $X = S \times \frac{1}{(1+r)^n}$ **which is a rearrangement of the compounding formula**.
- **Discounted cash-flow techniques** can be used to evaluate capital expenditure projects. There are two methods: the **NPV method** and the **IRR method**.
- The **Net Present Value (NPV) method** works out the present values of all items of income and expenditure related to an investment at a given rate of return, and then works out a net total. If it is **positive**, the investment is considered to be **acceptable**.

  If it is **negative**, the investment is considered to be **unacceptable**.
- The **IRR method** determines the rate of interest (the IRR) at which the NPV is 0. Interpolation, using the following formula, is often necessary. **The project is viable if the IRR exceeds the minimum acceptable return.**

  $$\text{IRR} = a\% + \left[\frac{A}{A-B} \times (b-a)\right]\%$$

Quick quiz

1 The formula for simple interest is...

Where X = ...
r = ...
n = ...
S = ...

2 The basic formula for compound interest is..

Where X = ...
r = ...
n = ...
S = ...

3 If Smita Smitten invests £250 *now* and a further £250 each year for five more years at an interest rate of 20%, which of the following are true if the final investment is calculated using the formula for the sum of a geometric progression?

	A =	n =
A	£250 × 1.2	5
B	£250 × 1.2	4
C	£250	5
D	£250	4

4 What does the term present value mean?

5 The discounting formula is $X = S \times \frac{1}{(1+r)^n}$

Where S =
X =
r =
n =

(a) the rate of return (as a proportion)
(b) the sum to be received after n time periods
(c) the PV of that sum
(d) the number of time periods

6 What are the two usual methods of capital expenditure appraisal using DCF techniques?

7 What is the formula used to calculate the IRR and what do the symbols used represent?

Answers to quick quiz

1 $S = X + nrX$

Where X = the original sum invested
r = the rate of interest (as a proportion)
n = the number of periods
S = the sum invested after n periods

2 $S = X(1 + r)^n$

Where X = the original sum invested
r = the rate of interest (as a proportion)
n = the number of periods
S = the sum invested after n periods

3 A $S = \frac{A(R^n - 1)}{R - 1}$

Where A = the first term
= £250 × 1.2 (as investment is made *now*)
n = 5 years (the number of periods)

4 The amount of money which must be invested now for n years at an interest rate of r% to give a future sum of money at the time it will be due.

5 S = (b)
X = (c)
r = (a)
n = (d)

6 The Net Present Value (NPV) method

The Internal Rate of Return (IRR) method

7 $IRR = a\% + \left[\frac{A}{A - B} \times (b - a)\right]\%$

Where a = one interest rate
b = another interest rate
A = the NPV at rate a
B = the NPV at rate b

Answers to activities

1

Value now	Investment period	Interest rate	Final value
£	Years	%	£
5,000	3	20	8,640.00 (1)
5,000	4	15	8,745.03 (2)
5,000	3	6	5,955.08 (3)

Workings

(1) £5,000 × 1.20^3 = £8,640.00
(2) £5,000 × 1.15^4 = £8,745.03
(3) £5,000 × 1.06^3 = £5,955.08

2 Using the formula for compound interest, $S = X(1 + r)^n$, we know that X = £2,000, S = £2,721 and n = 4. We need to find r. It is essential that you are able to rearrange equations confidently when faced with this type of multiple choice question – there is not a lot of room for guessing!

$$£2{,}721 = £2{,}000 \times (1 + r)^4$$

$$(1 + r)^4 = \frac{£2{,}721}{£2{,}000} = 1.3605$$

$$1 + r = \sqrt[4]{1.3605} = 1.08$$

$$r = 0.08 = 8\%$$

The correct answer is B.

3 (a) £8,000 × $1.10^3 \times 1.08^2$ = £12,419.83
(b) £10,000 × $1.15^4 \times 1.12^4 \times 1.09^2$ = £32,697.64
(c) £6,000 × 1.16 × 1.20 × 1.15 × 1.10 = £10,565.28

4 This is a geometric progression with A (the first term) = £1,000 × 1.08, R = 1.08 and n = 6.

If $$S = \frac{A(R^n - 1)}{R - 1}$$

$$S = \frac{£1{,}000 \times 1.08(1.08^6 - 1)}{1.08 - 1}$$

$$= £7{,}922.80$$

5 The value of the fund at the end of ten years is a geometric progression with

A = £A × 1.1
R = 1.1
n = 10

Therefore the value of the sinking fund at the end of ten years is £100,000.

$$\therefore £100{,}000 = \frac{A \times 1.1(1.1^{10} - 1)}{1.1 - 1}$$

$$A = \frac{£100{,}000 \times 0.1}{1.1(1.1^{10} - 1)}$$

$$= \frac{£10{,}000}{1.75311670611}$$

$$= £5{,}704.12$$

6 The final value of the loan (at the end of year 10) is

$S = £50{,}000\ (1 + 0.07)^{10}$
$= £98{,}357.57$

The value of the initial loan after ten years (£98,357.57) must equal the sum of the repayments.

The sum of the repayments is a geometric progression with

A = A
R = 1.07
n = 10

The sum of the repayments = £98,357.57

$$S = £98{,}357.57 \quad = \frac{A(R^n - 1)}{R - 1}$$

$$= \frac{A(1.07^{10} - 1)}{1.07 - 1}$$

$$= 13.816448A$$

$$\therefore A = \frac{£98{,}357.57}{13.816448}$$

$= £7{,}118.88$ per annum

7 Final value of mortgage $= £200{,}000 \times (1.09)^{25}$
$= £1{,}724{,}616$

Sum of repayments, $S = \frac{A(R^n - 1)}{R - 1}$

Where A = Annual repayment
R = 1.09
n = 25

$$\therefore £1{,}724{,}616 = \frac{A(1.09^{25} - 1)}{1.09 - 1}$$

$\therefore A = £20{,}361.25$ per annum

If annual repayment = £20,361.25

$$\text{Monthly repayment} = \frac{£20{,}361.25}{12}$$

$= £1{,}696.77$

8 £7,104

Working

Using the discounting formula, $X = S \times \frac{1}{(1+r)^n}$

Where
$S = £16,000$
$n = 12$
$r = 0.07$
$X = PV$

$$PV = £16,000 \times \frac{1}{1.07^{12}} = £7,104$$

9

Year	*Cash flow* £	*Discount factor* 10%	*Present value* £
0	(18,000)	1.000	(18,000)
1	6,000	$\frac{1}{1.10} = 0.909$	5,454
2	8,000	$\frac{1}{1.10^2} = 0.826$	6,608
3	5,000	$\frac{1}{1.10^3} = 0.751$	3,755
4	1,000	$\frac{1}{1.10^4} = 0.683$	683
		Net present value	(1,500)

The NPV is negative. We can therefore draw the following conclusions:

(a) It is cheaper to invest elsewhere at 10% than to invest in the project.

(b) The project would earn a return of less than 10%.

(c) The project is not viable (since the PV of the costs is greater than the PV of the benefits).

10 $IRR = a\% + \left(\frac{A}{A-B} \times (b-a)\right)\%$

Where
a = one interest rate = 15%
b = other interest rate = 20%
A = NPV at rate a = £50,000
B = NPV at rate b = –£10,000

$$IRR = 15\% + \left[\frac{£50,000}{£50,000-(-£10,000)} \times (20-15)\right]\%$$

$$= 15\% + 4.17\%$$
$$= 19.17\%$$
$$= 19\%$$

The correct answer is therefore D.

Formulae

FORMULAE

$$\textbf{FRACTION} = \frac{\textbf{NUMERATOR}}{\textbf{DENOMINATOR}}$$

A **percentage increase** or **reduction** is calculated as (change ÷ original) × 100%.

Percentage change $= \frac{\text{'Change'}}{\text{Original value}} \times 100\%$

Quadratic equations $y = ax^2 + bx + c$

Quadratic equations can be solved by the formula

$$x = \frac{-b \pm \sqrt{(b^2 - 4ac)}}{2a} \text{ when } ax^2 + bx + c = 0$$

Arithmetic mean of ungrouped data $= \frac{\text{Sum of values of items}}{\text{Number of items}}$

The **arithmetic mean of grouped data,** $\bar{x} = \frac{\Sigma fx}{n}$ or $\frac{\Sigma fx}{\Sigma f}$ where n is the number of values recorded, or the number of items measured.

The **semi-interquartile range** $\frac{(Q_3 - Q_1)}{2}$

Mean deviation $= \frac{åf\ Ix - \bar{x}I}{n}$

Probability of achieving the desired result $= \frac{\text{Number of ways of achieving desired result}}{\text{Total number of possible outcomes}}$

The expected value equation $E(x) = \Sigma xP(x)$

$E(X)$ = Expected value = Probability × Pay off

The normal distribution $z = \frac{x - \square}{\square}$

Where z = the number of standard deviations above or below the mean (z score)
x = the value of the variable under consideration
μ = the mean
σ = the standard deviation.

Correlation coefficient, $r = \frac{n\Sigma XY - \Sigma X \Sigma Y}{\sqrt{[nåX^2 - (\Sigma X)^2][n\Sigma Y^2 - (\Sigma Y)^2]}}$

Where X and Y represent pairs of data for two variables X and Y

n = the number of pairs of data used in the analysis

The **least squares method of linear regression analysis** involves using the following formulae for a and b in Y = a + bX:

$$b = \frac{n\Sigma XY - \Sigma X\Sigma Y}{n\Sigma X^2 - (\Sigma X)^2}$$

$$a = \bar{Y} - b\bar{X}$$

Where n is the number of pairs of data
$\bar{X}$ is the mean X value of all the pairs of data
$\bar{Y}$ is the mean Y value of all the pairs of data

Simple interest

$S = X + nrX$

Where X = the original sum invested
r = the interest rate (expressed as a proportion, so 10% = 0.1)
n = the number of periods (normally years)
S = the sum invested after n periods, consisting of the original capital (X) plus interest earned

Compound interest is $S = X(1 + r)^n$

Where X = the original sum invested
r = the interest rate, expressed as a proportion (so 5% = 0.05)
n = the number of periods
S = the sum invested after n periods

The formula for **compound interest** when there are changes in the rate of interest is as follows:

$S = X(1 + r_1)^y (1 + r_2)^{n-y}$

Where r_1 = the initial rate of interest
y = the number of years in which the interest rate r_1 applies
r_2 = the next rate of interest
n – y = the (balancing) number of years in which the interest rate r_2 applies.

The sum of a **geometric progression,** $S = \frac{A(R^n - 1)}{R - 1}$

Where A = the first term
R = the common ratio
n = the number of terms

Discounting formula

$$X = S \times \frac{1}{(1+r)^n}$$

Where S is the sum to be received after n time periods
X is the present value (PV) of that sum
r is the rate of return, expressed as a proportion
n is the number of time periods (usually years)

The IRR, where the NPV is zero, can be calculated as follows:

$$\textbf{IRR} = a\% + \left[\frac{A}{A-B} \times (b-a)\right]\%$$

Where a is one interest rate
b is the other interest rate
A is the NPV at rate a
B is the NPV at rate b

Index

Definitions are highlighted in **bold**